too costly for
indiv. purchase; probably
only libraries. Should that
spend 60 on this? I do not
know

ESL @ $2 per
copy

he made
I "   3

Raul Hilberg
Dest of European Jews

Cost of Greenwood
books! I once
paid $3.50 for book
w/ parallel columns "P.
citations ('q quotes) in
7 langs. Book selling
for $45 +

Banana Justice

Banana Justice

Field Notes on Philippine Crime and Custom

W. Timothy Austin

PRAEGER

Westport, Connecticut
London

Library of Congress Cataloging-in-Publication Data

Austin, W. Timothy.
    Banana justice : field notes on Philippine crime and custom / W.
Timothy Austin.
        p.   cm.
    Includes bibliographical references and index.
    ISBN 0–275–96204–0 (alk. paper)
    1. Crime—Philippines.   2. Criminal justice, Administration of—
Philippines.   I. Title.
    HV7108.5.A97   1999
    364.9599—dc21   98–41347

British Library Cataloguing in Publication Data is available.

Library of Congress Catalog Card Number: 98–41347
ISBN: 0–275–96204–0

First published in 1999

Praeger Publishers, 88 Post Road West, Westport, CT 06881
An imprint of Greenwood Publishing Group, Inc.
www.praeger.com

Printed in the United States of America

The paper used in this book complies with the
Permanent Paper Standard issued by the National
Information Standards Organization (Z39.48–1984).

10 9 8 7 6 5 4 3 2 1

to Philip

pub'd Aug 99 for $59.95!

Contents

Illustrations

TABLES

Preface

T he title of this book deserves some clarification. The use of the words banana and justice is somewhat metaphorical; however, it is not entirely illogical in the Republic of the Philippines. As will be discussed in detail later, the Filipino decidedly avoids formal mechanisms of social control and will often seek secluded areas in order to work out interpersonal disputes, hopefully in a peaceful manner. In the hinterland, if not under or near a banana tree, it is common for banana leaves to be used as a mat on which locals will sit and perhaps eat or drink. Important to this discussion of social control, about 70 percent of all people in the Philippines live in villages outside of the major urban areas. What the reader will find in this book is information based upon diaries kept by the author while conducting seven separate research excursions to the Philippines between 1980 and 1997. As the book chapters reflect, the research covered various topics but always emphasized aspects of crime and custom. The concepts of crime and custom overlap to some extent because what is criminal in the Philippines may also be customary. Also, what is customary and legal today may be inappropriate or criminal tomorrow. Issues of crime and custom are equally slippery throughout the world, but in the Philippines they appear particularly enticing as this small book will demonstrate. Some of the information in this book appeared elsewhere in a different form. That is, in some cases earlier versions of articles were first published in an assortment of professional journals and, as such, were meant for specialists in criminology or anthropology.

Scientific reporting is sometimes Spartan; in some instances terseness, comes at the expense of clarity. With the insertion of additional examples and case histories, the present format provides greater depth than the sometimes curt style of the earlier professional reports. A book format also allows findings to be interpreted with more creativity and a freer hand than is found in many professional report formats. Importantly, this synthesis allows the specific issues on crime and custom to be updated. In most instances, research completed in the Philippines in the 1990s allows for further rethinking of some of the issues previously reported in the 1980s. This book furnishes such an opportunity. Thus, this book presents a portrait of issues as they were observed and, in some cases, how they developed over a period of approximately twenty years. Any oversights or points of confusion which may have appeared in earlier publications are noted in this book, and attempts are made to fully amend them for a larger audience.

Each chapter relates to the others: General themes about peace and order in the Philippines are discussed, and they are sequenced in a meaningful order. When a specific issue in one chapter applies to subsequent issues elsewhere, the reader is so advised and cross-references are provided to diverse locations throughout the book for related reading or analysis. In attempting to unravel the crime themes—particularly in Part II—effort is made to go beyond a basic description of Filipino life ways and to untangle the relationship between crime and justice and the larger system of social organization in which they are found. Often, the celebrated writings of Donald Black provide a theoretical framework or launching point for explaining and clarifying specific justice-related topics. In this regard, the book consistently spotlights how law fluctuates between a meaningful cultural feature and something that can be laid aside. The concerns of crime and custom in these chapters reflect what the author felt to be particularly fascinating issues worthy of study. The research was funded by government agencies, adding some credibility to these topics of study, but they nonetheless represent themes for which this author held a fundamental curiosity. Filipinos were equally curious about the issues.

Giving recognition to others, and especially to various government agencies that helped support the research in this book, may appear at first to be a necessary tedium. However, this is of utmost importance in the research process, for it provides to the critical reader a historical connecting point for much of the work reported in these pages. It is germane, if not simply courteous, to give credit where it is due to those who helped the author along the way. A number of granting agencies were involved. In most cases they furnished not only funding for the original research but also much valuable critique and feedback.

The Fulbright-Hays program provided two separate Senior Research Awards, in 1980 and 1985. The first award, specifically for the Philippines, was aimed at analyzing rural courts. The second, for Singapore, was to study informal social control in that island nation, but the grant allowed for important side trips to the Philippines. The U. S. Institute of Peace must receive special thanks for a grant to study the general issue of peacemaking in the Philippines in 1993. The National Science Foundation funded this author's research in the Philippines in 1997 to further address the peacemaking strategies; this research produced spinoff studies of corruption, youth, and anarchy, and deserves special credit. In the intervening years, a variety of faculty development and/or travel grants were awarded by the State of Pennsylvania through either the State System of Higher Education, or Indiana University of Pennsylvania. These sometimes small grants were critical in filling in the gaps between the larger national research awards.

A number of people, both in the Philippines and in the United States, deserve acknowledgment. Some of the scholars who provided time and assistance in reviewing earlier manuscripts included Bruce L. Berg, Donald J. Shoemaker, and James Wallace. Also, for their listening patience and critical ears as Ph.D. students and dissertation advisees, thanks to Drs. Delbert Rounds, Shaun Gabbidon, Elizabeth Grossi, Peter Liu, Yingyi Situ, June Watkins, Glen Zuern, Nonso Okereafoezeke, Victoria M. Time and Aref Al-Khattar. Special appreciation for his analytical savvy goes to Steve A. Young, a Ph.D. research assistant who traveled with me for a time to Southeast Asia. I am also indebted to Donald J. Shoemaker who assisted me in writing Chapter 8 [Considering Youth]. Don Shoemaker and I attended graduate school together in the late 1960s and coincidentally found ourselves as researchers in the same area of the Philippines years later. After several decades, Frederick L. Bates must be remembered for instilling in many, including myself, the joy of research and the need to write. Filipinos who must be selected from the masses for recognition include Professor Rogelio B. Bandojo, Dr. Jerry Villacrucis, and most important, Ediberto and Trinidad Mugot. For early inspiration, personal gratitude goes to Willard F. Austin, one of my first and most esteemed teachers. Betty M. Austin, a scholar fluent in many Filipino languages, offered critical comments throughout the book and, during the field ventures to Asia, made numerous sacrifices. At Greenwood Publishing Group, two people standout. First, is Heather Staines, Acquisitions Editor, who provided early encouragement for the project. Second, during the final stages of completion, Betty C. Pessagno, Production Editor, guided the work to careful completion. The author alone is responsible for any faults within the book.

Asia and the Pacific

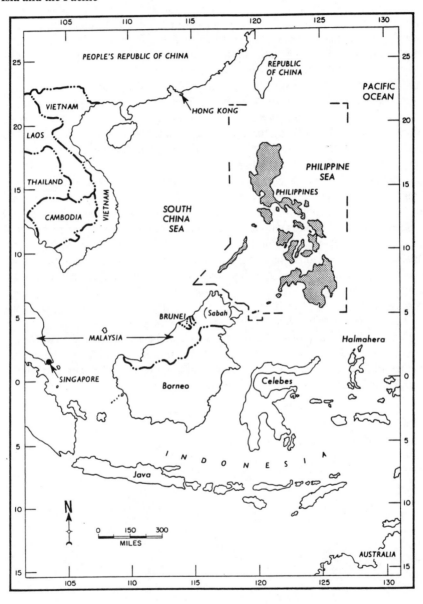

Introduction

The Republic of the Philippines is made up of over 7,000 islands although, as far as is known, fewer than 400 of these are inhabited. The islands extend over an area of about 1,000 miles, running north to south in the South China Sea. The country is situated about 400 miles south of Taiwan and the very southern tip of the Philippines nearly touches north Borneo. The Philippines is roughly clustered into three island groups. Toward the north is Luzon, the largest region and the site of Manila, the nation's capital and most populous city. The land masses of the central region comprise the Visayan Islands, and to the south is Mindanao, the second-largest island in the nation. If all the islands were squeezed together, they would form a land mass about the size of Arizona.

The islands are of volcanic origin and were likely populated as early as 30,000 years ago by peoples from the Malay peninsula and from what now forms Indonesia. Ancient archaeological influences from China have also been discovered. Early trade routes crossed the southern islands and brought a Muslim influence to the region in the fourteenth century. However, not until Magellan claimed the lands in 1521 were the mountainous islands referred to as the Philippines, named after King Philip of Spain. Even though Islam predated Christianity in the islands, Muslim groups only flourished in parts of Mindanao and today comprise a small but expressive segment of the Philippine scene. The total population of the nation has reached about 70 million after four centuries of Spanish rule, nearly a half century of occupation by the United States, four years of occupation by the Japanese during World War II, and the most recent half century as an independent nation.

With the highly segmented geography of the Philippines, and the majority of people residing in rural areas of provinces outside the major cities, much of the population rarely, if ever, has contact with the central government in Manila. The Philippines is subdivided into 74 provinces roughly equally distributed among the three island regions of Luzon, Visayas, and Mindanao. The scattered population and the lack of quick inter-island mobility have given rise to extremes in cultural diversity, as evidenced by about eighty-five different dialects spoken in the country. A Filipino not versed in multiple dialects, who travels widely throughout the provinces, will commonly have difficulty communicating clearly, if at all. This makes some knowledge of Tagalog [the national language, also referred to as Pilipino] or English increasingly necessary. Throughout the islands, there are a total of 60 cities and 1,523 towns [municipalities]. A majority of the citizens live outside urban areas in small villages colloquially referred to as barrios. There are about 50,000 barrios in the nation, each with an average population about 900. In many ways, a rural barrio existence forms the essence of Filipino life ways for most of the island folk, and much of this book will speak of barrio life.

Between 1980 and 1997 the author traveled widely in all three major regions. However, most of the research reported here is based on experiences in two provinces—one in Luzon and one in Mindanao—with references to other provinces, as warranted. The author's first experiences in the Philippines occurred during a five month period in 1980 in the province of Nueva Ecija, situated in the flat rice farming basin of Central Luzon. Although the central basin is known for fertile rice farming and the province is flat, one can see volcanic mountain ranges on the horizon both to the east and west. Other provincial resources include corn, sugar cane, tobacco, and coconut. Nueva Ecija has three cities and twenty-nine municipalities and, with surrounding villages, holds a combined population of about 2 million people. Just outside the municipality of Muñoz, in the north-central area of the province, is Central Luzon State University, where the author was attached for the first research venture. Very few roads were paved in 1980, and travel around the town of Muñoz, and to and from the university, was generally by motorcycle with attached side cars [often referred to as pedicabs or simply tricycles]. These would comfortably hold several passengers. In the hot, dry season, the farms are irrigated and travel is often on dusty rural trails. It was during this season that the author explored how many of the crimes and disputes were handled in the small towns and villages of the province. These research results are presented in Chapter 1.

A second province is Lanao del Norte from which a majority of the field notes discussed in this book were derived. Lanao del Norte stretches north and south for about 100 kilometers, forming part of the northwest coast of Mindanao. Iligan, its only city, is an industrial and agricultural seaport positioned on a secluded bay, which empties into the Mindanao and Sulu Seas and, eventually, into the South China Sea. About half of the province's twenty-two towns extend along the coast from Iligan. Others are located in the more mountainous inland area, reachable at times only with difficulty, even though they are merely 20 or 30 kilometers from the city. Numerous small barrios dot the provincial map. Isolated hamlets, called sitios [detached neighborhoods] are officially connected to larger villages or municipalities but are actually closer to rice, coconut, or banana fields convenient for farmers. The relevance of the isolated barrio and sitio for social control will be highlighted in Part I.

The region is culturally dynamic in at least three ways. First, it represents a mix of farming and city folk, many of whom congregate daily at the urban market places. A clear overlap exists between the rural population of the province and the more well-to-do city merchants and business people. Many of the city dwellers have not forgotten their rural origins and proudly boast of farming a small piece of land on weekends in the outlying regions to maintain local roots and supplement their income to maintain a costly urban lifestyle. Much of the city scene represents a composite of traditional rural and modern life ways. In parts of the city, farmers riding carts pulled by carabaos [water buffalo] compete side by side with motor vehicles for street space. Second, as a port city, Iligan is a hub of social and economic activity, with cargo and passenger ships docking at the harbor throughout the day and night. A transient character looms over the city and extends into the province, as people continuously move about by jeepney, bus, automobile, motorcycle, bicycle, and on foot. Third, the province has a near-notorious reputation as a periodic battleground for conflicting Muslim-Christian groups. In recent years, and even for generations, the research area has erupted into violence as religious antagonists clash within and outside the workplace (George, 1980; Gowing, 1988; Austin, 1989, 1996a,b). The transient and vigorous character of life in the province, which also reflects a mix of old and new values, provides a setting for examining most of the special themes of crime and custom in Part II.

The Republic of the Philippines, an island nation in Southeast Asia, holds a rich array of issues important to the student of comparative justice systems or to any serious reader concerned with peace and order. Here is a nation with special problems of bribery, extortion, terrorism, and Muslim-Christian conflict. At the same time, citizens choose their own ways to address these problems, whether peacefully [the norm] , or sometimes without peace. After substantial recent growth in the literature on comparative criminology in the Western Hemisphere, and especially in the United States, it remains difficult to decide how to approach the study of comparative justice systems, a course now available in most major Western universities. Given the approximately 190 independent nations in the world, an attempt to be comparative in any comprehensive sense must fall short. A number of ambitious comparative texts are available, containing a few examples of nations representing each of the major continents. Such needed and important works are limited. On the other hand, one can find eloquent anthropological monographs that report on a lifetime of study of specific issues centered about the life ways of a single village. Often, such findings may not be meaningfully generalized beyond the village. This book falls somewhere between these extremes. Admittedly, it sketches and analyzes a number of criminal justice issues as they have persisted in a single nation. In so doing, the work leans more toward the anthropologist's approach, although the book reaches beyond a single local community. Rather, it is concerned with patterns of behavior that cross multiple communities and provinces in several different regions of the larger Philippine setting. Where meaningful international comparisons make sense, contrasts are drawn between the Philippines and other cultural areas of the world. With the issues of terrorism or Muslim-Christian conflict, for example, ample citations are included to allow for further independent inquiry. Although the book is not meant to stand alone as a text on comparative justice, it will prove a useful supplement to those academics with interests in the particular justice-related themes represented so explicitly by Filipinos.

This book is straightforward in its organization. Part I includes three chapters that describe varied patterns of community cohesiveness and dispute resolution in the Philippines. Chapter 1 explains some of the pros and cons of island life with regard to personal security and how island life fosters community solidarity. Much of the chapter reports on the original development of a community-based system of informal and out-of-court dispute processing, now common as a government-imposed model, which, even if sporadically, operates throughout the Philippines. How well the system of resolving interpersonal conflicts is accepted by local Filipinos is addressed. Chapter 2 introduces the general topic of self-help and peacemaking practices in the Province of Lanao del Norte in Mindanao. This chapter builds upon some of the issues raised in Chapter 1 but is more detailed in organizing peacemaking strategies about culture and personality. The chapter also outlines a number of community-based peacekeeping organizations. Chapter 3 describes one field trip to the southern Philippines, which resulted in a number of surprising findings of cultural elements that tend to promote community security. These include *barangay,* or neighborhood organization, the absence of police, idle time, low technology, and the necessity of multiple personal follow-ups to finalize most business transactions.

Part II outlines four distinct, yet overlapping, features of crime and custom that have influenced Filipino life, particularly in the northwestern region of Mindanao, over the past several decades. Chapter 4 summarizes aspects of the conflict between Muslim and Christian peoples who live side by side in towns and cities in Mindanao. Chapter 5 addresses terrorist activity in regions of the Philippines and focuses on how such unpleasant activity impacts on the daily life of Filipinos in the northwestern region of Mindanao. Chapter 6 details what is meant by vigilante activity in the Philippines and examines a number of such enterprises observable in the country in the 1980s, with lingering presence in more recent years. Chapter 7 describes the rather omnipresent issue of bribery and extortion in the Philippines, an example of corruption that has become normal for some at the expense of many. Part III provides several interpretations of Filipino culture. Chapter 8, for example, clarifies the plight of some of the youthful population in the research area and draws upon the findings in the earlier chapters as they apply to youth. Also addressed are some of the government processes for managing Filipino delinquency whether by government or non-official procedures. Chapter 9 explains aspects of the folkways in the province of Lanao del Norte where near anarchy reigns, as shown by a lack of enthusiasm for the rule of law. Chaotic driving and queuing customs, among others, are discussed in light of their possible links to further styles of social deviance. Chapter 10 briefly retraces the book, attempts to weave a thread among all the previous chapters, and provides suggestions for further inquiry.

GOING TO THE FIELD

Going to the field means actually escaping the office or the library and traveling to the location where the issue under study can be observed, as much as is practical, in its natural setting. Thus, for example, if you want to study terrorism, or the impact of terrorism, you have to go where terrorism can be found and talk to people who have first-hand knowledge of such activity. Terrorism, Muslim-Christian conflict, vigilante activity, patterns of bribery, and anarchy just happen to be justice-related activities that could be found in the Republic of the Philippines. Because the Philippines contains these researchable issues, the author was drawn to the nation as a location for fieldwork. However, many nations of the world display the same researchable themes. So other factors favored the Philippines as a field-research setting. Importantly, that nation has been receptive to outside researchers since its independence in 1946. Some countries do not allow researchers to cross their borders; researchers who wish to explore socially or politically sensitive topics are particularly unwelcome.

Another reason why the Philippines arose as an attractive research setting is that most Filipinos speak some English, which is also the language widely used there in business, government, and educational institutions. The absolute necessity of speaking the Philippine language is less critical, even if understanding some of the local dialect is advisable. Further, the islands themselves are situated in the equatorial zone, and climate is temperate to hot year round, a preference held by some researchers—including this one—even though themes similar to those discussed here may be relevant in the more frigid climates of the world. Finally, the author was briefly introduced in the mid-1970s to a Filipino university official visiting the United States, who was willing to endorse original research to be conducted in the Philippines, with only minimal awareness of the author's background and plans. The first excursion to the Philippines was the most traumatic with regard to culture shock, but at the same time it set forth many new research questions requiring subsequent sojourns.

From the earliest of the seven field trips in 1980 to the most recent in 1997, the research goal was to develop firsthand awareness of how Filipinos think about, feel about, and react to issues of crime and justice. The aim was for a non-Filipino outsider to understand the themes, as outlined in the table of contents, as much as could be possible. If the author found it unrealistic to personally witness or experience the issue being explored, such as vigilante activity or terrorism, then the second choice was to locate individuals who had themselves been intimately involved in the activity and to spend sufficient time with them to promote unquestioned rapport. In some cases, multiple field trips over several years were necessary before friendships reached the point where both respondents and the author felt fully comfortable in discussing sensitive emotional topics. The field notes represent the written data that the researcher recorded while residing in the Philippines. This raw information is a product of watching people in their daily activities and listening to locals discuss the issues in question. Simply stated, the recorded notes themselves are a product of observation, participation, and listening.

Direct observations are similar in some ways to those made by tourists, since both may be looking at the same thing. However, researchers usually observe a scene for longer periods of time and generally on multiple occasions. Also, if researchers have done their homework, and have read widely in the subject areas being explored, then some of their observations should become more meaningful even at the raw observational stage. If observations are not instantly meaningful, they are nonetheless recorded. During the course of subsequent observations and recordings, it could only be hoped that significant patterns would emerge amid the raw data. A constant worry among field workers, and for this author, is that little could be made of the raw field-note data. Fortunately, this rarely occurs.

Occasionally, the observations in the Philippine setting were rather mundane. During one field visit, when the issues under study were bribery and extortion, this author would sit and observe social activity in open-air street markets for several hours each day for weeks at a time, making detailed records of interactions between customers and merchants. Similar observations, for example, were made in bank and post office lobbies, restaurants, various transportation depots, and government offices. Over the duration of the field trips, direct observations were made without, or with only minimal, verbal contact between the researcher and the people being observed. These observations, which could also occur spontaneously during the day or night, were first roughly recorded, when possible, on the spot in small notebooks. Even when walking the sidewalk or a village path, observations of local activity were made continually, mental notes taken, and later recalled. Each evening, without fail, all rough notes and recollections were carefully amplified and redrafted into more permanent handwritten diaries and journals. Computer technology now allows raw descriptions and accounts to be efficiently transferred to computer disk for quick retrieval and review. In the 1990s, a notebook computer replaced this author's portable typewriter. However, in making rather impromptu observations of local life, the jotting of pencil notes on table napkins still remains a most feasible practice.

Listening can take many forms. Casually overhearing conversations in a crowded room, a passenger jeep, or listening to people argue in the marketplace may provide random and sometimes imprecise information. Yet, even such accidental incidents can furnish insights and a basis for later asking more specific questions of selected locals. That is, more purposefully designed interviews with Filipinos who had long resided in the setting proved a most fruitful procedure for obtaining information. Research reported in this book involved several distinct forms of face-to-face interviews. A most informal style, and one often used during the field excursions, pertains to relaxed   conversations with rural villagers and city folk with whom the researcher had developed acquaintanceships or friendships over the years. Such conversations took place over coffee or lunch and might continue for hours. During these sometimes-lengthy discussions, and when the timing appeared right, the researcher would interject a prepared question to which a specific response was sought. Thus, the author routinely combined purely open-ended interviews with semi-structured ones.

This same style was practiced whether the subject under study was Muslim-Christian conflict, the impact of terrorism, or juvenile delinquency. In some instances, these casual interviews were audiotaped; more often, brief handwritten notes were taken during the interview, when relevant information was uncovered. If a question were to reap rich accounts from a particular respondent, then the issue would be reintroduced, even if in subsequent days, in order to gain additional facts and to clarify any misunderstandings. A major advantage of lengthy ethnographic fieldwork is that issues can continuously be reintroduced by the researcher to the same respondents.

Often a small group, rather than a lone respondent, would be present in the field setting, and an open exchange of information would occur at a fast pace, with one individual reacting to another group member's comment. Frequently, this required the researcher to ask that relevant statements be repeated or expressed differently in order to gain full understanding of the central arguments being made. At the request of the researcher,   it was common for particularly conversant groups to reconvene on multiple occasions and revisit issues of special importance (on focus groups, see Morgan, 1993). The local Filipino respondents generally were well aware of the researcher's identity and profession and realized that the subject matter would likely turn to crime and justice issues germane to the local region. Locals who knew the researcher from previous field trips to the area would occasionally volunteer information and ask if it might be useful in research. After several years, and multiple visits to the field setting, about six Filipino citizens became especially beneficial in continuously providing information pertinent to the subjects of study. These individuals were generally influential and longtime community members, with occupations allowing them special insights in a particular research area. These expert informants included educators, government workers, religious leaders, merchants, and farmers.

On infrequent occasions, as, for example,   while studying bribery and extortion [Chapter 7], a more formal style of interview was used. In this case, a list of prepared questions was administered to a selected group of respondents. Even in these instances, numerous informal discussions were also held with the local villagers or city dwellers to corroborate any findings derived from the more formal procedure. While participation in daily Filipino life in the field setting also requires both observing and listening as information-gathering procedures, the richness of the observations and discussions is enhanced when a researcher gains access to groups and organizations, and the label of outsider is, at least for a moment, partially laid aside.

During six field trips between 1985 and 1997, the researcher lived with a Filipino family on the outskirts of Iligan City in the Province of Lanao del Norte on the island of Mindanao. The author occupied a small room in a large house, which also had several spare rooms rented out to local college students. During these times the author had free access to the house and could come and go at will, but often stayed at the household for meals and occasionally helped with cleaning and general maintenance of the house. It was a busy location, and numerous guests would drop by during the day or evening to visit with one of the members of the house. The owner of the house was a government official of Lanao del Norte who supplemented his income with several passenger jeeps and a small rice farm. Jeep drivers would pick up the vehicles in the morning, return them in the evening, and give a percentage of the day's earnings to the owner. It was convenient from this location to hop a jeep to town or to a local village outside the city. The government worker traveled widely throughout the province in the course of his office activities, and the author would often be invited to accompany him to various business locations in towns and rural barrios of the province. This provided excellent exposure and insight into the Filipino work world at the provincial government level. This was particularly true because the government official was native to the area, was highly respected, and enjoyed acting as a guide and occasional interpreter for the researcher.

Contacts were also made with a number of local educators at a university branch campus, located in Iligan City. Over the years, the author became close friends with some of the faculty who were eager to have the author accompany them to their local service club organizations, to occasionally guest lecture, and to join them in local festivities, including roaming the local bars. Meeting with these friends, with whom great rapport was established after many months and years, strengthened the extent and quality of information collected pertinent to the research goals. Of particular importance, if these individuals were unable to adequately respond to a question regarding crime, justice, or some aspect of social control, they were able to suggest others in the community who could be of assistance. In any case, the old friends would introduce the author to the better informed individuals. In this manner, back-to-back field expeditions to the same area quickly established a growing network of respondents and specialists [on snowball sampling, see Berg, 1989; Curran and Renzetti, 1994].

Although the author is comfortable with the accuracy or validity of the information contained within these pages, it is true that with field research a question of reliability of data must arise. Will other field workers to the same area arrive at similar conclusions? Conceivably, others could talk to different informants and accumulate data that is also valid yet contradicts information reported here. To address this concern, the author made certain that expert informants were located who reflected, as much as was practical, a representative sampling of residents of the research area. Thus, care was taken to gain the views of women and men, elderly people and youth, professional and nonprofessional, and residents from both urban and rural areas. In this way, a more representative sampling of the population of the research area was approximated.

The field notes only embody the raw data accumulated over the years. Equally important is the sorting and sifting of the notes into a logical and organized response to the original questions. Some of the findings and patterns that emerged are presented in the remaining chapters of this book.

Republic of the Philippines

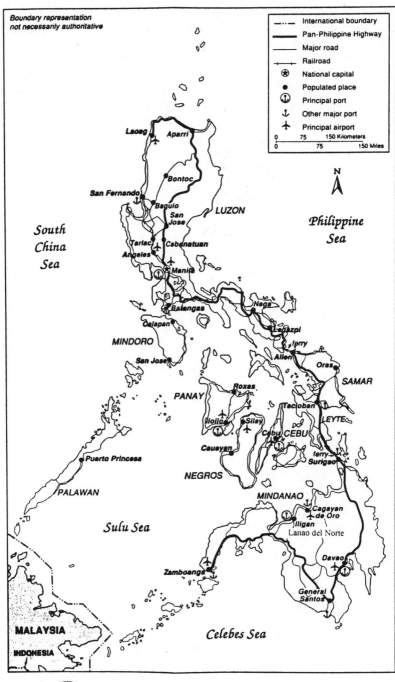

PART I

Community Atmospheres

This section describes and explains group and community dynamics that come into play as Filipinos try to resolve disputes and crimes without reliance upon the formal justice system. As will be seen, features of Filipino life inspire the emergence of uncommon styles of social order. Understanding these features requires scrutiny of Filipino culture, personality, as well as a number of situational variables which arise sometimes almost without notice. Chapter 1 ["Islands and *Barangays*"] explains how island geography, characterized by tight-knit communal life, tends to promote a social cohesiveness that makes strong government control less essential. Much of this chapter focuses on the origins of communalism in the Philippine islands. However, a most important theme is the tendency for the distinct island societies to reject the attempt by strong government to intervene in local affairs.

Although the government of martial law under Ferdinand Marcos could not be ignored when decrees emanated from the nation's capital, isolated villages could nonetheless give greater emphasis to local security and crime prevention practices long accepted as part of the local culture and personality. Chapter 2, "Peacemaking Filipino Style," presents a general overview of the self-help process that Filipinos have traditionally relied upon. These self-help strategies, found throughout the islands, appear to cultivate an orientation of peace and order, although with mixed success. The chapter also reveals how even the more formal governmental systems of order at the national level have picked up the banner of recognizing the importance of neighborhood-based social control.

Chapter 3, "Unexpected Faces of Social Control," elaborates upon the surprising dimensions of maintaining community order without reliance on government or formal law enforcement. An isolated community may reap the benefits of heavy emphasis on localism; yet several unanticipated, if not negative, consequences may arise. For example, what happens when police are physically absent from local villages and towns? What community structures emerge to maintain peace and order? What is the impact of technology, or the absence of such, in the social organization of security during a time of unrest? Several positive features are addressed as well as the potential for a few negative consequences. In this chapter, special scrutiny should be given to the work of Donald Black, whose theoretical influence is introduced here and will re-appear in subsequent chapters.

Chapter 1

Islands and *Barangays*

I f creating a community atmosphere is a goal, then it is a big advantage to begin with an island. Geographic detachment and isolation place restraints on people by naturally limiting mobility and forcing social interaction, sometimes for long periods. A small island is similar to a ship. If you irritate someone while on board ship, as on an island, there are not many places you can run or hide. This geographic feature may, in part, engender or necessitates a sense of conciliation on the part of the inhabitants. Even with the well-known exceptions of mutiny, the process of reconciling differences nonviolently is most typical of seafaring people. Close confinement requires that shipboard conflicts be worked out through mediation. Extreme punishment or incarceration within the ship's hulk would deplete a small seagoing community of needed human resources. Also, the ship's captain is the logical choice as mediator of interpersonal conflicts. To the extent that the Philippine island groups were populated by boat people, it should not be surprising that a pattern of mediation by a village leader or captain would remain intact. For centuries, then, a process of settling community problems amicably emerged at the local community level in the Philippines (see Vreeland, 1976).

Cohesive communities do exist elsewhere and can even be found as cultural oases within large urban areas. Yet, there still appears to be something special about the seclusion of naturally isolated islands. It is with the reality of island life that we must begin any discussion of Philippine culture, and certainly any examination of the nature of social control among Filipinos. Photo 1 shows a beach scene at the research site in Lanao del Norte, Mindanao as it appeared in 1997.

Some archaeological evidence (Zaide, 1990) and scattered historical accounts suggest that the seeds of communal life were already partially planted prior to the development of societies in what are now the Philippine islands. That is, the

Photo 1. Beach scene at research site in Lanao del Norte, Mindanao

islands were populated originally by people sailing from the Malay archipelago in boats [called *balanghais*] that held about fifty people. These distinct groups, tightly organized by kinship around a leader or captain, settled among the islands and atolls, forming communities that were called *barangays* [meaning community], a word probably derived from the Malay term *balanghais* [thus, "boat communities"]. During the more than three centuries of Spanish rule, the Malaysian term for community was phased out in favor of the Spanish word "barrio." In 1978, then president Ferdinand Marcos decreed a return to the official use of the early Tagalog term *barangay* as part of an effort to cast off the last vestiges of Spanish influence, a directive that appears to have been relatively successful. Today the expression *barangay* is the official political designation for community, although barrio can still be heard, especially in the rural areas of the provinces.

More recently, others have also shown keen interest in the neighborhood-based community structure referred to as the Philippine *barangay* system (Orendain, 1978; Silliman, 1985). The *barangay* system provides an organization of political boundaries at the submunicipal level, resulting in approximately 50,000 distinct communities spread throughout the nation. Other regions of the world have also structured their population into increasingly smaller political units—in particular Singapore, Japan, and Korea—but the Philippines appears to have carried the structuring of neighborhood boundaries to the extreme.

The average population of a *barangay* is 900 persons. These people may reside in a detached and isolated village, far removed from another people, or they may appear clustered together, with multiple *barangays* forming an urban base for a municipality or city. In a true sense then, no matter where you are in the Philippines, you are standing in a political boundary called a *barangay,* whether in a remote jungle or in the center of Manila. Thus, a rural village one would have called a barrio would now, at least technically, be referred to as a *barangay*. For example, what was barrio Santiago would now become *barangay* Santiago. If the earlier barrio was large enough, it might be subdivided into two or more *barangays*. Manila, a city of about 9 million people, comprises approximately 1,900 *barangays*. To complicate matters, even for local Filipinos, the political boundary called a *barangay* is actually subdivided into smaller units called *puroks,* which are often further split into even smaller units called *sitios*. These will be discussed more fully in Chapter 3.

A GOVERNMENT-IMPOSED COMMUNITY JUSTICE SYSTEM

In 1978, President Marcos signed a decree mandating that throughout the nation *barangay* captains attempt to solve all minor disputes at the neighborhood or village level. Specifically, disputants in cases that could, if taken to court, result in jail terms of thirty days or less, or fines of 200 pesos ($25 U.S. in 1978) or less, must meet with the village captain, where an informal process of amicable settlement would be initiated. The time-tested and casual process of amicable settlement became officially labeled *"barangay* justice," or *Katarungang Pambarangay* [community justice] in the national language of Pilipino [Tagalog].

In essence, with the stroke of a pen, the captain, already wielding formidable informal influence and authority at the village level, was made, at least administratively, a functionary of higher government. Hence, in the Philippines, a system was set on course that appears to have the potential, if not the effect, of formalizing what had been a rather pure informal and traditional process of dispute settlement. A legal mandate that two persons in dispute are obliged to attempt to solve their civil or criminal altercation informally, rather than having the immediate option of going directly to a formal court is rare around the world. Some wonder whether the formalizing of a traditionally informal process was an example of a totalitarian administration trying to include the settlement of minor neighborhood disputes under the umbrella of a strong martial-law-government regime. That is, it is unclear if the Marcos administration was purposefully establishing a local network of government-controlled dispute-settlement patterns in order to keep closer tabs on the citizenry, or if tighter control was just part of an ongoing trend in the Philippines.

A second argument advanced to explain the 1978 presidential decree is that the Philippine government reasoned that by requiring the captain to hear and, hopefully, resolve minor disputes within the *barangays,* and outside town and city courts, a great deal of congestion would be eliminated from the formal judicial system. Minor thefts and assaults could then be relegated to the neighborhood and would most likely not reach higher court. This second argument has some appeal to many nations, including the United States, seeking to lessen the burden of crowded courts (Berger, 1982).

Notwithstanding the political motives of the Marcos administration in restructuring local justice processing, researchers stilll need to identify more clearly the way the new system alters basic social interaction patterns within the community. Several questions arise. First, how did the system of dispute settlement, as mandated in 1978, modify the justice process with regard to the daily life of Filipinos at the *barangay* level? For example, what were the characteristics of the various groups and the roles that comprised the new *barangay* organization and through which disputes were then processed? Second, what indications, if any, suggest that a tendency persists for the local villagers to resist change and to revert to the informal patterns of dispute settlement traditional to pre-martial law? The following procedures of settling disputes according to the new national model were first revealed to the author during field work in 1980 in the province of Nueva Ecija [Central Luzon] in several *barangays* just outside of the town of Muñoz. The system mandated by presidential decree was officially established throughout the islands. In the 1990s, remnants of the system can still be found in some of the more rural regions of the country.

BARANGAY JUSTICE PROCEDURES

Prior to the 1978 decree establishing a new form of village justice, two basic alternative methods of dispute processing were available to local citizens. First was the traditional, and relatively informal, system of amicable settlement. This process was generally implemented by the captains, who used their influence in relation to the disputing parties to persuade the conflicting members to desist in feelings of hostility toward one another. Such a process of mediation or reconciliation, fostered between the aggrieved parties, was indispensable if community harmony were to be maintained, especially in rural settings where victims and offenders remained in close contact with each other and stayed in the same community. The focus of the captain was not on a determination of guilt but more on ways in which the disputants could resolve their differences.

A second alternative method of dispute processing was available to local citizens through the town or city court. The formal judicial setting, patterned, in part, after the U.S. court system, was characterized by a trial judge who heard testimony from the accuser and the defendant [respondent]. Adversarial proceedings between attorneys were common. The aim of the judge was essentially to determine the guilt or innocence of the accused and to pronounce sentence. To date, no formal trial-by-jury system exists in the Philippines.

Whereas the process of amicable settlement was typically resolved quickly and informally, the court case involved formal proceedings that were often time-consuming, expensive, and stigmatizing to one or both parties by leaving a permanent court record. Both judicial processes persist today in Nueva Ecija and throughout all provinces, and continue to be alternatives available to local citizens pursuing justice. However, what is now observed at the *barangay* level is a third alternative method of dispute resolution, which synthesizes the informal process of amicable settlement and the formal court (Pe & Tadiar, 1979).

Although the captain retains the initial role of mediator or persuader for disputants to reach amicable settlement, the post-1978 system of *barangay* justice appears to have the effect of superimposing upon the amicable-settlement process a more elaborate set of judicial procedures. The new rules extend the informal process beyond the single role of the captain and officially involve other *barangay* members, who make further efforts to ensure that an out-of-court agreement is reached when the captain, acting alone, is unsuccessful. At the heart of the organization of justice at the *barangay* level is the *Lupon ng Tagapayapa* [i.e., a group of persons who initiate peace and order]. The *lupon* comprises a minimum of ten up to a maximum of twenty *barangay* citizens, appointed for two-year terms. Any willing and mature citizen, not expressly disqualified by law [for example, an ex-felon], may be considered as a potential appointee by the captain, who also serves as the *lupon* chairperson.

When a petty crime or dispute arises in the village, and is not successfully resolved through amicable settlement within fifteen days by the *barangay* captain, the *lupon* assembly may be activated. The disputing parties are all presented with a list of *lupon* members by the captain, and are directed to choose three members who will act as a subcommittee of the *lupon* to hear their individual complaints. The disputants choose the three-member panel through a process of alternatively removing one name at a time from the *lupon* membership until only three members remain. Should a stalemate occur as to the third and final member, the captain will choose a member to complete the panel. The resulting subcommittee, referred to as the *Pangkat ng Tagapagkasundo* [i.e., "committee which initiates arbitration"], is charged with hearing and judging the grievances of both parties. At this point the *pangkat* members attempt one last time to rekindle the prior frustrated attempts of the captain to pressure the disputing citizens to reconcile.

The functional importance of the *pangkat* as an extension of the amicable-settlement process is seen in the relationship between the committee members and the disputants. The three members are most often of the same village as the accuser and respondent, are frequently friends or relatives of one or both parties, and can thus exert substantial power of persuasion over their behavior. This is especially true since the *lupon* members represent the more established and influential elders of the community. The original *barangay* justice philosophy argued that friends or kin of the disputing parties might serve as *lupon* members and be able to encourage reconciliation better than would strangers or mere acquaintances. However, the "striking off" process tends to negate this, in that one disputant would obviously remove a *lupon* member who is closely related or sympathetic to the opposing party. A disputant who resides outside the *barangay* may not know the *lupon* members and would therefore be at a disadvantage, apparently a price one must pay for getting into trouble in another's territory.

The *pangkat* has the authority to move from mediation to arbitration and to levy penalties upon the party judged to be at fault. The three-person subcommittee will listen to each dispute in private. After both sides are heard, the *pangkat* may convene and decide whether to accept the explanation of the accuser or the respondent. If a final arbitration is necessary, and all attempts at reconciliation fail, then a majority vote of the *pangkat* will decide the dispute. Penalties are often enacted in the form of restitution and can be in the form of money, property, or labor. Chicken stealing, for example, was rather common in the *barangays*, and often a villager would have to repay the aggrieved party a chicken for the one stolen, plus the bonus of a second chicken. Regarding minor assaults, one or both parties of a dispute may be required to apologize to all residents within earshot of the disturbance. Even in cases that suggest fault of one party or the other, the overriding concern is on re-establishing good-will between conflicting residents. However, once the disputants agree on a *pangkat*, any decision is final. Disputants may appeal a case to a formal town court, but they must be able to prove that they were the victims of coercion or threat. Should a case not be resolved by a *pangkat* decision, it may be taken before the municipal or city court by the captain.

It would be very rare that a *pangkat* would not carry out its official duty. Moreover, town judges were known to quickly throw petty cases back to the *barangay* for settlement, occasionally leaving disputants in limbo. Highly assertive and respected captains would generally make every effort to see that disputes were resolved within the *barangay*. To have many conflicting citizens leave the *barangay* unsatisfied would be a sign of a weak captain, and captains were elected by popular vote.

EFFECTIVENESS OF *BARANGAY* JUSTICE

The official government rationale for the *barangay* justice system was to provide a "paralegal alternative" for the resolution of personal disputes. Various secondary justifications include speedy dispensation of justice, the alleviation of crowded court dockets, and increased monetary savings. Furthermore, the Bureau of Local Government Supervision argues that the paralegal system of *barangay* justice fosters a perpetuation of the honored Philippine tradition of settling disputes amicably for the maintenance of peace and harmony (Ministry of Justice, 1983).

In an astute demonstration of success, the Philippine government published a multicolored brochure with charts and tables asserting that the new system of dispute resolution was a resounding success. Between 1978 and 1983, a total of 179,398 disputes were brought for action to some 41,411 *Lupon ng Tagapayapa*—representing over 800,000 members in *barangays* all over the nation (Ministry of Justice, 1983). Of these *lupon* cases, 87.25 percent [156,527] were reported as amicably solved, and 5.11 percent [9,167] were pending in various *lupons* in 1983. The remaining 7.64 percent [13,704] were forwarded to the courts. Considering the nation had a backlog of 450,000 court cases in 1983, the system of *barangay* justice did, in fact, appear to rid the courts of a substantial additional burden. A savings in court costs of 155,900,892 pesos [about $12 million U.S.] was reported in 1983, compared to a five-year cost of only 14 million pesos [about $1 million U.S.] for the implementation of the *barangay* justice program.

POINTS OF CONCEPTUAL CONFUSION

It appears likely that the *barangay* justice organization, initially set up in 1978, has been variously accepted around the islands and that the more modern urban centers depend less on traditional modes of dispute settlement than in the hinterlands and outlying islands. In the research settings, this author found a number of ideological stumbling blocks for the smooth acceptance of the formally imposed government procedures. Rural Filipinos tended to prefer more traditional pathways to justice.

Formality Versus Informality

In reference to interpersonal disputes, the Filipino has traditionally chosen informality over formality. The rule seems to be that only as a last resort should one go before a formal town judge. With the inception of the 1978 decree requiring the initiation of out-of-court dispute settlements, several features appear at the village level which tend to give the amicable-settlement process an air of formality. Prior to 1978, barrio residents would resolve their interpersonal grievances with the aid of their captain without much regard for a specific setting. A group might convene in someone's backyard, at a kitchen table, or in a local beer parlor in order to iron out differences between disputants. A favorite gathering place during the heat of the day was under banana trees, which bordered the rice fields of the villages just outside the town of Muñoz.

During the first five years of the *barangay* justice program, the Ministry of Local Government spent 2.5 million pesos to construct in each *barangay* small concrete buildings designated as *barangay* justice halls (see Photo 2). Although the villagers dutifully erected the halls, they were rarely used for processing disputes and crimes and, by 1985, weeds had overgrown the small rectangular-shaped buildings at the research sites. By 1997, many of the *barangay* halls were painted and carefully maintained, although their function was more as health and recreational centers than for holding court. The national government also printed and distributed the rules and regulations regarding how disputes should be processed. However, given the diversity of Philippine languages and dialects, getting the printed word to the people was difficult. Over 12 million pesos were reportedly designated for this purpose.

As early as 1980, one could find the booklets in many homes of *barangay* families (see Ministry of Justice, 1983; cf. Orendain, 1979). Captains, *lupon* members, and other influential citizens would likely have a copy or two of the regulations, sometimes in several dialects. Even in 1980, however, villagers interviewed were quick to offer as a gift a copy of the *barangay* justice philosophy

Photo 2. Small town *barangay* hall above drug store

and regulations. The comment "We do not need it" was regularly heard. A sense of its uselessness was suggested in the way the booklet was flipped on a table. The publication of *barangay* justice regulations also included numerous pen-and-ink sketches or artist's renderings of the interior of *barangay* justice halls. A formally styled courtroom arena was illustrated with a male judge seated behind the bench, flag draped in the corner of the room, and opposing tables for accuser and respondent. Drawings of emotionally charged disputants were depicted. Interestingly, the original *barangay* justice philosophy disapproved of the use of lawyers in the new amicable-settlement process, suggesting it would be better to keep legal jargon and argument clear of the court. However, the Ministry of Justice felt the villagers should be trained by outsiders in the art of mediation and dispute settlement. This seems to be an indirect way of patronizing locals to suit the government's objective. After all, the villagers had settled disputes locally for generations prior to the 1978 mandate. No cases of locals being trained in mediation were ever reported. It was not surprising that lawyers interviewed in Lanao del Norte were not happy with the *barangay* justice philosophy, which discouraged formal legal representation.

Although a reported purpose of the national government was to perpetuate informal dispute processing, in reality the printed regulations, along with the physical structures of *barangay* halls, gave the appearance of a formalization of community dispute-resolution patterns. In one *barangay* visited during the course of the research, a debate arose as to the appropriateness of uniforms for *barangay* captains, which would have made the captain look more like a sheriff or town police officer. As of 1997, no case of uniformed captains has been reported. To the extent that these formalizing features were not readily or fully accepted, the Filipino villager tended to favor informal settlement of disputes.

Ignoring the Rules

Although the captain is given fifteen days to persuade disputants to reconcile, on occasion captains do not strictly follow the *barangay* justice rule book. For example, there is some leeway as to when the captain begins counting the fifteen days. Captains may know of a grievance that has been brewing for some time and may informally act on the problem by using their powers of influence prior to the dispute being formally processed. More often, captains may talk to their compatriots, who may happen to be *lupon* members, and request their aid in helping resolve a particular dispute. This is especially true when several *lupon* members are known to be friends or relatives of one or both disputants, and who may be in a position to exert pressure based on kinship obligation unavailable the captain. Such a common-sense maneuver may or may not take place within the fifteen-day period. Thus, the captain is seen as avoiding use of the more official *lupon* and *pangkat* process. Should one of the disputing parties be from outside the *barangay*, it is much more likely that the case would be handled by the *lupon* and *pangkat* procedure, and not resolved through mediation by the captain (for similar patterns see Ynvessen, 1978; cf. Todd, 1978). If *barangay* captains are going to preserve their own credibility as strong and efficient leaders, they must be able to resolve disputes. The statement "A good captain is able to take care of things" was commonly heard.

Setting a fixed and seemingly arbitrary time limit of fifteen days for the captain to either generate an amicable settlement or turn the case over to the *lupon* undermines the captain's use of non-action. However, some disputes within a neighborhood or community are best dealt with by doing nothing. In the eyes of the captain, non-action may be deemed the best course—that is, to let things cool down. In many cases, such a cooling-off period may certainly extend beyond the fifteen days.

Given the likelihood of rule-bending by captains, it makes sense to assume that the statistics on the number of amicable settlements reached through the *lupon* structure are misleading at best. In fact, the records of the Ministry of Local Government clearly do not refer to the number of disputes resolved through a *pangkat*. When the data show extreme success of the *barangay* justice program through use of the *lupon* [i.e., 87 percent of cases resolved amicably], this can be interpreted as a combination of cases handled by the more formal *pangkat* structure and an unknown proportion of the cases actually resolved very informally by simply calling on friends of lupon members. This would distort the official data as to the effectiveness of the 1978 *barangay* justice program.

Guilt versus Non-Guilt

According to the *barangay* justice philosophy, the captain and *lupon* are not supposed to be directly concerned with determining the guilt of one party or another engaged in a dispute, but with persuading the disputing parties to "get along with one other," even if it is simply a matter of "peacefully agreeing to disagree." In reality, interpersonal conflicts often return to the basic question of whether or not one individual is at fault, or more at fault than another. Is one of the parties lying? To reach the truth, the captain and members of the *lupon* or *pangkat* frequently conduct fact-finding and evidence-gathering missions. This runs counter to official *barangay* justice policy, which strongly urges *barangay* officials to be mediators first and arbiters last. The early juvenile court philosophy in the United States maintained a similar stance toward child offenders. Do not be concerned with determining children's guilt but with how to help those children solve whatever personal or social-adjustment problems they may have. This ideal soon gave way to the immediate dilemma of fact-finding and determining guilt (Platt, 1969). Also, one must keep in mind that as soon as a guilt-orientation becomes evident, it is most likely that one of the parties in dispute will remain angry after the arbitration process. Such a "win-lose" game does little to maintain harmony in the village compared to the earlier mediational process which often resulted in "win-win" outcomes between disputing parties.

In the Philippine research setting, *lupon* members typically engage in some detective work prior to making a final decision. The captain and *lupon* members feel free to ask questions of any witnesses in the *barangay*. Also, *lupon* members may discuss the case with members of the village security force. This strictly informal group of citizens operates much like a neighborhood watch group, and often provides an information link between village disputants and the captain or lupon.

Evolution of a Jury

Although a jury is not discussed in the Philippine Constitution, and does not appear in formal judicial proceedings, the elements of a jury system are found, even if only in embryonic form, in the *lupon* and *pangkat*. In theory, if not in fact, the *Lupon ng Tagapayapa* forms a jury pool with the subsequent three-person *pangkat* representing the jury, although admittedly small. Given the historic absence of jury hearings in the Philippines, the establishment of a *lupon* and *pangkat* during the height of martial law seems ironic. These observations of *barangay* justice were made at distinctly different times in the recent era of Philippine politics. During the initial field trip to Central Luzon in 1980, the new community-justice procedures were still being implemented, and some rural residents were still unfamiliar with *barangay* justice law, but many seemed anxious to have an opportunity to be involved in village operations and decision making. The *barangay tanod*, for example, all carried cards proudly identifying themselves as official members of the security force. The new law allowed an increasing number of locals to have a more active voice in the community.

In 1985, just prior to the fall of Marcos, local affairs and justice processing were overshadowed by national politics. The military either united with city and town police or, in as many instances, military and municipal police were antagonistic toward each other. Consequently, the *barangay* justice system could not be easily observed in its pure state. In the *barangays* studied, the *barangay* justice process slowed down in the later years of the Marcos regime for one of two reasons: fear of locals to take any kind of active stand, or a disenchantment of many local leaders with anything associated with higher levels of government.

These findings nevertheless suggest a tendency to resist the impersonal aspects of *barangay* justice law. Captains were able to retain a sense of autonomy by bending rules to suit village-level needs rather than explicitly following national guidelines. The motives underlying the *barangay* justice law are murky. What is clear is that if officials of the Marcos regime were prompted by a wish to keep tabs on local affairs [i.e., crime and disputes] through the monthly *lupon* reports to Manila, they were only partially successful. In fact, the formalization of dispute processing through *barangay* justice law may have actually pushed the resolution of interpersonal conflicts underground to the sub-*barangay* neighborhood level. Dispute processing became increasingly informal.

What may be viewed as an implicit move by the autocratic martial-law government of 1978 to scrutinize local activity through the guise of *barangay* justice actually resulted in introducing democratic features of impartial juries at the village level. The subsequent Aquino and Ramos presidential administrations have retained a Mandatory Conciliation Act (ABA, 1986). However, it appears that the national government is giving less concern to publication of reports touting the extreme success of the program. In the southern Philippines, and particularly in the Mindanao research settings, the *barangay* justice procedures discussed here are rarely talked about. It may be that they are destined to fade from the scene entirely. The more important point is that the informal systems traditional to the Filipino are still alive and well. Chapter 2 will address a number of these more traditional systems.

Chapter 2

Peacemaking Filipino Style

T his chapter explores the relationship between self-help activity and village security networks in the Philippines. Two levels of inquiry are developed. First, we examine a variety of behavioral features, which underlie fundamental patterns of altruism seemingly widespread in the Philippines at the family and neighborhood levels. What is it about the Philippine sociocultural structure and Filipino individuality that fosters the emergence and remarkable durability of security-related self-help patterns? At this level, emphasis is on the manner in which familism, friendship, and other features of Philippine daily life generate good will and a corresponding condition of small-group and neighborhood security. A second level of scrutiny focuses on the apparent extension of altruism from family and friendship patterns to include an assortment of more structured and official styles of village-watch or vigilante-type organizations that have flourished in the Philippines in recent years. We take a look at how these more formalized self-help activities connect with official agencies of social control.

One might presume that the relationship between altruism and volunteer-type organizations is simple and direct, but is not the case. Reasons other than altruism may prompt the emergence of self-help organizations aimed at providing village security. Therefore, this chapter therefore attempts to untangle any confusion by responding to several categories of questions. First, what basic altruistic features are associated with Filipino life ways, and how do they informally provide security at the most local level? Indeed, does an altruistic tradition tend to thrive primarily within villages and rural barrios or does it extend into the more urban regions?

Second, what kind of activities comprise the more formally organized civilian-volunteer associations popular in the Philippines in recent years? Do these groups represent extensions of basic Filipino characteristics of good will toward one's neighbor, or do they stem from other factors such as a reaction to inadequate government social control? As the chapter unfolds, we begin to view volunteer-security patterns from different stages of localism by observing self-help activities in both rural and urban settings and from behavioral as well as organizational levels. As shown in Figure 2-1, culture and personality are important variables or axioms, which may be viewed as building blocks of behavior. Through social interaction, these elements coalesce and influence, or are expressed through, various levels of group activity. Separate discussions of each variable yields a clearer picture of altruistic and security-oriented activity in the *barangay*, whether at the individual family, neighborhood, or community level.

Figure 2–1 Social Structure and Village Security Systems

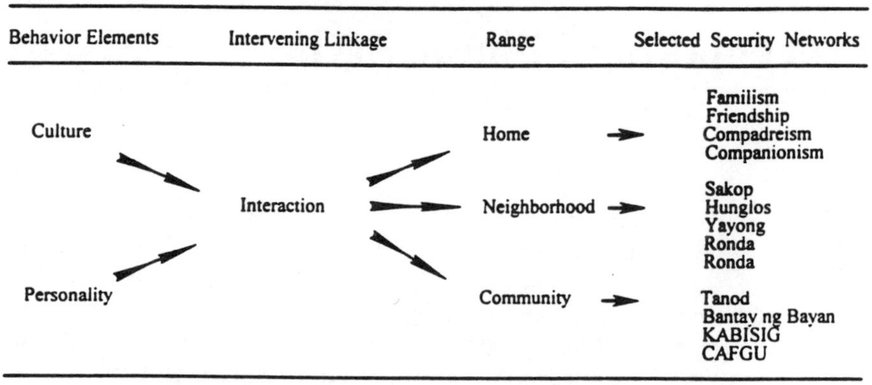

Behavior Elements	Intervening Linkage	Range	Selected Security Networks
Culture		Home	Familism Friendship Compadreism Companionism
	Interaction	Neighborhood	Sakop Hunglos Yayong Ronda Ronda
Personality		Community	Tanod Bantay ng Bayan KABISIG CAFGU

Source: Adapted from Bates and Harvey (1975), Nix and Bates (1962) and Austin (1989, 1991, 1995a)

CULTURE

By focusing on Philippine culture, a number of normative patterns may be identified which appear to underlie village-security efforts. At the most elementary level, these patterns are grounded in a sense of altruism that gives rise to self-help activities aimed at protecting the immediate family, but which occasionally extend outward to the larger neighborhood and community. These traditional patterns may be roughly categorized under familism, friendships, status obligations, and cooperative schemes.

Familism

Filipinos adhere to a rigid code of filial piety. Although devotion between siblings and between children and parents in Philippine society is clearly documented (Andres & Ilada-Andres, 1987), it is not widely understood that a by-product of such family cohesion is increased security against intruders. That is, the immediate household [often numerically large] automatically creates a formidable protective household shield (Sorokin, Zimmerman, & Galpin, 1930;

Smith and Zopf, 1970). This tendency is especially noticeable in the Philippines where a number of married or unmarried children remain attached to a large family unit, often until adult ages. Exceptions exist, but it was routinely found in Lanao del Norte and Nueva Ecija that even among adult children who marry and depart the immediate household, most remained within the same *barangay* or in a nearby village. Indeed, it was common for a father to build an extra room onto a house as new nuclear families were formed; small single-room dwellings would regularly be constructed a few feet from the main house for growing families. All the families would still convene for meals, even if some worked outside the house.

Such a stable pattern of familism and localism customarily includes an obligation for family members to assist each other in time of need. This pattern is more generally noted in economic terms, as when older siblings aid younger brothers or sisters with educational expenses or in finding employment, but the assistance may also take on more of a group territorial function, as when members convene to provide household protection. Family members can readily be mobilized should any member of the nuclear or extended family send a call for assistance.

During the summer of 1990, in one closely observed family, a father sent for his five sons to defend private property against squatters. The father, an employee of the provincial government, had rented a family-owned house and the renters refused to pay the rent or to leave the dwelling. The father had earlier attempted to resolve the matter through the courts, but the formal proceedings had bogged down and months had passed with no rent from the squatter family. Within hours the brothers convened, some from a nearby village. Several of them arrived with firearms, fully prepared for potential hostilities. The show of force effectively repelled the recalcitrant tenants. No questions were ever asked by the assisting brothers, who simply appeared to react in a reflex manner. Other neighbors, who were surely well aware of the confrontation, asked no questions and considered the situation a private matter. Since this case had already been filed in formal court with no timely resolution in sight, it was technically out of the hands of the *barangay* captain. In this particular case, the *barangay* captain was, in fact, informed of what was going to take place, and he allowed the show of force, even with the potential for hostilities. Cases of house or land squatting are among the toughest kinds of disputes to resolve.

In another case, a brother and sister combined forces, armed with firearms, to assure the protection of a third family member who was feared to be targeted for ambush by a local extremist group. The endangered family member was to give a speech on local politics, which might, it was feared, inflame the opposition groups. The family head asked a community leader about the safety of the potentially targeted relative, but it became clear that no official action was going to be taken to protect the family member. The brother and sister therefore positioned themselves in an automobile outside the hotel where they suspected an

ambush would most likely occur, and were readily prepared to shoot it out with
any ambushers or kidnapers.

Families in the research area still commonly rely upon family for protection
of the household or family members and would not likely depend solely upon
formal government agencies. Official control agencies are present, but in recent
years in such a politically unstable region, families place greater confidence and
trust in themselves for protection.

Friendships

If immediate kin provide the first order of household defense, it is quickly
followed by extra-familial relations in the form of a vast kumpadre/kumadre
system of obligatory relationships. Hundreds of years of Spanish occupation
gave rise to a pattern whereby adult men proudly boast of numerous kumpadre
relationships resulting from being requested to be a godfather by sponsoring a
birth or to officially witness a marriage (Arce, 1973; Hart, 1977). In either
case, the kumpadre, simply referred to as a "p're" by locals [or a "maré," in regards
to women], provides additional associates who could reliably be called upon
for assistance in family matters or problems including security.

A Filipino would typically choose as a kumpadre one considered as a close
friend, thus reinforcing an already existing friendship with religious sanction.
Moreover, the kumpadres are imbued with a set of obligations toward the
individual or family requesting the relationship. Such extra-familial affiliation
may result in eventual economic assistance, but on a daily basis the close and
continuous connection between the two adults united by the kumpadre bond is
immediately apparent. One will spend a substantial amount of time associated
with those who also happen to be kumpadres.

Even more widespread than the kumpadre relationship is the companion
concept. In the research setting, if not in Philippine culture generally, an adult
male or female should not be alone while going about everyday routine activity,
especially in recent times of heightened illegal activity and even terrorism.
The comment, "Where is your companion?" is commonly asked of
unaccompanied individuals. Locals, as well as outsiders, are expected to have
same-sex companions to provide either friendship or, for the outsider, to act
as guides. The value orientation against solitary activity tends to endorse
companionship and indirectly provides the individual with ready access to
assistance should any threat or danger occur.

Status Obligations

Filipinos are also bound together through status obligations. That is, every
work role carries with it a certain status or prestige. At the same time, the function
that one performs in the work world places one in a hierarchy of prestige with
others in the same occupation. Persons lower in the workplace are obliged to
assist those higher in the status hierarchy. The higher or more prestigious an

occupational position, the more persons one can potentially rely upon for assistance, either at the workplace or in the community at large. Such a network of duty-bound subordinates is referred to as the *sakop*.

The Filipino concept of *sakop* roughly translates as "in-group" and transcends kin, kumpadre, or friendship relationships. A *sakop* relationship originally pertained to persons subordinated to another, as in serfs to landlords. The feudal system maintained during the Spanish occupation required the lower-status subjects to provide household security to the landowner, should the need arise. All persons obligated to a landlord comprised the landlord's *sakop*. As a cultural artifact of the earlier pattern, one still hears the term *sakop* used today, but it generally encompasses various persons in one's employ who may be counted upon to provide assistance [typically outside the workplace]. Indeed, some respondents in the research area suggested that *sakop* now referred to all persons in a community considered as allies and with whom one would expect reciprocal obligations. *Sakop* members may indeed be friends or family, but the network extends beyond family and friends to include persons holding only an employment affiliation.

In the research setting, such work-related networks can represent a private security reserve associated with an individual in the community or *barangay*. Moreover, a sense of hierarchy prevails in that an individual could be considered the head of his own *sakop*. As in the case of kin and kumpadre networks, individuals who maintain large *sakops* are even more secure because they have at their beck and call a cadre of persons obligated to provide aid or protection.

Cooperative Schemes

At the level of community organization in Filipino culture is the tradition of neighborhood cooperation. Several examples of cooperative behavior persist throughout the provinces. In the research setting, a notable illustration of such cooperation is seen as villagers group together to assist a neighbor in moving a *nipa* [thatched] hut from one location to another; the process is referred to as *yayong* in the Cebuano language. This pattern is not as frequently observed as in the past, given the more permanent housing styles. However, the cultural ideal underlying *yayong* remains, and respondents in the research area are well aware of their responsibility to aid neighbors. After the work is completed, the person needing assistance is expected to provide food and drink as part of the festivities.

Rice farmers in *barangays* to the south of Iligan City report an equivalent cooperative spirit of assisting one another in the maintenance of crops, a system referred to in earlier years as *hunglos* and translated from the Cebuano as "one after the other" or "taking turns." A scheme such as *hunglos* was necessary because a lone farmer could not complete the time-consuming task of planting seedlings or harvesting. A plan evolved whereby farmers grouped together and quickly planted a single farm before the entire group moved on to the next farm. The pattern of *hunglos* has generally given way to one involving professional field workers, often women, who are paid according to the number of seedlings they plant [referred to as a *pakyaw* system]. Consequently, the work is rapid and a farm may be planted in a single day. The team of hired workers retains some of the same spirit of helping the individual farmer as the early *hunglos* system. Farmers today also voluntarily convene on other matters such as group efforts to save a crop from drought, insects, or rat infestation. Such a continuing example of interdependence, especially when it comes to rice farming, helps to create in the research setting a sense of neighborliness and unity. Each farmer knows well all the other farmers in the immediate vicinity [within about twenty farms]. The routine pattern of daily social life among rural villagers presumes a strong sense of community cooperation, although it is beneath the surface and not often the topic of conversation. A few local farmers had difficulty understanding why one would inquire or be interested in the reasons why farmers pull together to help maintain the rice farm.

A cooperative scheme more immediately associated with village security is found in the cultural tradition of the *ronda* [literally a "raid" or "round-up"] to investigate noise or commotion in the immediate area, perhaps associated with rowdy youth or drunken villagers. One local suggested that the word implies the encircling of another as if persons were linking arms and moving to encapsulate another. The local felt the word may derive from the English word "round." The *ronda* pertains to a group of close associates—or, more likely, family or friends—who gather after a hue and cry to investigate disruptions in the immediate neighborhood. One is tempted to draw an analogy between *ronda* and "posse," but they appear to differ in that the *ronda* would not commonly pursue or chase intruders in any organized manner but would more simply deal with localized skirmishes. The custom for community residents to mobilize in order to investigate neighborhood disorder persists, even if the label traditionally given to such a custom has begun to fade. It appears that the *ronda* is a phenomenon more common in the isolated barrio. In the city, neighbors are reportedly less apt to spontaneously pull together in order to investigate local disturbances. The existence of terrorists groups, which ordinarily make raids at night, stifles *ronda* activity. Thus, especially in the city, residents seem more inclined to peek out of their windows or from behind bushes to check out disturbances. On the other hand, in the rural area a *ronda* would more likely be successful because of the close proximity to kin.

PERSONALITY

Three other behavioral features also comprise part of Filipino culture, but because of their impact upon individual dispositions may be more clearly aligned with the element of personality. These are *utang kabubut-on, pakig-uban-uban,* and *ka-ulaw.*

Utang kabubut-on [literally, "inner-debt" in the Cebuano language] has been suggested as the principal cohesive force in the Philippine society (Vreeland,

1976). The Visayan term *utang kabubut-on* is in the Tagalog language referred to as *utang na loob*. Indeed, what is published about the Philippine concept of "inner debt" is generally cited under the more widespread Tagalog designation (Kaut, 1961:268, see also Jocano, 1966, Lawless, 1966). The issue of Filipino values continues to interest researchers (Hennig, 1983; Ligo-Ralph, 1990). A flurry of scholarly attention to personality issues and intrinsic values emerged in the 1960s, including the work of Frank Lynch and Alfonzo de Guzman (1970; cf. Hollnsteiner, 1963). Vitaliano R. Gorospe (1966) compiled a detailed bibliography on Filipino values, which should be consulted by interested researchers.

This behavior pattern refers to a system of reciprocal obligations whereby a villager is expected to repay a gift or, just as likely, a service. Such reciprocal exchange patterns instill a perpetual bond among in-group or *sakop* members, or even citizens outside the *sakop*. Many of the celebrated exchange systems among South Pacific societies incorporate more economic or market oriented principles, whereas the *utang kabubut-on* appears more generally to be a social debt one is obliged to repay. By combining sociological and anthropological works, Alvin Gouldner's early report (1960) provides a complete discussion of many reciprocal systems and forms a fitting basis for those interested in comparing the *utang kabubut-on* with other patterns. This particular feature directly pertains to "expected obligations," but it still carries with it a profound psychological and emotional connotation by providing the giver and the receiver with a sense of satisfaction and pride at being able to perform reciprocal obligations. If service or assistance is needed, one might approach another from whom a favor is due.

Even though the *utang kabubut-on* is well known for its economic and social functions, it has not been noted in the literature as an underlying means of enhancing security within the barrio. Nonetheless, if one owed a debt to a fellow villager who was in need of assistance, as in the form of a household or farm protection, the individual holding the inner-debt would very likely be obliged to assist in any reasonable way. Thus, it appears that *utang kabubut-on* may apply to mutual obligations to others in the style of protection as well as economic or other social debts. All respondents expressed vivid awareness of the responsibilities of *utang kabubut-on* in the research area, even from early childhood. According to longtime residents in the research area, the idea of intentionally stockpiling favors is inconsistent with the value of *utang kabubut-on*, but theoretically the possibility of such an action is not far-fetched. A custom of mutual obligation is not consciously pursued. That is, one would not purposely sit and target the people in the village with whom one would like to develop an *utang kabubut-on*. Nonetheless, the greater the number of debts owed to oneself, the greater the number of people who would likely assist, should an alarm be issued. Such a feature, which draws people together, logically enhances the security of a community. On occasion, a resident of the community may oppose such a pattern of mutual obligation. One respondent in the research setting was known to remark to her children, "Do not take any gifts or favors from anyone; we do not want to have an *utang kabubut-on* with them." It is plausible to presume that the tradition and disposition of *utang kabubut-on* would diminish with increasing transiency and urbanization. Indeed, elderly urbanites reared in farming communities emphatically claimed that *utang kabubut-on* is less prevalent in the towns and cities than it was in the barrio.

Pakig-uban-uban, on the other hand [literally meaning "to go along with" as in "camaraderie" in Cebuano] refers to the desire to avoid placing others in stressful or unpleasant situations. One who agrees to go with friends or to assist another, even though alternative activities may be more personally pleasurable, is said to have *pakikisama* [a Tagalog term in common usage throughout the Philippines]. Such a person can always be counted on for help, for example by neighbors, even when the request might involve something potentially disagreeable or even dangerous. This value orientation may seem dubious or absurd to one adhering to a strict individualist mentality. By contrast, the quality of readily agreeing to go along with another, or generally trying to maintain another's favor by being agreeable or compatible, even at the expense of one's own personal preferences, can also be identified as a most admirable trait. Such a fundamental quality of altruism serves to draw people together. In a society composed of thousands of distinct *barangays*, it is not surprising that a cohesive style of community—with high degrees of esprit de corp—has prevailed, if imperfectly so, at the village level. The benevolent trait of *pakikisama*, which is frequently characteristic of other isolated, rural or island communities, was undoubtedly accentuated in the Philippines by the over 300 years of monastic conditioning by Spanish Catholics. Although it cannot be fully developed here, the presumption that strict adherence to Catholic, or other pious creeds, would expectedly lead to *pakikisama* appears a logical conclusion. For example, the Protestant conviction would hold that *pakikisama* [surrendering personal appetites for the hungers of others or, in another sense, "self-sacrifice"] found its purest expression in Christ.

The affiliated concept of *ka-ulaw*—the Cebuano term for shame—relates indirectly to both *utang kabubut-on* and *pakig-uban-uban*. That is, one will be shamed and lose face before significant others should an obligatory debt go unreciprocated or should one fail to assist another who has previously rendered assistance. The motivation to remain untarnished by *ka-ulaw* strengthens the desire to extend assistance without it being requested and to offer aid when asked. *Ka-ulaw* [or *kahiya-an* in the Tagalog] is the flip side of *utang kabubut-on* and *pakig-uban-uban*. To a distressed neighbor in need of assistance, a wide assortment of behavioral traditions binds citizens together and thus creates an interactional protective network. If kin are unavailable, one's kumpadres can be summoned. If these mechanisms cannot be mobilized, one might call upon *sakop* members, or, indeed, rely upon an earlier *utang kabubut-on*. One may find it necessary as a last resort to place faith in the good nature of community members, their *pakig-uban-uban* and *ka-ulaw*. It is worth reiterating that respondents in the research area did not ponder or consider the array of self-help mechanisms in any premeditated way. That is, only from a distance, and perhaps by an outsider, does it appear to be the case that troubled villagers would have, at least potentially, a wide range of support strategies. The issue of which mode of self-help is to be mobilized first, or in what order, is yet to be fully addressed.

These three complex moral imperatives persist in Lanao del Norte, and reportedly throughout the nation, and clearly provide a behavioral base upon which more structured self-help security networks may be built. The cultural and personality features provide a fertile sociocultural foundation for the emergence of self-help groups at the *barangay* levels. Three styles of more formally structured citizen-based volunteer patterns were observed in the Lanao del Norte region and deserve elaboration: the *tanod*, the *Bantay ng Bayan*, and the CAFGU.

The *barangay tanod*, simply referred to in the research areas of Nueva Ecija and Lanao del Norte and throughout most of the Philippines as the *tanod* [translated as "guard" from the Tagalog] pertains to a group of male citizens charged with keeping watch, generally at night, over the *barangay*. The *barangay* captain appoints a chief of the *tanod* who, in turn, selects from a group of volunteers approximately ten men—trusted individuals—to perform the task of walking guard in the village. Although it remains to be more fully explored, the *tanod* does not appear to maintain a rigid social structure but is rather loosely organized. *Tanod* members, having been reared in the same village, usually know each other from childhood.

In rural settings, the *tanod* does not generally walk scheduled patrols; instead, *tanod* members casually station themselves at strategic places in the *barangay*, often favorite drinking establishments. On occasion, the guard also takes part in drinking. The *tanod* are not thought of as police officers, wear no uniforms, and do not commonly carry weapons, but it is to them that the villagers customarily turn should a fellow drinker become unruly or should a brawl erupt. Indeed, when asked what the *tanod* does, respondents smile and say "Take care of drunks." This is no small task in the barrio, with so many unemployed and underemployed people easing their depression through alcohol [often via *tuba*, an inexpensive liquor distilled from coconut tree sap]. A number of Manila *barangays* use the *tanod* members to assist police in directing traffic on the secondary streets. After a decade of marginal acceptance, the *tanod* is now viewed as a legitimate, government-authorized organization. As a result, there is now an assembly of individuals, even if ambiguously organized in rural areas, to be initially called upon in the event of a neighborhood disturbance. The *tanod* member would generally be expected to deal with conflict only until more formal control agencies arrive [if necessary, the *barangay* captain, municipal police, etc].

Operating within the same villages and towns as the *tanod* is a more recently organized "self-help" styled security force called the *Bantay ng Bayan* [Tagalog for "watch of the country"]. This organization emerged in the research setting of Lanao del Norte about 1988 as a network of local community-minded citizens who also had access to two-way radio communications. With the growing accessibility of small, hand-held radio transceivers, citizens at the sub-*barangay* neighborhood level have organized themselves into a radio net that now reportedly extends throughout the Philippines. Almost overnight, vigilante groups, which had earlier depended upon coconut tree climbers tapping messages on coconuts with bolos, now rely upon sophisticated high-frequency communications equipment. Very few accounts attest to the role of the coconut tree climber as a gatherer and transmitter of intelligence-type information, but locals are well aware of their special tree-top advantage. During outbreaks of terrorism, some of the climbers volunteered as outpost observers and provided information to local vigilante groups or occasionally to military units [see Chapter 6 on vigilante activity for more detail].

The extensive dependence on modern technology has been dramatic and many of the affluent private citizens can now be seen with a walkie-talkie-type radio fastened to their belts. Citizen applicants to the *Bantay ng Bayan* must pass radio examinations and also undergo screening by police and military officials to ensure loyalty to the government. A municipality might provide up to six transceivers, but membership in the *Bantay ng Bayan* generally requires one to supply the radio, excluding all but the relatively well-to-do. Some trusted non-radio owners may be seen accompanying regular members. As in all countries, one can acquire a hand-held radio transceiver and go on the air without a license, thus pirating the airwaves. This practice is also widespread in the Philippines, where enforcement of such regulations in rural areas would be hopeless. Supposedly, the members of the *Bantay ng Bayan* abide by the regulations. Police and military units assigned to the research area maintain close ties with the radio net although it clearly remains citizen controlled. In some instances a municipality may provide a motor vehicle for *Bantay ng Bayan* use as well as a base radio station. Military operations in the region may also include several *Bantay ng Bayan* operators positioned in military vehicles sidebyside with official personnel. The electronic self-help movement continues to expand in popularity and remains strongly dependent upon unpaid volunteers interested only in increased local security. News reports attest to the success of the *Bantay ng Bayan* in solving inter-*barangay* crimes such as "carnapping" (Padilia, 1989).

A third organizational style, also composed of civilian volunteers, is the CAFGU [Civilian Army Force Geographic Unit]. The CAFGU replaced the earlier Civilian Home Defense Force [CHDF] around 1988. Indeed, the CHDF was itself an outgrowth of the even earlier Barrio Defense Force, a neighborhood-watch system analogous to todays *barangay tanod*. Although the CHDF was quite popular, its casual organization allowed for corruption and inconsistency in function. It occasionally operated more as a *barangay*-level, violence-prone, vigilante force and caused some embarrassment at the national level (Jones, 1987a; cf. Serrill, 1987; Austin, 1988). The new CAFGU is more of a civilian-oriented military auxiliary. Citizen volunteers are now screened and trained by the

Philippine Army and receive a small allowance. CAFGU members nonetheless remain tied to local *barangays*, more as reserve units, and continue to uphold civilian jobs, including farming. When activated, they carry high-powered rifles and occasionally wear fatigue-type uniforms. Respondents noted that the CAFGU volunteers were used as point troops ahead of regular army personnel in communist rebel areas. CAFGU volunteers reportedly know the local, rural areas better than the regular army. Another explanation given by the locals was that the CAFGU volunteers were believers in, and wearers of, protective amulets [*anting-anting* in Cebuano], which some believed would even repel bullets. Nonetheless, the success of the Philippine military in countering rebel attacks now appears to be due, in part, to the willingness of locals to volunteer for the civilian army force. Each *barangay* carries up to six CAFGU volunteers, providing a sizable cadre throughout a province. CAFGU members, who also know local *tanod* members, patrol in hot-spot areas at night, relieving—if not replacing—the *tanod*. A critique of the history of the CAFGU, and of several of these comments about the volunteers, can be found in Nadeau and Suminguit (1996; cf. Austin, 1995a).

This chapter followed two levels of exploration. First, it examined several traditional ways Filipino culture and personality patterns set the stage for the emergence of volunteerism and altruistic convictions. Second, we have described a variety of more official self-help groups in what appears to be an extension of benevolent principles. In several cases, these more official groups reportedly evolved in recent years at the neighborhood level in response to political and religious terrorism. By reviewing accounts of longtime residents of Lanao del Norte, examples of transitional and formalizing volunteer activities have been described. Arguably, some of the same traditions that grew out of natural and selfless responses to maintain harmony and close neighborhood ties—familism, friendship, and the like—now underlie the success of more structured voluntary security networks in the community. It may be that the CAFGU is the least altruistic and the most mercenary-like. As in many parts of the world, people join police forces for many reasons, some because they genuinely want to assist their fellow community members, while others seek to exert authority over others.

At the most rural level, one finds the most consistent presence of all styles of self-help. The integrative forces of familism and friendship are notable, as are the *ronda* and *sakop*. Moreover, with the relative absence of official police, one finds the *tanod* to be intact and working in unison with the *Bantay ng Bayan* [radio net]. The CAFGU is apt to be consistently identifiable in the more rural areas than in the towns and city. Simply stated, the rural areas of the province are considered more dangerous than the town or city because the terrorist-prone, extremist groups tend to hide out in the hinterlands. It is also clear that in the densely populated regions of Lanao del Norte, the *ronda* and *tanod* have all but disappeared, their function having been replaced by the local law-enforcement agencies. In the more semi-rural *barangays*, formal police officers rarely appear, unless purposely summoned. A *Bantay ng Bayan* appears to be well known and considered quite functional and necessary given the distance from inner-city police. Furthermore, a *tanod* and even CAFGU may likely become part of the local scene in the semi-rural regions. While countless people hang about the downtown area of Iligan City, especially at night, the multitudes appear less orderly than those smaller and more familiar groupings at neighborhood gathering places. The formal and official police agencies patrol the inner city, but the outlying areas, and surely the rural regions, increasingly rely upon citizen volunteers.

Citizen-oriented volunteer groups persist at varying levels of influence. The *tanod*, for example, remains strictly attached to the *barangay*, and any connection to government is indirect through the locally elected *barangay* captain. The position and function of the *barangay* captain is of fundamental importance to any community-based self-help activity. Since captains are elected community leaders, known by all in the area and invariably most popular citizens, they are in touch with all activities of the community. As representatives to municipal, city, and provincial government, captains can play an integral part in any self-help movement. Officially, captains appoint a chief of the *barangay* tanod who would, without question, be a trusted associate.

Whereas the *Bantay ng Bayan* originated at the most local level and continues to operate within the smallest barrio, it is interconnected by radio networks to other, more distant, civilian operatives of the province. The *Bantay ng Bayan* of one village would not, however, normally maintain contact with similar groups beyond the immediate province. In the more rural sections of the research area, the hand-held radio net is limited by low wattage to maintaining its security functions with Illigan City, the province's only major urban area. Another civilian-operated radio network would take effect in an adjacent province. With the ascent of the *Bantay ng Bayan*, the earlier and more notoriously renegade vigilante movements common in Mindanao several years earlier (1970s to mid-1980s) have radically diminished or disappeared entirely.

The Civilian Army Force Geographic Unit [CAFGU] is unquestionably tied more securely to government military operations. Yet, CAFGU volunteers preserve their home base in the barrios while at the beck and call of outside controls. Moreover, the CAFGU stands as a voluntary community group that, still maintains military links throughout the islands to all provinces. Even so, a local CAFGU unit would rarely serve far from its home base. Keep in mind that even the CAFGU must be considered an example of self-help social control, even if imperfectly so. CAFGU forces represent a more formal organizational style than any of the other local self-help groups. Respondents in the research area claim that CAFGU members are provided with some meager training by the military, receive a modest stipend, and wear fatigue-type uniforms. Moreover, locals are quick to add that the CAFGU represent honorable citizens and are perhaps the bravest of the soldiers. In U.S. history, a counterpart to the CAFGU appears to be the scouts who volunteered to go ahead of the military, assisting in clearing a path for the regular troops. The scouts were often reared in the local area, knew many of the residents, as well as the territory, and were quite effective in battle.

On occasion, local self-help campaigns receive a stimulus from national leaders, as illustrated by the *Kabisig* ["linking-arms" in Tagalog] movement. Toward the waning months of President Corazon Aquino's administration, she rather boldly denounced the "traditional politicians" [*trapos*] who were reluctant to approve monies for *barangay* social programs. The abbreviation *trapos* was used by Aquino to mock the hard-nosed conservative politicians she viewed as outdated. *Trapos* is also the Tagalog word for "rags," and thus a slap in the face to the old-time elected officials. The term is now widely used in political commentary and cartoons. Rather than fight Congress, she established a funding program from her own office and bypassed traditional political authorization. The *Kabisig* funds were to be used as seed money to support local civic organizations that were eager to help clean up neighborhoods, sponsor employment opportunities, and volunteer to indirectly provide greater security to local regions hard hit by communist insurgency and religious conflicts. The *Kabisig* people's movement connects the national government to local self-help initiatives and appears to have remained healthy (Jimenez-Magsanae, 1993; Danao, 1997; De La Cruz, 1997) into the administration of President Fidel V. Ramos. Distinct civilian security networks layered one on top of the other, are now found in the research area, albeit with varying geographic scopes and disparate links to formal government control.

Chapter 3 will explore several unexpected features of Filipino society—outside the realm of culture and personality—which tend to result in increased social control.

Chapter 3

Unexpected Dimensions of Social Control

Whereas culture and personality remain critical features that combine to reflect the behavior of people or groups, one feature sometimes neglected is "situation." The actual geographic, demographic, or general environmental surroundings in which culture and personality interact to trigger a behavioral outcome are often ignored [see Bates & Harvey, 1975, for a detailed review of situational variables]. We note in this chapter that situational features of the Filipino landscape frequently create a condition of security, even if that happens purely accidentally or unintentionally. The field notes describe five situational features that clearly supplement the unofficial or informal processing of grievances—and sometimes crimes—in the research settings.

A CLOSER LOOK AT *BARANGAY* ORGANIZATION

Further evidence of the Filipino's pattern of avoiding formality is revealed by probing more deeply into the social structure of the *barangay*. Whereas the *barangay* is often referred to as the smallest political entity or boundary, this is not entirely true. Perhaps so from the perspective of national government officials, and in their quest for official reports, but in fact, the *barangay* is further sub-divided into what are called *puroks* [roughly translated from the Tagalog as "clusters of houses"]. A *purok* might represent in a small *barangay* a subdivision of twenty to thirty households, and a *barangay* may comprise many *puroks*. Some large-city *barangays* may have extensive *puroks* that are themselves larger than some rural *barangays*. Some *puroks* may be neatly organized and immediately contiguous to another *purok*. Thus, as you walk along a street in a town, you might pass every two or three blocks a permanently placed placard announcing which *purok* you are entering. To complicate matters, some *puroks* are distantly separated or isolated from each other by natural boundaries—mountain

Photo 3. Bulletin board at entry of *barangay*

ridges, valleys, rivers, farmlands, and the like—and form relatively disconnected
or distinct communities. When such a cluster of households is detached from the
more populated center of the *barangay*, it is referred to as a *sitio* or *sityo* [meaning
"site" or "place" in Cebuano]. If one comes upon a cluster of houses or a detached
hamlet when walking down a country road, one may have to inquire if it is a self-
contained *purok* or a part of a nearby *purok*, and to which *barangay* the cluster
of homes belongs. Photo 3 shows a bulletin board listing *barangay* officers.

Importantly, a *purok* or *sitio* typically maintains a local political organization
separate from the larger *barangay* political organization. The *purok* organization
is highly structured, with elected officers and neighborhood meetings held at least
once a month or when needed. The *purok* is concerned with all social problems or
issues of interest to the neighborhood, including issues of education, sanitation,
water supplies, recreation, and peace and order. In other words, a venue is
available for any resident to bring a concern to the *purok* without having to go
before the larger *barangay* organization.

This is a simple but important point regarding informal social control. All
citizens know to which *sitio, purok*, or *barangay* they belong. The significance
of the clearly defined boundaries is that every resident is linked to a community of
citizens that paves the way for, or optimizes cooperation and participation in, the
numerous voluntary self-help programs for which Filipinos are well known. Stated
in proposition form, *Tight connective boundaries of a community facilitate close
identification of citizenry and informal social control*. Although the point is a
subtle one, attempts to process interpersonal conflicts through private, social

networks and third-party mediators are met with situations whereby villagers know each other—likely from distant kinship affiliations—and as a rule acknowledge or appreciate the unofficial or, at times, quasi-official roles held by *sitio* or *purok* officers. First, however, and fundamental to an efficient process of informal justice, is the linkage of all residents into a cohesive core of citizens. Such a connective web, as provided by *barangay, purok*, and *sitio* organizational boundaries, joins citizens—no matter how isolated—and provides a path for the promotion of cooperation.

A dilemma often voiced in more urban nations such as the United States is that people residing in the same immediate neighborhood are strangers. Until a true neighborhood is created, possibly by a community organization, attempts for crime prevention and security programs at the most local level will likely collapse. A community is necessary in order for a citizen-based program to succeed. A first step toward community building is to give the local citizenry an identity. The Philippines serves as a model of this kind of social cohesiveness.

POLICE ABSENCE

Filipinos have a long tradition of distrust of government and particularly of police agencies. The preference for local and unofficial resolution of disputes or crimes at the *barangay* and *purok* level likely originates with established reliance on family and community networks typical of island or self-contained communities. Yet, such a distaste for uniformed police is not unusual on the world scene and certainly, for example, not in the United States. Some of the aversion to formal authority in the Philippines likely received a boost from the half-century of American occupation (see Reckless, 1960). In addition to a homegrown tradition of dependence on community cooperation and cohesiveness within the *sitios* in the research setting, and likely throughout much of the Philippine hinterland, police agencies are simply not to be found.

Reasons are rather straightforward. First, in the past several decades formal police agencies have associated with the military in near-continuous attempts to extinguish communist-inspired political radicals [New People's Army] and fierce religious skirmishes between Muslim and Christian rivals, particularly in Mindanao. Consequently, local towns and notably isolated villages or *sitios* must make do either without police or with only an occasional and brief visit by a representative of the nearest *barangay* or municipal police precinct. Second, if formal police are only available in the isolated *sitios* on a case-by-case basis and when available, then the situation is compounded by poor long-distance communications and transportation routes. Should one want to notify the police, even in an emergency, rapid communication from most *sitios* to the nearest town is typically difficult or hopeless, and at times rural trails are impassable, even by four-wheel-drive vehicles.

What has actually transpired in the rural region of Lanao del Norte has been a clear example of what Baumgardner called "de-policing" (1980). In proposition *duh!*

format: *The withdrawal of formal police from a community creates opportunity for self-help patterns to flourish.* In the research setting, the absence of formal agencies of law enforcement from the *sitios* has been associated with a rise in unofficial or informal styles of conflict resolution. In this case, it is not purposeful de-policing but rather a matter of priorities. Any police outpost positioned near an isolated *purok* or *sitio* would commonly give the local policing function [and certainly minor disputes and petty crimes] lesser importance than the more intense combat typical of the communist insurgents or religious rebels. Regardless, this situational circumstance results in increased attention being given by locals to private, out-of-court processing of grievances or disputes.

IDLE-TIME

Idleness is generally noted for its negative qualities. Certainly, lack of meaningful employment generates low self-esteem and despair, and eventually may motivate one to anger and even violence. Filipinos suffered a fifteen percent unemployment rate in the early 1990s and as much as fifty percent of the population are estimated to remain below the poverty line (National Census & Statistical Board, 1993). Many who do have jobs work only parttime. In 1997, in the larger cities, youthful beggars could still be seen on the streets. About a quarter of a million young adults—many college graduates—flocked to nearby Asian nations to work, often as servants. These overseas contract workers are discussed more fully in Chapter 8. Easily observed in the research setting are households filled with young adults even in their late twenties or thirties who remain at the home of their parents because they have nowhere else to go.

Curiously, such a negative pattern reveals at least one positive consequence. The *sitios* teem with activity during the day and far into the night. Rather than having the luxury of leaving home for a workplace, many adult males commonly fritter away the hours at one of the numerous curbside *sari-sari* [literally "variety-variety"] stores (see Photo 4). Such family-run, closet-sized shops, situated at the front of about every fourth or fifth home, sell five-and-dime-type sundries, some food items, and alcoholic beverages (beer, rum, and low-cost *tuba*). Each store invariably provides several benches where locals, usually men, congregate. The gathering place offers two indirect benefits to informal social control. First, the presence of local adult men provides a ready-made neighborhood watch. Any stranger is quickly detected and scrutinized, if only in a casual manner. Crime by outsiders appears minimal in such sitios. Second, and more indistinct, when amicable settlement is sought (see Chapter 1; cf. Jardiniano, 1989), friends and kin of any disputing parties can generally be readily located in the *sitio* to assist private mediators or perhaps *purok* officials striving for reconciliation. Predictably, therefore, *Idletime increases the number of adults remaining in the neighborhood and facilitates local security as well as third-party mediation.*

Photo 4. Neighborhood *sari-sari* store

Admittedly, this proposition is surprising and strains believability. One would expect, and generally finds, a relationship between idleness—often stimulated by unemployment—and a motivation toward illegal conduct. It appears, however, that if the idleness is contained within a community, the residents may cope with frustration in ways other than violence or theft. Alcohol and drug use is prevalent in the Philippine *sitio* but the crime rate in the same locale may remain low. A similar pattern emerges on American Indian reservations, where illegal conduct remains low among idle and unemployed Indians but increases when Indians venture off the reservation (Austin, 1984). Even so, within the Philippine *sitios* and on the Indian reservations, the strain is undoubtedly increasing and it may be only a matter of time before traditional cohesiveness and altruism break down.

LOW-TECH ENVIRONS

Without question, for the poor of the more remote *sitios*, the research setting is at the low end of technological efficiency. Only the well-to-do city folk tend to have private telephone and television. Even for these people, frequent electrical blackouts and unreliable equipment make contact outside the immediate area extremely problematic. Mail delivery is slow and intermittent. Often the only means of electronically communicating with the rural residents of the research area is by telegraph. This style of communication is functional for short messages only, is relatively expensive, and is also of uncertain reliability, due to dependence (as late as 1998) upon radio transmitters abandoned by the United States after World War II. Facsimile transmission (FAX) was generally unheard of in 1994 by rural provincial government officers. By the mid-1990s, FAX was beginning to appear in Iligan City but with mediocre efficiency. In 1997 only select government workers and a few university faculty had Internet capability and had begun to use e-mail.

Locals with any important business transactions must rely on face-to-face contact. Ironically, this is precisely what Filipinos are good at and have traditionally striven for, particularly for any kind of sensitive negotiations involving dispute settlement. In the research setting,the near absence of quick communication tends to promote face-to-face meetings, which usually call for [according to custom] entering a private dwelling and partaking of refreshments or a meal, often taking hours. The amount of time consumed is not typically of major concern but simply an expected aspect of visiting another's living quarters and of doing business. Such meetings are generally unannounced due to lack of rapid communication.

Respondents claim that any person who can establish a connection through kinship, regardless of how distant, who is a *"kumpadre,"* or who can avow friendship linkage would not be considered an outsider and would be welcomed into the *sitio*. Individuals seeking personal audience do not appear to feel uncomfortable standing and bellowing out a greeting at the front gate of a house until acknowledged. Residents constantly watch or listen for callers and usually drop whatever they are doing to greet, scrutinize, spend time with, and invite visitors for food and drink. Only after lengthy greetings and refreshments would the guest finally drop a hint as to the real reason for the visit. Stated in proposition format: *Low-tech regions deprive citizens of rapid communication but function to facilitate face-to-face interaction and informal social control.* Interestingly, in the mid-1980s to mid-1990s, a growing number of hand-held radio transceivers could be seen carried by some of the more upper-class citizenry in the urban area of the province. Such mobile "walkie-talkie"-styled devices provide security as well as a convenient means of carrying on business. Also, a sense of comradeship is induced by the quick, informal means of communication and, as amateur radio operators have known for decades, frequent users of two-way radios often become friends. Thus, increased use of the pocket transceiver could allow wealthier urbanites to return to informal and personal relations now regularly found only in the most rural *sitios*. A pattern of moving from total dependence on informal social control can be seen in the rural sitios where technology is least developed.

As some technology begins to reach the research area, a shift away from extreme informality is observed, only to be followed by a potential return to informal control with advanced electronic technology, which provides immediate personal, though indirect, contact. In 1997, among the well-to-do, the two-way radios were rapidly being replaced by cellular phones. These were totally out of reach to the average citizen and certainly to the poor. The future will undoubtedly bring a mixture of high technology and informality, eventually even to the more isolated areas.

THE *PALO-APON* PHENOMENA

Nothing in the research settings happens automatically. Decision making within the government bureaucracy, as well as negotiations or mediations of disputes taking place in private meetings, require personal revisits or follow-ups to iron out any details. The follow-up [literally "to follow upon"], pronounced colloquially as the *palo-apon* by local Cebuano speakers, is a regularly used expression pertaining to any matter for which the status must be progressively verified or checked out. In northwest Mindanao, few transactions or decisions are processed smoothly or as a matter of due course. Instead, every arrangement or agreement invariably demands that the interested parties make sequential efforts to determine the ongoing status of bureaucratic processes or private negotiations. In the *sitios* this means personal follow-ups, more visits into local residences, and more serving of beverages and food.

Several reasons account for the lack of automatic processing of social or business transactions after an initial meeting. First, at a manifest level is the inability [due to low technology] in the rural regions to make any kind of quick follow-up, such as a telephone call, to learn of the latest progress on any earlier decision or transaction. A second and more latent explanation provided by reliable informants was that continual requirements for the *palo-apon* enhanced opportunities for bribery.

With some embarrassment, locals emphatically claimed that offering and receiving bribe money has reached epidemic proportions. So much so, that handing over money to speed up sluggish or delayed bureaucratic processes or to clinch private deals appears to be conventional. Those Filipinos who are embarrassed by the widespread practice of bribery are undoubtedly the more traditional villagers who long for a return to earlier years of economic prosperity and tranquility. A situation whereby locals are expected to make under-the-table payments must strain the ideals of altruism. The offering of alms to the poor, which has also been prevalent in both Muslim and Christian regions of the research setting, was based on voluntary charity. Requesting bribes, no matter how commonplace, involves coercion, even if slightly so. It remains to be seen how such expected or compulsory handouts will impact on the traditional altruism common in the isolated villages.

Payoffs flourish whether in the case of several hundred pesos [about $8 U.S. in 1997] to convince a traffic officer to overlook a citation, a travel agent to search more diligently for special airline tickets, or indeed, to encourage one party of a private grievance to cool down in regard to an antagonist. The situations for bribery are limitless. Of concern here is the specific issue that a face-to-face follow-up allows a party involved in a grievance to hint for monetary encouragement. Respondents believed that one could more surreptitiously solicit bribe money in private, face-to-face encounters than indirectly, for example, over a telephone or through correspondence. Personal encounters could allow for sotto voce-styled utterances, which, when combined with facial cues, could suggest a receptiveness to bribery. Also, face-to-face encounters enabled an on-the-spot payoff without elaborate plans to meet at a later date for bribe transactions. The passing of money under a table or the half-secretive pushing of cash into another's hand is not only rampant but anticipated in the research setting, even though in many cases it remains illegal.

Locals suggested that mediators would not be expected to pay or receive bribes, but it would be common for one of the disputants to privately suggest to a mediator that money may ensure his or her acquiescence. In proposition form it can be predicted that *All else being equal, face-to-face follow-ups facilitate bribery.* Given the near-abject poverty in many areas of the research setting, the assumption that a few pesos might change hands does not appear in most circles of the region to be considered deviant, even if the act is technically criminal. Even those fortunate enough to have jobs, including low-level government workers, barely manage between paydays. Thus, it is easy for most to rationalize receiving bribe money or, in some cases, delaying a bureaucratic or private transaction until a payoff is offered. Chapter 7 will give detailed attention to the bribery issue in northwestern Mindanao.

When returning to this topic during a subsequent field trip to the area in 1997, it was learned that the *palo-apon* had become sufficiently prevalent to require the emergence of a new occupational specialty. Now available, to those who can afford them, are skillful persons who "follow-up" unfinished business or incomplete paperwork which had bogged down between any party and business or government enterprises. These individuals are somewhat analogous to mediators and are not necessarily high in formal education but very knowledgeable in the workings of government and aware of which persons, behind the scenes, need to be contacted in order to get papers processed. Such occupational types were referred to in the Cebuano language as *Tigs*. The word *"Tig"* is likely a corruption of *"taga"* which means "someone who." Thus, for example, *Tigs* could be expert in "following-up papers" *[Tig-atiman sa papeles]*. They may also be able to "speak on another's behalf" *[Tig-say-say* or perhaps *Tig-sulti]* or to "attend a meeting on another's behalf" *[Tig-salmot]*. Local newspapers would advertise for *Tigs* who may, in some instances, be allied on a permanent basis with a private business. Locals figured that *Tigs* were often retired government or business workers who had previous executive experience. An ex-police official would also likely make a successful *Tig*. It was unknown to what extent *Tigs* involved themselves in bribes, but such was presumed to exist. In fact, a *Tig* hired by a private citizen would often be paid from money the private citizen needed to pay under the table in order to get any paperwork processed. Although there are certainly respectable *Tigs*, respondents were quick to point out that more often than not the specialty carries with it a negative connotation of one who is a "runner" [or "go fer"] for another and in a subservient position. The term "boot lick" was used by one respondent. This negative suggestion bolsters the presumption that the specialist must engage in sometimes unsavory activity, or at least practices preferably avoided by the employer.

This discussion explains how Filipino social patterns, pertaining to informal control, are influenced by situational conditions. Earlier discussions of the well-established tradition of amicable settlements and avoidance of the official control agencies neglected to adequately describe environmental or daily situational factors that tend to fall outside cultural and personality variables. It is acknowledged that the boundaries separating culture, personality, and situation are blurred. Some overlap exists between these independent variables. The spillover among the variables results, in part, from situational features eventually being accepted as part of the culture. For example, the necessity of a "follow-up" is stimulated by a lack of rapid communications, but the multiple revisits become expected aspects of daily behavior or part of the culture of Lanao del Norte. As well, the constant need to follow up any business or social transaction also impacts on individual dispositions of citizenry, thus introducing personality as a further complicating variable in understanding social patterns of the research setting. Yet, the situational links [for example, *sitio* boundaries, police absence, low technology, etc.] have been neglected in past years and deserve further scrutiny.

Whereas this chapter's discussion was not originally designed as a test of specific theory, several of the findings clarify predictions set forth by Donald Black (1976). For instance, the judgment that intricate connections and boundaries function to unite members of a community and facilitate informal social control magnifies Black's prediction of a direct relationship between organization and law. Furthermore, the finding that in Lanao del Norte informal social control, including amicable settlements, is necessitated by the withdrawal or absence of official police provides corroboration for the projections of Baumgardner (1980) on de-policing. The high unemployment rate from the 1980s to late 1990s resulted in idletime and a retention of adults within the villages. This appears to enhance security and extends the theoretical conclusions of Stark (1987) regarding neighborhood ecology. That is, citizens who congregate in the streets and stoops of the ghetto may be stereotyped by police as problematic, but such a gathering of neighbors, at least in Lanao del Norte, may also provide the latent function of community security.

Finally, the Filipino response to low-tech communications provides a distinct example of Black's discussion of the general relationship between culture and law. Furthermore, Black's relatively ignored predictions on anarchy appear to apply in the case of Lanao del Norte. For example, anarchy [absence of law] is approached at the most extreme *sitio* level. Also, as inexpensive hand-held transceivers are made available to growing numbers of citizens, presently owned by the wealthy, anarchy may again be approached as urban citizens tend to increasingly depend on self-help, through instant communication via radio transceiver or cellular phones, rather than to depend on the unpredictable arrival of police to assist in conflict resolution. It appears clear that the recent discussions by Felson (1998) concerning the importance of "routine activities" is relevant in the Philippine community. That is, the variety of rather purely situational factors, including "idletime" and "*palo-apon*," arise to impact upon the life ways of Filipinos and influence their pursuit of village-level security and justice. It may be that the routine activity patterns have an effect on village behavior at least as much as the more-often-discussed issues of culture and personality. The issue of growing anarchy in the research setting is more fully developed in Chapter 9.

PART II

Special Themes

A s would be true in many regions of the world, the special themes of crime and custom in the Philippines are many. However, in the research settings, and particularly in Lanao del Norte, four subject areas arise which are of intrinsic interest as well as of theoretical significance. The four chapters of Part II are not set forth in any necessary order and no single chapter is more important than the others. Yet, because of their recent notoriety on the Philippine horizon, Muslim-Christian conflicts are addressed first. As a most complex subject, this issue could be approached from diverse social-science viewpoints. Here, attention is given a social-psychological perspective, in that disputes between Muslims and Christians are discussed as they arise in the workplace and consequently influence behavior at the individual and small-group level. Case studies illustrate some of the theoretical assumptions addressed in the previous chapters and especially the ongoing avoidance of formal government control.

Though some may object to a highlighting of terrorist activity in northwestern Mindanao, any serious probe into crime and custom cannot ignore its impact over the past several decades on Philippine sociocultural structure. Employing the Bates and Harvey model of behavior causation (1975), a series of propositions are arranged which explain how terrorism impacts on Filipino citizens and their society. Also, vigilante activity is certainly of both historical as well as contemporary importance. Some of the organizations portrayed here now remain dormant but help provide an overview of how the Filipino has responded to unrest in previous decades and into the present. Finally, a rare glimpse is provided of how corruption arises and operates in the research area. An intricate system of likely universal behavior, emphasizing bribery and extortion, is shown as activity generally outside the reach of formal agencies of social control. Several of Donald Black's theoretical principles provide conceptual clarity to some of the near-normative and persistent corruptive practices found in Lanao del Norte.

Chapter 4

Muslim-Christian Disputes

It is difficult to pinpoint the beginning of Muslim-Christian conflict. Disagreements and some violence occurred between advocates of the two religions during the four centuries after the death of Muhammad in A.D. 631. Nevertheless, much of the period was peaceful. The avid proselytizing of Christians likely compounded the intermittent state of belligerence between the two rivals. However, when Pope Urban II urged in 1095 that an all-out crusade be organized against the spread of Islam in the Middle East, the conflict increased in intensity and organization. To the great embarrassment of Christianity, the Holy Crusades failed dismally. Indeed, the Muslims took Constantinople in 1453 and thereafter generally managed to parallel the Christian expansion step by step. Today, various styles of crimes and atrocities continue between Christians and Muslims in such places as Algeria, Bosnia, Egypt, India, Iraq, Lebanon, Turkey, and the Philippines, among many others. In Mindanao, the two religious antagonists have been at each other's throats since Magellan, a Catholic, claimed the islands for Spain in 1521—even though Muslim colonies, referred to by the Spanish as Moros—were already well-organized there. Historically, the Moors, a warlike north African tribe of Arab and Berber extraction, invaded Europe, conquering Spain in the eighth century. Defiant natives of Mindanao [Muslims] appeared as fierce as the African Moors and were called Moros by early Spanish troops in the Philippines. The region was stereotyped as Morolandia. The term Moro appears to have lost its earlier derogatory connotation and is used rather openly, sometimes with pride, in modern speech by Philippine Muslims.

Today, nearly 500 years later, the two old foes persist in terrorizing each other (Balacuit, 1994; Gowing, 1971, 1975, 1977; Rodil, 1994; Saber & Madale, 1975). Daily reports graphically relate incidents of ambush, robbery, murder, and kidnaping. For instance, in 1992 at least 119 kidnapings involving religious extremists were reported by the news media (Anderson & Vokey, 1993; Feleciano, 1993a, 1993b; Flores and Agnote, 1993; cf., Roces, 1997b; Soliven, 1997a; Tamano, 1973).

A substantial literature base has developed in recent years regarding the political and religious turmoil in the southern Philippines (see, for example, George, 1980; Gowing, 1988; Gowing & McAmis, 1974; Lacar, 1987, 1988, 1993; Macalangcom, 1974; Madale, 1990; Man, 1990; Molloy, 1988). These publications, and others, generally emphasize historical, political, and ideological patterns of the conflicts in Mindanao. Conspicuously lacking are ethnographic accounts of the daily tensions and infighting at the local level, especially in mixed Muslim-Christian communities. Whereas nationally appointed task forces abound to address the peace and order crisis in the Philippines, the precise descriptive nature of the Muslim-Christian struggle at the small-group level receives only scant attention other than occasional newspaper features (Marapao, 1991; Regalado & Bagares, 1997; Rodriguez, 1993). Such grass-roots personal accounts are implicitly understood by longtime village residents. Yet, the absence of such ethnographic detail in the contemporary literature precludes adequate qualitative analysis.

This discussion partially fills the research void by furnishing case studies as models of local conflicts in which the Muslim-Christian variable is ingrained. The case-study approach provides an initial explanation of some of the styles of discord between Muslims and Christians in the research area and the manner in which hostilities are resolved. Particular attention is given to how locals attempt to peacefully manage grievances and law-breaking without total reliance on official control agencies. Such detailing of the conflict resolution process in a volatile Muslim-Christian region offers needed clarification of the precise role relationships between antagonists and mediators. Until now, this relationship in the southern Philippines has remained at best a gray area.

The observations and accounts were gathered while residing in the province of Lanao del Norte. Several of the highland or mountainous towns of the province are populated by Maranao Muslim citizens, whereas residents of the lowland coastal towns tend to be Cebuano-speaking and Christian. Also, some towns and parts of Iligan City have mixed Muslim and Christian people living in the same neighborhoods. This creates a logical environment for the study of Muslim-Christian interactions and particularly a focus on cross-cultural conflicts. It should be noted that Muslims in Mindanao are also officially Filipinos although most, in fact, do not identify with the label Filipino (Lacar, 1993). They distinguish among themselves less bassed on religion than on other ethnic lines [i.e., Maranao, Maguindanao, Taosug, etc.]. However, the Visayan and Luzon Filipinos of the central and northern islands tend to lump all Arab-linked Filipinos together under the label Muslim. Throughout the Philippines the Muslim [rather than Filipino] label carries a jaded insinuation, perpetuated after hundreds of years of Spanish Catholic rule and fifty years of American, and primarily Christian, occupation. Both colonial powers considered Muslims as foreigners in their native land (Casino, 1988:43; Guerrero, 1972; Majul, 1966; Noble, 1977). Remaining intact is the unfortunately religious-based conceptualization of Muslim versus Christian. Even if this may logically be viewed as a false dichotomy, it is firmly embedded as a reality in everyday speech and actions.

For centuries, tempers have flared between the highland and lowland folk who typify distinct cultures separated by language and, to a large extent, socioeconomic status. The Muslim groups are poorer and represent a minority population of about 2 percent, or 1.5 million residents of the Philippines, mainly in Mindanao. Over the years, each group—lowlanders and highlanders—have stereotyped each other as the inferior culture. Yet, for centuries trade and commerce united the two regions, intermarriages occurred, and members of the different groups often competed for the same jobs. Several of the towns of the province, as well as Iligan City, have sizable integrated communities. Regardless, local skirmishes and intermittent military-style clashes have erupted between the antagonists.

Conflict between the rivals can be seen at two levels. First is the more radical attempt of some Islamic groups and organizations to create an autonomous region and, for some, to press for secession from the Philippines. In 1989, through a highly publicized and controversial open election, voters in four Mindanao provinces chose to create the Autonomous Region for Muslim' Mindanao [ARMM] (Noble, 1976; Pano, 1997a, 1997b; Rodil, 1994). These provinces are Maguindanao, Sulu, Tawi-Tawi, and Lanao del Sur. The research site of Lanao del Norte, a mixed Muslim-Christian area, failed to approve entry into the autonomous region. Rather than providing a homeland, many Filipinos are fearful the autonomous region—in many ways still dependent on the national government—would create a situation similar to American Indian reservations of the United States. By 1997, the ARMM was intact with elected officials [Governor, etc.] and prepared to receive tax funding from the National government. News reports reflect that payments are delayed causing some animosity within the autonomous region.

This level of turmoil has bred in past years a civil war-like atmosphere, with the national militia [predominately Christian] joining the struggle against the Muslim secessionists. In recent years, artillery shells commonly exploded in some parts of the research area, and the region gained a well-deserved reputation as a terrorist-prone land. At another level, and of primary concern in this chapter, is the friction observable not on the battlefield, but among small groups in the form of intimidation, threats, and occasional hostilities detectable in the daily workplace. Focus is placed on the strained interactions between Muslims and Christians in and around the offices of local government, both at the provincial and municipal levels. Here, heated relationships surface as Muslims and Christians seek elected offices and as the two cultures clash in everyday pressures of the job.

CASE STUDIES INVOLVING MUSLIMS AND CHRISTIANS

The field observations and extensive discussions with locals furnished a series of case studies. Some were more richly detailed and significant than others. However, at least four personal accounts clearly reflect how native grievances or law breaking may be further complicated in the southern Philippines by the addition of the Muslim-Christian variable. The first two cases illustrate styles of nonviolent intimidation; the remaining accounts profile actual violence. Also, the personal accounts constructively reveal how attempts are made to resolve local conflicts informally and often outside the boundaries of official control agencies. Special care is made in each case study to highlight and contrast deviation style, political ramifications, resolution format, and outcome.

The Case of the Harassed Ballot Counter

My name is Nina and I work in the town of Palang, which has about 20,000 people and is more than 90 percent Muslim. I am employed in the office of local government which has fifty-two employees and only seven Christians. I am one of the Christians in the office and work as a bookkeeper. Jobs are hard to find in the province, and I have been reasonably content, even being very much in a cultural minority. In 1992, the election of the municipal council took place and I was assigned the task of tallying the votes. The election occurs every three years, and eight council members were to be elected. Being a member of the municipal council assures a monthly income of 8,000 pesos [\$300 U.S.] and gives the council member a significant boost in social status. Also, a member could wield some influence on important municipal matters directly impacting the community.   Following established voting procedures, the top vote getters of more than one hundred candidates were announced. All winners were Muslim and male. However, the candidate receiving the ninth most votes, a Muslim woman, was unwilling to admit defeat. She claimed improper tallying of the votes, which directly placed blame on me. The irate loser argued that I falsely tallied the votes in order to give the number-eight candidate sufficient votes to win; thus, bumping the number-nine candidate. The number- eight candidate, although Muslim, was the father of the town treasurer who was a mestizo [mixed Muslim-Christian heritage]. The treasurer was my boss. It was implied that if I could please my direct superior by allowing her father to win a seat on the council I could myself gain a better position in the local government. Moreover, it so happens that the mayor is also a distant relative of the number-eight candidate, which makes it appear even more like political favoritism. Rumors circulated that I had better watch myself, for the angry loser would seek revenge. I am not married and, being alone, could exert little or no influence in the community over the established Muslim family. I have heard that it was actually family members of the losing candidate who were the real instigators in seeking revenge against me. The pressure has become so great that I fear for my safety. The family of the successful Muslim candidate who received the eighth most votes tried to intervene on my behalf. Although I believe their intentions were sincere, their efforts seemed unbelievable to the angry candidate and her family. After all, according to the resentful candidate, the eighth vote getter was improperly declared a winner and as the father of my boss is not a credible person to try to settle the grievance. The mayor, *barangay* captain, and Muslim Imams [religious leaders] of Palang, for whatever reason, were not of much immediate assistance and did not pursue the case. As it turned out, the problem was coincidentally resolved by my accepting a temporary bookkeeping assignment in the nearby town of Tago. For a year I worked at this indefinite position. However, when a new mayor was elected in Tago, a shakeup occurred in the office of local government and my impermanent position was terminated. Now I find myself in the position of losing the Tago job but still feeling unsafe in Palang. To make matters worse, I have learned that if I do not return to Palang, I risk losing that job also.

It was at this time in the sequence of events that Nina's problems came to the attention of the researcher. She was visiting Iligan City to seek out a Mr. Manisco, who had many years in government service in the province and knew the town mayors in both Palang and Tago. Also, he was himself half Muslim and spoke the Maranao language as well as Cebuano. Furthermore, Nina was a distant relative of Mr. Manisco [who was a third cousin of Nina's father], which likely made her feel more comfortable approaching him. During the researcher's interview with Mr. Manisco, he outlined three potential remedies to Nina's plight.

As I see it, Nina has a college degree in accounting and holds government work experience. She ought to be able to compete successfully for vacancies in the provincial government. If she can be relocated, her problem could be solved without having to test the anger of the losing candidate and her family in Palang. I have written a letter to the regional director of local government proposing that Nina's position in Tago be reactivated or that she be fitted into some vacancy in that office. This would be one solution. Second, I know that the municipality of Munoz has a vacancy for the office of Assistant Treasurer for which Nina should apply. She is qualified for that position, although she would have to reside in that town for six months prior to taking office. Also, she would have to be endorsed by the town mayor and the municipal screening committee [*Sangguni-an*], a panel appointed by the mayor. If Nina were to be approved for this position, she could reside in the town for the six-month period and would be allowed by law to retain her salary from the Palang job until final appointment in Munoz. As a third option, I will accompany Nina to Palang and confront the angry Muslim candidate in the presence of the mayor. I will ask the chief of police of Palang, whom I know, along with several of the town council members, other than number eight, to sit in on the meeting. I would first send someone ahead of me to set up the meeting and to see if the bitter candidate is willing to attend the meeting. In such a setting it may be that

the candidate and the family will back down and promise to leave Nina
alone.

Mr. Manisco related that ideally, Nina would return to Palang and await the
outcome of the vacancy in Munoz. He also added that he had earlier provided a
favor to the mayor of Munoz by recommending his son-in-law for the position of
provincial treasurer. Assuming the truthfulness of Nina's account, as did Mr.
Manisco, her case provides a distinct example of the power of intimidation and
subtle threats in the research setting. Although the criminal nature of intimidation
may be cloudy, it is plain that it can radically alter a person's lifestyle. It is both
interesting and significant that the right of the provoked candidate to try to
intimidate Nina was never questioned. Rather, it is as if such facedowns are simply
part of the daily struggle for status, and that if the heat were too much for Nina, it
would be her place to step back. Several key informants agreed that the action of
the losing candidate and her family should not be surprising, due to the need, or
even duty, to protect a Muslim's self-esteem [or *maratabat*]. If a Maranao Muslim
believes herself to have been wronged, as in the case of the losing candidate, she
and her family can rationalize, through the built-in cultural mechanism of the
maratabat, taking a vengeful stance against many purportedly blameworthy
non-Muslim opponents.

No data exist on the frequency of use of the *maratabat* to neutralize vengeful
reactions, such as intimidation, which may otherwise be inappropriate.
Unquestionably, however, *maratabat* is alive and well among the Maranao, one
respondent poignantly remarking, "It may be all we have left." Revenge is
mandatory, even though the time frame is secondary, illustrated by examples of
children, once grown, avenging wrongs reportedly inflicted on parents or long-
since deceased grandparents (Baradas, 1974, 1977; Saber, Tamano, & Warriner,
1960). The phrase "We do not get mad, we get even," periodically heard in the
province, takes on new significance. Were the situation reversed, with a Muslim
ballot counter in the minority, an angered lowlander [Christian], not having
maratabat, would likely have to resort to civil court or some strategy of informal
dispute resolution. Personal revenge may be more difficult to rationalize for
Christians. Several passages in the Qur'an can be interpreted as justifying revenge:
"Fight in the cause of God, those who fight you" (Chapter 2:190), and "Fight them
on until there is no more tumult or oppression" (Chapter 2: 193). Old Testament
scriptures suggest similar actions with the "Eye for an eye" passage (Exodus
21:26), but the doctrine is reversed for Christians in the New Testament "Turn the
other cheek" passage (Matthew 5:39).

Regarding conflict resolution, two important factors arise. The first is a
strong dislike of official control agencies, especially the police, and the second is
an active reliance on a third-party mediator. When possible, Filipinos avoid
interaction with official social-control agents. In cases such as intimidation, when
hard evidence may be lacking, the necessity of resorting to unofficial solutions
increases. Also, *barangay* officials or religious leaders in the community appeared

ineffectual, probably because such functionaries also reside in the town and must consider any long-range ramifications of opposing a Maranao seeking vindication.

As noted in Chapter 1, government-imposed *barangay* justice procedures have received mixed reviews. Whereas it does offer a rather ornate but clever system for managing small crimes and disputes, no comprehensive analysis addresses its nationwide effectiveness. Locals in the Mindanao research setting appear to respect *barangay* officials but do not typically place much faith in their capability and regard their operations simply as an additional semi-formal clerical barrier en route to official court. If true amicable settlement is sought—especially in mixed Muslim-Christian areas—one must find a purely informal "fixer" [third-party mediator] with influential personal contacts. In the case of Nina, even as a permanent resident and government worker, she was an outsider in the eyes of the Muslim majority and was in a weak position to exert influence by herself.

On the other hand, Nina was lucky to have Mr. Manisco to call upon. The fact that he was a distant relative provided an additional stimulus for him to intervene. Searching one's own kinship lineage to locate people of influence, no matter how distant, is an established and acceptable practice among Filipinos. Loyalty to kin is generally regarded as a first line of defense and is relied upon whenever possible. Also, Nina was fortunate that Mr. Manisco's many years of service in the provincial government had provided him with numerous personal and professional contacts which could be activated to assist Nina. Importantly, Mr. Manisco was willing to use his influence to create options for Nina, even to the point of setting the stage so that a local town mayor could help her and simultaneously return a favor owed to Mr. Manisco. Reciprocity in the form of giving and receiving favors, or *utang kabubut-on*, is strongly etched in the local culture. Favors not yet reciprocated can be called upon, even if very subtly, as bargaining chips. In a real sense, helping others increases one's personal influence or power by allowing the accumulation of favors which later can be called upon. A sizable amount of attention has been given reciprocal gift exchange among Pacific islanders, but less focus has been given the offering and receiving of favors (see, however, the comments of Enriquez, 1988; Gouldner, 1960; Kaut, 1961; Morais, 1980). What appears unique in the research setting is that favors may be held somewhat in a back pocket, only to be pulled out when one is in need of assistance or if a favor can be used to help another, as in the case of Nina.

In the province, the third-party mediator is commonly referred to as a "fixer." Nina's fixer, being a bilingual mestizo, possessed qualities allowing him to straddle the fence between the two cultures. Still, he maintained that even if he could defuse the heated issue, it would be at best only temporary until Nina could be relocated. The mayor of Palang wished for the return of Nina but refused to guarantee her safety. The time frame for these resolution strategies extended over the duration of the research project, and the wait was frustrating for Nina. The fixer believed that patience may in the end pay off for Nina by providing a cooling-off period for the irate loser, permitting Nina to quietly and officially compete for the other vacancies. Also, time would allow for the *utang kabubut-on* to take its course. As a final note, it became clear that Mr. Manisco was not entirely happy with Nina. He had observed her in the office as relatively meek and unassertive. He felt that as a single woman, it would be best if she were ultimately relocated to Munoz, which was incidentally also closer to Nina's home, where she could be nearer to family. Living far from the extended family made her vulnerable and was, in the fixer's perspective, part of her original difficulty.

Four years later, when visiting the area, Mr. Manisco was asked what ever happened to Nina. He replied that for several years she had been residing in Munoz, but eventually returned to Palang, the original problem location, and married a police officer. She was apparently now reasonably content.

The Case of the Procrastinating Governor

Rico related the following scenario, describing how social interaction between government officials may become strained and lead to unseemly and possibly abusive behavior, due in part to mixed religious allegiances of the government workers.

> I worked in government service for more than forty years and am now anxious to retire. After so many years I have a sizable government terminal leave pay [bonus] due me or about 200,000 pesos or $8,000. Unfortunately, necessary approval of superiors is not always automatic. In fact, I stopped receiving my regular government salary last October, and here it is nearly April and the final approval of my accumulated bonus has been delayed. I was attached to the accounting office, where I was an official. Persons who work with large sums of money must be audited carefully before they are allowed to receive terminal leave money to make sure that all funds they managed have been verified. The books and financial transactions for which I have been responsible over the years have always balanced. However, the present provincial governor has chosen to delay signing final approval for my bonus. The governor argues that one piece of inventory which I had a hand in processing had never been officially cleared. That is, a certain speedboat—or actually a boat, an engine, and a trailer for hauling the boat—were not fully accounted for by the usual process of vouchers and checks. An ex-governor who was an opponent of the present governor had arranged for a speedboat to be assigned to his office. The only role I ever played was to sign papers indicating that the engine had been borrowed from one government agency [Philippine National Police] to another [the Office of the Governor]. However, the ex-governor kept the speedboat at his house, and when he met an untimely death some months ago his family did not return the boat. Because the deceased ex-governor, a Christian, and the present governor, a Muslim, engaged in a fierce political rivalry it is not surprising that after the death of the Christian governor the family was in no hurry to return the property. The governor has several reasons for delaying my terminal leave pay. First, he wants me to file a legal suit against the family. This would make the keepers of the speedboat squirm and it would please the present governor. However, I really had very

little to do with it and am in no reasonable way the person to file suit. Second, the governor wants me around to help settle a complaint filed against him by the ex-governor who believed the election was fraudulent. Since I was an official observer in the last election, the governor would like me to remain attached to the office to help clear up the complaint which looks bad even if the person who filed it is now dead. The speedboat case is just being used as a controversial case to retain me. A government worker who is party to a legal suit cannot receive terminal leave monies until the case is settled. It would be less appropriate for the governor to delay my retirement based only on his need for my assistance in the election law violation. That dispute is more of a political move against the governor and with no implication of me. The present governor is a Maranao Muslim from a very powerful political family in the province. I have some Muslim heritage but have long since converted to Christianity. Although we are cordial and respect each other, the governor would not likely delay my terminal leave bonus were I a full-blooded Muslim or held kinship allegiance to the family.

Rico's plight illustrates a different type of intimidation from Nina's. Whereas Nina was a young adult beginning a career, Rico was of retirement age, hoping to quietly end a long and satisfying career in government service. It is a matter of perspective who was, in either case, the victim or the offender, whether the Muslim or the Christian. Still, both Nina and Rico believed they were victimized by powerful Maranao individuals and families. Both suffered the disruption of career plans. Relatively little attention has been given to the concept of intimidation by criminologists, yet its emotional impact can be as disruptive and visceral in the lives of the victims as the more conspicuous forms of violence. Intimidation, as a disturbing force, usually parallels if not precedes the sequence of threat and assault leading to battery. Regardless, it is clearly as emotionally wrenching as other modes of nonphysical harassment. Long-term intimidation appears analogous, in these Filipino accounts, to the emotional concept of mental cruelty. Distinctions can also be drawn between Nina's and Rico's circumstances with regard to the immediacy of interaction with their adversaries. Because Nina departed the area, she avoided confrontation with her perceived treacherous accuser. Rico's situation did not carry the same mood of hostility, yet often he was forced to interact agonizingly with his antagonist.

Methods used in attempts to resolve the two cases differ. Nina's situation involved a third-party intermediary, but one who attempted first to resolve the issue without forcing confrontation with the accuser by altering Nina's workplace. Rico did not have ready access to a third-party fixer. The introduction of a mediator might have inflamed a confrontation at a time when the governor would have denied that any problem existed with Rico. Instead, he chose to swallow his pride and avoid an open quarrel with the governor. At the same time, Rico combined accommodation with soft negotiation. That is, he agreed to work, even while no longer on government salary, to assist in clearing the governor's name of the voting-fraud charge. However, Rico persisted in denying any fraudulent involvement in the speedboat incident. In fact, Rico did succeed in convincing a local fiscal [prosecutor] to write the governor, stipulating that Rico was not the appropriate person to bring formal charges against the family of the deceased governor.   Rico resigned himself to relying on his personal qualities of perseverance, combined with his wish to avoid any kind of formal judicial case against the powerful Maranao governor.

Key informants were vociferous in contending that Rico was not in any way directly involved in wrongdoing by the deceased governor. However, because Rico could still be a political pawn of the present governor, the door was open for him to be coerced. Without question, Rico suffered both emotionally and economically. Rico, having scheduled for many years to retire only to have his plans abruptly put on hold, temporarily was forced to seek alternative funding for retirement. No official data is available on such cases in the Philippines, but respondents consistently report that dilemmas such as Rico's are widespread in the research setting. Locals are quick to recognize the need to stay in the good graces of a superior when approaching retirement age. One interviewee noted that problems could even arise "if one's friends or close associates were in disfavor with a superior, thus indirectly tainting their own image and possibly resulting in delayed clearance of retirement plans." Although it is possible for a government official to be formally charged by a subordinate with "abuse of office," townsfolk vouch that such cases are notably rare. The formal judicial process could take years which, unless used as a last resort, somewhat defeats the purpose of a retiree awaiting the pension. Also, if a subordinate were to lose such an obviously sensitive case against a supervisor, which appears probable, the superior may find reason never to sign the clearance.

Rico's case was further complicated by both local politics and cultural alliances. Recent years have seen extreme bitterness between the families of two gubernatorial candidates, one being Maranao Muslim and the other Cebuano Christian. Rico's position was not a political appointment, yet he was required to work closely with and take orders from the governor. If he chose to remain totally independent and not indulge or accommodate the empowered governor, he would place himself in an insecure and vulnerable position. If Rico refused to bend a few rules when requested by the governor, which was Rico's decision, then he might have to suffer the consequences of such a stance, no matter how honorable.

When the researcher returned to Lanao del Norte in 1997 and talked to Rico, five years had elapsed since his retirement and he still did not have clearance from the governor for his terminal-leave pay. The speedboat case was finally taken to a Manila court and Rico testified and told his story. In fact, he also talked to the governor and Rico feels that soon his pay will be released. Some locals aware of the situation are not optimistic. It is true that many interpersonal conflicts in the research setting persist as long-term and brooding intimidation. Others, however, reach a flashpoint where intimidation turns to more overt forms of violence. In northwest Mindanao, as illustrated in the following account, terrorist-style property destruction and sometimes murder prevail, incorporating political and religious variables.

The Case of the Burning Bus

In a semi-rural region of Lanao del Norte during November of 1992, a modern, air-conditioned bus was hijacked by passengers, taken to a remote area, and firebombed. Although no one was injured, property damage was substantial and the dramatic event was a major news story for months. Mario, a native to the area and a longtime companion of the researcher, provided a summary of the political and cultural ramifications underlying the incident as well as his own involvement.

> For generations several factions in the province have antagonized each other, particularly around the municipality of Karomatan. The Maranao Muslims have been at odds with the Maguindanao Muslims and both have generally opposed the Christian people of the area in various ongoing squabbles usually concerned with land rights and/or who has the greater political clout. In late 1992, the provincial governor, who was Christian, also happened to have maintained closer ties to the Maguindanos. This angered the Maranaos, who were campaigning to win the governorship of the province in the upcoming election. A full-fledged feud developed between the Christian governor and a powerful and politically astute Maranao family of the area. It occurred that when a member of the Maranao family was visiting Manila, he was ambushed and fatally shot. The Maranao Muslim family presumed the Christian governor to be responsible. Some weeks later the bus-burning incident occurred. Although it was true that the Christian governor owned the land on which the bus terminal was located, he did not, in fact, own the buses. Thus, if the bus burning was an act of reprisal by the Muslim family as revenge for the ambushed family member, then they missed their target. However, the Christian family who leased and managed the buses suffered and wanted the matter resolved. As a mutual third party, and fluent in the Maranao language [although now Christian], I was asked to intervene. I am acquainted with the angered Muslim family as well as the owner of the buses. I spoke to several Muslim town mayors who resided near the location of the firebombing and knew the people who ostensibly ordered the burning. As it turned out, one of the mayors agreed that he would inform the responsible parties of the misdirected bus burning, but expected payment for such action from the owner of the buses. Not surprisingly, the owner refused to pay any money. I was also asked to inform the bus owners that if there is another bus incident the damage would be more extensive.

Mario further explained in the interview that it was certain that the Christian governor remained abreast of the highly publicized case and may or may not have been intimidated. From a purely economic point of view, the owner of the firebombed bus was the unfortunate loser. No more buses were destroyed, although some months later the Christian governor was shot dead at a local gasoline station. At the next election, a member of the powerful Muslim family was chosen as governor. Even though there were witnesses to the firebombing of the bus, the controversial and publicized case never made it to court and no arrests were made. Clearly, the bus-burning case differs from the two less-abrupt styles of conflict and deviation. An innocent bystander became entwined in a political clash between contesting political and cultural camps. Victimization of the bus owner was spontaneous and obviously disruptive to his business. Misinformation [presuming the governor to be the bus owner] resulted in abuse to a previously uninvolved citizen. At the same time, the bus owner became resentful, fearful, and intimidated. Although the bus owner refused to give money to confederates of the saboteurs, unlike Nina he had the ability to opt for heightened security. Respondents later affirmed that private police could be seen stationed at the bus depot. Furthermore, the bus owner now always keeps his house gates closed, drives a van with fully tinted windows, and, according to one interviewee, "Drives directly from home to work with no side trips." Mario remarked that he believes that the bus owner, who also owned a gas station, was providing free gasoline to a police officer, suggesting a payoff for special protection.

The bus-burning incident was obviously a violation of law, yet *barangay* officials and local police were unsuccessful in resolving the politically connected case. The only recourse for the bus owner was to rely on a private fixer, and again the go-between had to be a mestizo who was allied with both sides. Mario defused the case in the sense that no more property destruction befell the bus owner, although he plainly remains intimidated, as shown by his new private security measures. Indeed, it was Mario who suggested to the bus owner that it might be wise for him to seek additional security for the buses. The fixer could only call a truce between the bus owner and the vandals. He did not stop the fatal ambush of the governor.

The Case of the Benevolent Princess

Criminologists have given comparatively little attention to the act of kidnaping, yet from a social-psychological perspective few events are as damaging. In Lanao del Norte, and throughout the Philippines, anxiety over being nabbed off the street or from one's home for ransom—particularly for expatriates and wealthy merchants—demands constant alertness. Although both Muslims and Christians were equally guilty of inflicting atrocities, in past years one antagonist bombing Mosques and another churches, it was the Muslims who gained a reputation as skilled kidnapers. As of 1993, the Philippine literature lacked any systematic examination of the flurry of kidnapings, whether of offenders or of victims. Local and national police forces seemed frustrated in attempts to solve kidnap cases, and strong warnings from government law-enforcement agencies and the military were customarily disregarded by organized kidnap gangs. Certain regions of the research setting were to be entered at one's own risk, and locals emphatically cautioned of impending capture if one were to ignore the warning.

The following personal account of a kidnap victim provides an example of how political and religious distinctions complicate an understanding of kidnaping in the Lanao del Norte vicinity.

> I had resided at a provincial university in the Lanao area for several years and worked as a Christian missionary. As an American working with the Maranao Muslims I was aware of the kidnap danger. The rule was not to trust opening the door to even your closest friends, for they may have a gun at their backs. We kept the gate locked and a dog to forewarn of encroachers. Yet, late one night our front door was knocked in and I was taken at gun-point and forced to walk to a nearby lake and board a boat destined for a small island hideout. There I was confined for six days while my kidnapers announced my capture. They apparently sought both publicity and money. As it turned out, my captors were angry because they had lost their university jobs due to political reorganization resulting from the dethroning of a Muslim university president, along with many of his political cronies. Also, the Muslim kidnapers were furious that then President Corizon Aquino had remarked in a speech that the real problem in Mindanao was the communist insurgency, not the Muslim uprisings. This comment slighted the Maranaos, who decided to send a return message to Aquino and the nation through a series of kidnapings. Although the U.S. Embassy encouraged strong police and military intervention to gain release, it was in fact the Muslim daughter [princess] of a powerful sultan who stepped in on my behalf. She had political aspirations and approached the tribal leaders of the kidnapers. She had reportedly collected a sum of money for my release, though I am unsure of the amount. I am not certain if it was the money or the fact that the negotiator was a sultan's daughter that won my release. I was only thankful to have gained freedom when I did, for I was beginning to suffer from loss of sleep and intestinal disorders.

As with the previous accounts, this case emerged from political unrest in the workplace. The fear of kidnaping as well as the act itself comprise aspects of intimidation and abuse. Any person thought to have money, and virtually any foreigner, was vulnerable. Kidnaping may have an impact on the pocketbook and the body [through torture or fear of torture] and must be included as a type of violence. Respondents emphasized that most kidnaping involves competition between political and religious factions. In such cases, some form of revenge against a perceived harm is apparent, and it is through kidnaping that the Muslim sufferer can seek vindication. When one Muslim group pursues revenge it is referred to in the research area as "redo," in the sense of "repeating" an earlier harm which had been inflicted upon themselves by others. In fact, kidnaping may simply be one means to avenge prior hurts imposed by years of oppression. Theoretically, at least, *maratabat* is at issue in the kidnaping cases and predictably in all acts of Muslim revenge.

The plight of the kidnaped missionary was eventually resolved through the efforts of a private fixer. In this instance, the fixer not only acted out of compassion but also had political motivations. Nonetheless, for the princess to intervene against an avenging Muslim group which was in allegiance with a powerful Muslim family required substantial fortitude. The kidnap victim related that in the months that followed his ordeal, he became friends with the Muslim princess who, drawing on her image as a peacemaker, won the next election for provincial governor. Clearly the victim of a violent act, the missionary volunteered that he eventually realized that his captors had meant him no bodily harm. Though they did threaten his life to ensure his compliance, it was later revealed that his captors were willing to protect him from other renegade bands who may have wished to steal the prized missionary for themselves.

When an individual is kidnaped by a small, loosely organized group of rebels, the victim may be held only for a short time. If ransom is not forthcoming, the victim may be turned over to a more powerful and better organized kidnap band who may have the means to care for the victim for an extended period as well as superior skills in negotiating for a ransom. Once a ransom is received by kidnapers, a kickback is paid to any rebel groups who may have previously held the victim or who may have made the initial capture. Such contracts between kidnap bands may involve up to three separate transfers. Some rebel groups camping in mountain bivouacs are themselves quite destitute and barely able to care for and feed themselves, let alone to safekeep and feed a prisoner for any extended time. Respondents knew of some cases where unsophisticated kidnap groups appealed to victim's families for expense money if ransom was not going to be paid. Such networking between variously organized kidnap gangs provides opportunity for some impoverished but angry rebels to become bounty hunters by snatching well-to-do persons off the street and handing them over to kidnap gangs in hopes of receiving future kickbacks.

Interestingly, when kidnapers release their victims, the intimidation may linger on if the victim remains vulnerable. It is possible another group could target the same individual while avenging their own long-festering wounds. Whereas the missionary stated that he "continued to pray a lot," others resorted to more secular security measures, such as carrying weapons and fortifying their homes. Three conclusions emerged from the data which, though at times only suggestive, do provide new insights and needed focal points regarding Muslim-Christian discord in Lanao del Norte.

Prevailing Mood of Prejudice and Hostility

Clearly, the research setting represents a region beset with prejudice between lowlanders and highlanders who stereotype each other as deficient, vengeful, and malicious. Simply stated, with few exceptions each distrusts and dislikes the other. Without question, interpersonal skirmishes between Muslims and Christians in the workplace are prevalent and diverse. Virtually all respondents could cite examples where they were directly or indirectly involved in religion-based discord.

Whereas the four case studies furnish examples of conflict in workplaces linked to local government, many other illustrations of interpersonal conflict involving Muslim-Christian groups were provided by locals; these, too, corroborate the detailed cases presented. Also, much information pertaining to Muslim-Christian turmoil was interesting and important but related to areas outside the workplace setting [marital and family problems, land-claim conflicts, vehicular accidents, etc.].

A condition exists which appears roughly analogous to the relationship between American Indians and non-Indians, particularly observable near reservations where the two cultures daily intersect (see Austin, 1984). In Lanao del Norte, religion has developed into a most unique negative label used mainly by Christians against Muslim's. A Christian does not typically say, "There goes a highlander or a Maranao;" rather, "There goes a Muslim." That a person is acting "just like a Muslim" is frequently expressed with derogatory inflection. Automobile passengers were overheard commenting about a jaywalker, "Don't hit that lady, she's a Muslim and her family will retaliate." On another occasion, a Muslim woman broke into a long grocery checkout line ahead of her turn. A bystander remarked, "She is Muslim and realizes that the others in line [Christians] will be afraid to interfere with her." Thus, the religious stereotype overrides other cultural distinctions of speech, residence, dress, or socioeconomic status. Being dirt poor and living in squalor is associated with Muslim lifestyle by Christians, though many lowland Christians live in identical circumstances.

The Muslim individual also uses derogatory labels for Christian lowlanders [dirty pigs, swine eaters or *kaper* in the Maranao and Arabic languages], but the label "Christian" does not appear to be a slur in the same fashion as the label "Muslim." Yet, the religious terms Muslim and Christian, as used in the research setting, must be considered misnomers and their use illogical (Casino, 1988) because neither side is really much concerned with the theological or spiritual leanings of the other. Rather, over the years the religious label [of being either Muslim or Christian] has stuck, and it is used by each side as a symbol of inferior, offensive, and even criminal behavior. Except for a few local intellectuals, the early origins of the cultural conflict between Filipino Muslim and Christian groups, extending back through the centuries, seems to have been forgotten or of little concern to contemporary townspeople. There is no concerted effort to achieve proportionate representation of the two cultures in the workplace, especially in municipal or provincial government. Instead, representatives from each culture compete for influential government positions, such as mayor or governor, and citizens rely upon political favoritism from the winning candidates for jobs.

Nature of Muslim-Christian Deviance

The heated competition for lucrative positions in the workplace only adds to the prevailing backdrop of distrust and disrespect between the religious antagonists. The four case studies underscore diverse styles of deviant and sometimes illegal behavior in Muslim and Christian interaction. The accounts portray both similarities and differences in that all contain aspects of intimidation or harassment of one culture by the other, while several cases illustrate specific styles of brutality [sabotage and kidnaping]. Efforts to rank the types of rule breaking and victimization according to severity are awkward at best. Severity of victimization becomes blurred, and attempts to prioritize the degree of discomfort fail, depending on one's point of view. That is, from a purely legal perspective, kidnaping plainly results in steeper penalties than does destruction of property or intimidation. However, if long-term disruption of lifestyle in northwest Mindanao is of prime consideration, then severity of victimization becomes obscured.

As a victim of harassment and threat, Nina was compelled to seek job relocation elsewhere in the province, involving many months and potentially years of uncertainty and torment. Similarly, Rico's plight of being denied his lifetime accumulated terminal-leave pay because of personal ploys of a government superior could be easily viewed as just as disruptive and perplexing as the typically fleeting but more sensational crimes of sabotage or kidnaping. An understanding of deviance and crime in the research setting as portrayed in the four examples requires scrutiny of both political and religious allegiances. Each case involves a complex interplay of actors, some of whom are jockeying for political advantage and all of whom happen to have been born into either Muslim or Christian families. Religious persuasion or political aspiration alone appears insufficient as an explanation of conflict. Being Muslim or Christian does not, in and of itself, generally motivate one to wrongdoing. However, in the scramble for political office, if one's opponent is viewed as heretical, then ruthlessness is more easily justified. The case of the angry Muslim who sought revenge against a Christian to soothe a loss of self-esteem [*maratabat*] also illustrates a failed attempt to enhance one's political stance. The presence of the inflammatory religious component provides further pretext for initiating or perpetuating reprehensible behavior in the research setting, sometimes resulting in criminal victimizations.

Key informants contend that the styles of friction observable at the local level are reflective of Muslim-Christian tensions and violence throughout Mindanao. Reportedly, a vast majority of the Muslim population continues to experience oppression, and most Christians residing in Muslim areas remain intimidated in the presence of religious minorities, whom they fear will resort to violence too quickly if provoked. Throughout the field study, respondents and the daily print media corroborated such a conclusion. The brief profile of personal accounts in the specific research setting plausibly represents a microcosm of conflicts in the larger Muslim-Christian community in the southern Philippines. Longtime residents of Lanao del Norte concurred that infighting and anxieties at the interpersonal level, as outlined in the case studies, may spread quickly throughout the larger community from *barangay* to town to city. Locals remarked that what may appear as office skirmishes involving Muslim-Christian factions competing for prized job vacancies, may quickly ignite entire tribes and regions, eventually requiring military intervention [as illustrated in the case of the benevolent princess]. Several of the seemingly localized accounts discussed here received periodic national coverage in Manila-based newspapers.

Resolution Strategies of Muslim-Christian Conflicts

As noted in Chapter 1, the social organization of the dispersed and isolated Philippine islands from their earliest origins appears to have resulted in the formation of a unique complex of tightly-knit, village-based community networks. The cohesive and relatively independent island communities coincidentally gave rise to a social structure for resolution of local conflicts. Private management of Muslim-Christian skirmishes at the most local level has capitalized on these village-based networks, as illustrated in several important ways by the four case studies.

First, and rather ironically, in a region awash with interpersonal Muslim-Christian conflicts, a rich tradition of altruism lingers. Sources of self-help usually begin with kin and are likely followed by compadreism [among Catholics], companionship [friendship cliques], and finally work-group associates. Kinship is of primary importance, but, when necessary, victims may probe other potential sources of assistance. Private fixers, who may act as negotiators or mediators, always appear to be available, but it is often up to the victim to seek such operatives through word of mouth. Some victims have more extensive kinship or alternate networks than do others, placing them at an advantage when assistance is needed. Also, some fixers are more efficient than others. In the same way that one may choose a lawyer after much shopping around and then hope for the best, the outcome of seeking the private fixer is often uncertain.

Second, a fixer's accomplishments appear to be influenced in part by persuasiveness, believability, and connections [both private and official]. Personal attributes of persuasion are difficult to assess; but believability of a fixer, at least in the research setting, was decidedly a function of being mestizo (see Photo 5). Possessing mixed heritage and bilingual ability allowed for the immediate capacity to relate to Christian as well as Muslim antagonists. To both Muslim and Christian parties involved in conflict, the mestizo tended to carry an air of respect, or a sense of being esteemed, probably resulting from holding intimate or exclusive knowledge of both cultures. This observation would seem at least somewhat problematic because to convert from Islam to Christianity places upon the convert the label of infidel, even if not overtly noted. Yet, possessing some knowledge of Islam, for example, still provides one, even if a convert, with special knowledge of the culture which appears to override the negative stereotype of infidel in the research setting. In addition, mestizos may be related by kin and also may have friendship ties within the religious camp from which they departed.

Although somewhat speculative, the data suggest that effective fixers are unbiased in their quest to achieve subjective understanding of each adversary and opposing perspective. In the research setting, fixers commonly strive for reconciliation rather than retribution and avoid implying blame or favoritism. Even

Photo 5. Researcher, left, with Muslim-Christian mestizo

though a fixer may hold kinship or friendship linkages with one of the troubled rivals, no assumption is made that one adversary is necessarily right. Rather, the ultimate aim is to defuse the conflict, even if only through a temporary truce. A fundamental assumption is that one's closest allies should be most anxious to heal wounds rather than to seek retaliation. Since this appears to fly in the face of the *maratabat* attribute of Muslims, the fixer must be especially enterprising and realize the impermanence of any reconciliation.

Admittedly somewhat of an interpretive leap, it appears that successful mestizo fixers tend to be what Richard Quinney described as "seekers of the way of peace through compassion and service" (Quinney, 1991:8–9). Being able to feel the suffering of both antagonists must be viewed as a positive trait by contesting parties. Following Quinney's argument, an acceptance of "patience" as a virtue appears to be of fundamental importance to the fixer ideology. Patience of the fixer implies slowness to anger and willingness to wait for the interjection of compassion and sympathy to take hold. This Eastern ideal is elaborated by Udarbe (1989: 75–76). The situational features which fostered informal social control and were outlined in Chapter 3 apply here. That is, citizens rely heavily on personal interaction and seek face-to-face contact for any consequential transactions. In the search for fixers, and in any subsequent negotiations or mediations, participants involved in the resolution process travel frequently and with some difficulty throughout the province in order to directly, but informally, converse with one party or another. The meetings are time consuming and invariably call for serving of refreshments including food, coffee, beer, or rum.

It is clear that as confidence in the government system of justice declines, a reliance on private and informal networks of control increases (as cogently argued by Black, 1976). This proposition is confirmed by the Lanao del Norte circumstances discussed in this chapter.   When it comes to highly sensitive Muslim-Christian conflicts in the research setting, official control agencies either ignore the cases or do not vigorously mobilize all resources. Locals contend that among police agencies, when such delicate crimes occur, a lackadaisical mood of "Go round up the usual suspects" prevails. A worst-case scenario, which is believed prevalent in Lanao del Norte, is that government-control agencies, particularly police, are themselves often parties to much wrongdoing and may be willing participants in crimes, especially kidnaping. Such a near-anarchic atmosphere demands the emergence of informal controls if any semblance of peace and order is to be found.

Chapter 5

The Impact of Terrorism

intensity

It is difficult to arrive at a definition of terrorism which will please all scholars. Some prefer the concept of "low intensive warfare" when terrorist activity goes on for years between two identifiable antagonists as appears to be the case in Mindanao. Regardless, during the decade of the 1980s, and with less turbulence into the latter half of the 1990s, much of Mindanao experienced substantial terrorist activity. Because locals use the term "terrorist," it seems appropriate to continue its use in this discussion. As is the case with crime in general, terrorism allows a wide variety of perspectives. On the surface, and surely in a behaviorist context, crime and terrorism and even war may appear nearly synonymous. All may involve a sizable amount of violence and destruction and may victimize seemingly innocent and unknowing citizens. However, distinctions become more clear as the circumstances—especially offender-victim relationships—and the goals of terrorism are considered. Although terrorism has been interpreted in numerous ways over the past several decades (see, for example, Greisman, 1977; Simmons & Mitch, 1985; Turk, 1982; and Walter, 1964), the recent analysis by Gibbs (1989) seems best suited for clarifying terrorism as it appears in the Philippines. That is, terrorism pertains to illegal interpersonal violence, including threats of violence, linked to political or political-religious extremism and subversion. Furthermore, an essential goal of terrorist activity, and one observed in the Philippine scenario, is to alter some aspect of the prevailing sociocultural order by incorporating secretive, furtive, or clandestine methods. Such tactics work to conceal the identity and location of participants in the terrorist enterprise.

In recent decades, the Philippines has presented an unusually volatile but opportune arena for the study of terrorism. Three reasons have accounted for this. First, the Philippines has witnessed a persistently armed conflict between a communist-inspired and supported insurgence. The NPA [New Peoples Army] is the military arm of the Communist Party of the Philippines [CPP], and into the late

1980s maintained a troop force estimated at 25,000, with 5,000 believed to be located in Mindanao (Bergonia, 1988). Assassination teams or death squads known as "sparrows" have operated throughout the nation with relative success (Capadocia, 1988; Espino & Sampana, 1988; Giron, 1988). Although the NPA remains active into the late 1990s, its fury has been minimized, at least in part, as a result of the military campaigns authorized by President Ramos (Pano, 1997a). This is especially clear when the Ramos political regime is compared to the rather fragile but perseverant, democratic republic of the earlier Aquino administration which suffered, but survived, numerous coups d'etat (Bergonia, 1988; Francisco, 1988; cf., Whitehall, 1981).

Second, and mainly in Mindanao, are the lingering, hostile disagreements between Filipino Muslims and Christians, nervously residing side by side, in rural and urban areas of the southern Philippines (Magdalena, 1977, 1990; Noble, 1976; Tarroza, 1997; Timonera, 1988). Muslim organizations, including the MNLF [Moro National Liberation Front], uphold a force of about 90,000 and are heavily situated in southern and northwestern Mindanao. An offshoot organization of the MNLF is the MILF [Moro Islamic Liberation Front] which has been most vocal in recent years and in 1997 began peace negotiations with the Philippine government. Muslim Filipinos have pursued a mission of Mindanao independence for decades (Almonte, 1988; cf. Usman, 1997; Chapter 4, this book). The ferocity of religious warfare, as history confirms, can be as malevolent and destructive as more purely political confrontation (Kelley, 1982; Lebow, 1978; Lee, 1984; Tarroza, 1997). In Mindanao, even into the late 1990s, religious altercations have bred kidnaping and murder on a pace with the communist/democratic conflicts more active in the 1980s (Timonera, 1988; Zwick, 1984). In 1997 Fortune Magazine dubbed the Philippines the "kidnap capital of Asia" (Soliven, 1997a).

Third, and finally of waning significance, yet an enduring cause of unrest and occasional hostility, are the devoted followers of the deposed and now deceased ruler, Ferdinand Marcos. Certain of these frustrated and sometimes rebellious supporters are reportedly prepared to initiate, encourage, or to affiliate with a coup d'etat of the existing government. This issue has been of less concern to the Ramos administration than it was to the Aquino presidency. These forms of sociopolitical turmoil have been compounded by the relatively high level of poverty evident in much of the Philippines. Extreme pauperism sporadically evident throughout the Philippines likely promotes an abnormally high level of property crime, if not violence, and fuels motivations of latent terrorists.

Rates of terroristic violence are difficult to assess because much victimization is never reported to the police. Local journalists argue that there are at least twice the number of kidnapings occur victimizing wealthy business persons or foreigners that are reported to police. In a four-month period (January to April, 1997) police reported ninety-seven kidnapings nationwide, with Mindanao accounting for a majority of cases. Of these, twelve victims were killed, fifteen remained unaccounted for, fifty were released for ransom, ten rescued, and seven escaped (Locsin, 1997b). In this chapter, focus is placed upon the impact of terrorism upon citizenry of Lanao del Norte. The related and equally critical issues of the causes of terrorism and the nature of terroristic activity itself fall outside the scope of this discussion. In order to explain how the daily life of Filipinos may be influenced by terrorism, a conceptual model was used which was previously constructed by Bates (1963, 1982; cf. Bates & Harvey, 1975; Nix & Bates, 1962). The earlier work by Bates (1963) analyzed the social and psychological impact of a natural disaster [hurricane Audrey] at the individual, group, and community levels. Borrowing the natural-disaster model, this discussion reflects similar structural impacts of terrorism at the same three levels.

Also, this chapter explains how the perpetuation of terrorist activity in northwestern Mindanao applies to cultural, personality, interactional, and situational features of behavior (see Figure 5-1). An assortment of twelve propositions and explanations are set forth which predict the influence of terrorism and describe the outcome of behavior at the individual, group, and community levels.

Figure 5–1
Theoretical Consequences of Terrorism at Diverse Social Levels

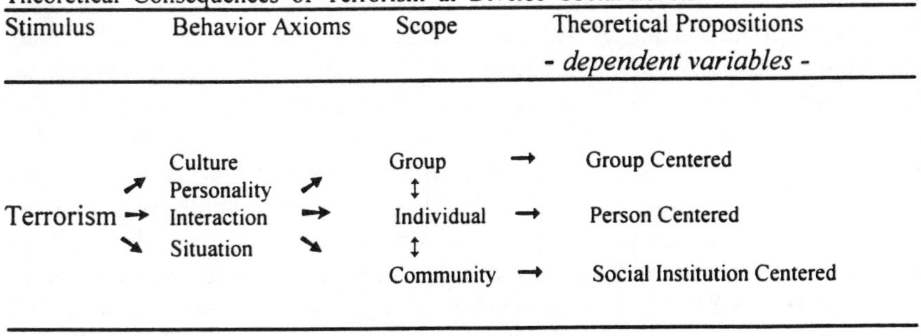

Stimulus	Behavior Axioms	Scope	Theoretical Propositions
			- *dependent variables* -
	Culture	Group →	Group Centered
↗	Personality ↗	↕	
Terrorism →	Interaction →	Individual →	Person Centered
↘	Situation ↘	↕	
		Community →	Social Institution Centered

Source: Adapted from Austin (1989); cf. Bates & Harvey (1975) and Nix & Bates (1962).

CULTURE

In this discussion, culture is viewed in the context of nonmaterial or normative perspectives of individual behavior. That is, the norms or behavioral expectations comprise a primary variable for understanding and predicting behavior. Field notes were analyzed to uncover specific instances whereby the prevalence of terrorism affected the rules dictating how Filipino *barangay* residents went about their daily lives. Although this represents a rather fundamental assumption, it deserves elaboration. Terrorism and the fear of terrorism exists in the research setting as a constant. Furthermore, as in the case of natural disasters such as hurricanes or earthquakes, it is presumed that most citizens in a terrorism-prone area will suffer its consequences, whether directly or indirectly. Thus, an obvious relationship is inferred between terrorism and normative fluctuations. Nonetheless, not all citizens adapted to terrorism in an identical manner, and not all citizens necessarily behaved similarly prior to the advent of terrorism. Regardless, the field study reveals a variety of distinct ways in which Filipino villagers adjust their traditional patterns of behavior in the face of terrorism. Simply put, the rules of daily life were altered. Three propositions predict patterned ways terrorism relates directly to culture.

Proposition 1: *Life in a terrorist-prone area tends to polarize citizenry between activism and passivism.* Both city dwellers and villagers feel a climate of terrorism and tend to react by choosing between two extremes. On the one hand, a smaller but vocal number of respondents seem to express ill will toward any group or ideology that runs counter to traditional beliefs. These individuals represent residents of the province who are quick to become political activists themselves and openly speak their views, even to outsiders, without apparent regard for potential reprisal. Similarly, these individuals would openly admit their allegiance to various political/religious counter-organizations. Such individually rebellious responses appear to be in the minority. However, this does not preclude such individuals from pooling resources into a larger corps of vigilant and vocal citizen activists.

On the other hand, it became clear toward the end of the author's fieldwork that a substantial portion of villagers reacted in an opposite fashion by openly acknowledging few, if any, consequences of terrorism. Although it was common knowledge that terrorist acts, such as ambush and kidnaping, were rampant in the area, most villagers went about their day-to-day activities, at least on the surface, in a nonchalant, "life as usual" manner. Many locals tend to display a sense of having become "habituated" to terrorist violence. For example, citizens would often speed defiantly through highway checkpoints without slowing down or walk about during reportedly unsafe night hours. This reaction style appears not so much as brave or misguided but simply as a means of adapting to turmoil by disregarding terrorism as a significant feature of the environment. Such individuals seem to disregard, or be unaware of, local newspaper headlines which regularly report killings or kidnapings, or to disregard the continuous radio broadcasts of local skirmishes. Unlike the activists, these individuals would rarely, if ever, take part in political conversations. Whereas both these polar types appear to have adapted differently to continuous terrorist violence, it is the activist reaction that represents the most conspicuous change in normative patterns.

Proposition 2: *The prevalence of terrorism in an area is associated with a heightened sense of personal vigilance.* A concern for immediate personal safety or survival increasingly replaces, for example, what some would envision to be a life of tranquil, routine-oriented rice farming. In the Philippines, this conclusion may be somewhat puzzling, in that one could argue that given the constancy of turmoil in the area over the decades, the citizens have actually developed a tradition of community vigilance. Although this appears true to some degree, interviewees repeatedly emphasized the increased need in recent years to "remain ever alert to danger and to continually watch over their shoulder." In a community characterized by a mix of political extremist groups, all capable of kidnaping, assassination, or intimidation, one had to avoid being labeled or targeted by a particular radical group. Of course, exceptions to this assumption do exist, as in the case of the activist who defies ideological opponents by publicly denouncing them.

Personal vigilance, which in this context pertains to the way individual Filipinos have redefined or accented the rules governing daily behavior, is observed in three ways. First is the struggle for immediate survival. For example, the lone farmer must now be concerned for safety on the way to the rice field in the morning. This is obviously notable in those instances when armed insurgents are embattled or carrying out maneuvers on or near the farm. Second, the concern over safety is logically followed by a vigilant mindset. Personal vigilance results from the fact that numerous citizens are likely to be labeled, if not targeted, by one extremist faction or another, given the proliferation of fanatical splinter groups. One cannot simultaneously be an advocate of all groups. The passivist may try to ignore all camps but even this becomes difficult. Third, many citizens have gone the extra step to prepare themselves either for escape from the area, in the even of battlefield conditions, or to ready themselves for a fight. Many citizens in the research area possessed some kind of weapon, even if only a homemade firearm. The point is that the rules of the game have changed, as shown by citizens who openly talk of escape plans, or who would protect themselves in time of skirmish or combat. Such an enhanced flight/fight response increasingly appeared as part of the normative culture of the area until the early 1990s. Although those who choose the "activist" response to ongoing terrorism are likely to be openly vigilant and perhaps to join vigilante groups, it would be a mistake to presume the "passivist" to be nonvigilant. That is, whereas villagers who are seemingly habituated to violence may not "get involved" in politics, they nonetheless are, except in rare cases, certainly mindful of potential danger. As noted by one respondent who resided only twenty miles from the immediate research setting, "Going to bed at night while listening to shooting in the distance has become routine." It must be inferred that most were aware of danger but responded in different ways.

Proposition 3: *Terrorist settings are associated with an increased cognizance of compelled decision making by the citizenry.* The nature of terrorism in Lanao del Norte, motivated by political and/or religious subversion, necessarily forces individuals to rethink traditional norms and values. In the research setting, increasingly characterized by an unusual mix of ideologies, individuals are pressured to make decisions often far removed from established family expectations. This is particularly evident when residents are part of a highly integrated community, where changing ideals is unusual, and they are now impelled to take a stand on multiple sociopolitical and religious doctrines. Individual family members, historically adhering to a pattern of filial piety, may be encouraged or coerced to change from traditional family beliefs. Hostile elements, competing to win the will of the citizenry through persuasion, intimidation, and/or treachery, take their toll. It no longer appears as easy for young Filipinos to follow smoothly in the footsteps of their parents.

In one family, which had resided in the research setting for about thirty years, an aging mother admitted with some embarrassment that her daughter now disagreed with her with regard to the political climate of the region. The daughter, a kindergarten teacher, was actively, but surreptitiously, involved in the local communist party organization. However, the daughter continued to reside in the mother's house but with some nervousness, especially toward outsiders.

INTERACTION

Behavior is directed toward, or influenced by, another person through the process of interaction. Although a single individual can feel the impact of terrorism, the consequences of terrorism, as noted in earlier examples, quickly reach the social or group level. Accordingly, by specifically focusing on the connection between terrorism and the variable of interaction in the research setting, additional distinctive propositions emerge.

Proposition 4: *Terrorism tends to enhance the extent of fluctuation in group membership.* Enhanced shifting in group structure results from the prevailing climate of nervousness permeating the research setting. Again, the data do not allow a precise measurement of the extent of change, only that it is occurring. This is particularly noticeable considering the traditional cohesiveness of agricultural villages in the Philippines. Field notes reflect two rather distinct ways in which terrorism affects group structure. First, it follows that given a condition of timidity and suspicion among the citizenry, the frequency of daily interactions between people would be voluntarily minimized. Distrust and fear keep people behind closed doors and limit interaction between the unacquainted—often even among friends. One respondent stated flatly that she no longer felt comfortable talking about sensitive issues with people she did not know. This was particularly disappointing to the elderly woman for she was an avid reader of big-city newspaper editorials and had always enjoyed engaging in debate on many social and political issues, even with chance encounters with visitors who might drop by her home with friends.

As expected, after a prolonged restraint of interaction, a group tends to dissolve. Members choose to isolate themselves in the safety of their houses. This process of decay in frequency of interaction would first be noted in the more loosely structured encounters typical of the marketplace. Social gatherings might be avoided or else they would be rather bland, as sensitive issues are sidestepped. Similarly, some individuals may become disenchanted with a group's seditious mission and drop out. One rather well-known and respected professional in the area sadly remarked, with something of an unconvincing laugh, "Sometimes you just have to give up your friends." Without question, even if a group remains intact, it is clear that the positions held by members become increasingly distinct as members were more aware of each other's allegiances. That is to say, conversational boundary lines are drawn across which one should not stray.

On the other hand, the terror-prone region influences group structure in a second and opposite fashion. Contrary to the consequences of avoiding contact with others, interaction in some cases may be stimulated if activists are present in a group and anxious to gain converts to their cause. In these cases, persons may be either forced out of the closet regarding their political views or else pushed into the presumed safety of silence. Regardless, an open appeal for converts functions to alter group membership while at the same time putting friendships in jeopardy. Outsiders, including the researcher, are put on the spot in the presence of activists who are quick to bluntly ask one to disclose or comment on politically sensitive issues.

Proposition 5: *The persistence of terrorism provides increased opportunity for the citizenry to use terrorism to their own advantage.* Although one would think it rather unorthodox, locals readily acknowledge that terrorism now provides Filipinos a ready outlet for venting revenge against a fellow citizen. That is, a nonterrorist may seek to avenge an old grievance or dispute by causing injury or property damage to a fellow villager and feel immune from retaliation knowing that blame can be diverted to the unpredictable terrorist activity in the region. Using terrorism as a pretense for personal revenge was recognized as a widespread concern. An even more bold use of terrorism to one's own advantage, acknowledged by some respondents, is the case of a local villager who actually joins a police, military, or vigilante group as a masquerade, thus allowing access to firearms and the waging of private battles to resolve past rivalries or feuds. This parallels the long-held concern about determining someone's true motives for entering police work anywhere.

PERSONALITY

Because personality is so closely intertwined with normative culture, the two are difficult to separate. Nonetheless, the prevalence of terrorism in the research setting clearly modified personality traits of disposition and temperament in several noteworthy ways. It is likely the personality traits associated with the impact of terrorism evolved from [or paralleled] the changing behavioral norms.

Proposition 6: *Normative changes resulting from ongoing terrorism generate feelings of anger and resentment among the citizenry.* This is most obvious as focus is placed on the polar types of normative culture—activism versus passivism. The activist reaction was associated with a rather profound spitefulness or indignation directed against any terrorist elements demanding an unwelcome shift in the traditional life ways of local residents. Such resentment led to outrage, even maliciousness, against the persons or groups forcing cultural change. Malice may be toward one's friends and acquaintances who themselves may become less trustworthy, toward the activist and, more likely, toward outsiders who are immediately looked upon with suspicion. The extreme case would be the resentful Filipino who carries a grudge against extremist groups and who would take any opportunity to verbally attack another's ideology, either directly, as in face-to-face confrontations, or more likely, indirectly. That is, ridicule of another's political views are quite common, and this leads to a daily occurrence of backbiting. Locals talk of personal "intrigues" at the office, which are often associated with resentment against another's political or religious allegiances. Politics and religious affiliation reportedly represent primary features in upward mobility at the workplace. Success at the office often appears to be associated with possessing the right political/religious leanings and connections. Muslims and Christians in the research setting display wide-ranging cultural differences, extending from belief systems to speech and dress patterns. Christians appear to be more concerned about Muslim economic ventures, power bases, and potential for corruption than any differences of purely religious concern. Both groups distrust each other and mutual discrimination typically prevails.

As a visiting researcher to the area, the author readily observed and occasionally felt the animosity. Even for one with established community ties, it is especially difficult to continuously undergo scrutiny by locals. It is virtually impossible for an outsider to remain aloof in terror-prone areas and to claim ideological neutrality. As in a war zone, one cannot chance being associated with the enemy. By experiencing the vocal inquiries and occasional insinuations, an outsider soon realizes the nature and intensity of the distrust and resentment. Regardless, the activist mentality or, in this case, the resulting personality trait of malevolence and anger helps account for the unrehearsed massing of 70,000 civilians into various bitterly emotional vigilante groups in Mindanao (Austin, 1988; Pascual, 1988).

Although the "malicious activist" is by nature most vocal and more likely to be the topic of discussion in local newspapers, the bulk of the citizenry appear to maintain a passive stance. Such a response is associated with a disposition of timidness or a hesitation to become involved in any way with extremist politics. In a terrorist area, the Filipino, historically depicted as outgoing and friendly, understandably upholds a certain disquietude toward others, because in recent years only the closest of friends or family members can be trusted. Such a fear is evident in the way individual families react to visitors knocking at the front gate. Ever-present dogs are allowed to bark incessantly at any intruder into the living space; this gives time for the resident to scrutinize encroachers from behind shutters until safety is assured. Thus, adjusting to a dangerous community situation not only alters the cultural expectations but, to a certain extent, individual temperaments. This extreme caution conflicts with the equally basic cultural pattern among Filipinos of being able to drop in on a neighbor even if unannounced. Consequently, in a terrorist-prone land—or when terrorism flares up—neighbors are especially careful with face-to-face meetings or "follow-ups." Such voluntary seclusion would make "follow-ups" [the *palo-apon*, as discussed in Chapter 3], or the seeking of third-party mediators particularly difficult. Undoubtedly, this role-conflict only enhances the stress of community residents.

Proposition 7: *Involvement in terrorist activity is associated with varying levels of guilt by participants and citizen reactionaries.* Although it appears inappropriate for Filipinos to blame themselves for the presence of terrorists in the region, it is common to detect a mood of culpability or shame in the reaction of locals toward ongoing terrorist activity. Such a display of guilt appears to take two forms. First, viewing the province or nation as a whole, some citizens express a genuine embarrassment that their homeland is the target of such chaos and destruction. When *Fortune* magazine printed the feature article naming the Philippines as the "kidnap capital of Asia," national newspapers wrote editorials for weeks afterwards commiserating over the negative publicity. Conversations regularly begin by a local villager acknowledging the sorrow felt by the Filipinos undergoing such turmoil. This is no doubt accentuated toward outsiders who locals feel are unable to appreciate the natural beauty and earlier tranquility of the area. Such statements as "You should have seen this area before the hostilities" are common.

At a more personal level it is obvious that an increasing number of Filipinos in the research setting have close friends or even relatives who hold allegiances with extremists or terrorists groups. When, by chance, a family member or friend opposes the political or religious stance of an intimate, then it is understandable when one expresses a sense of family shame or embarrassment. Such a dilemma is heightened when the ongoing terrorist activity involves increasing numbers of local citizens clashing with fellow residents, or even neighbors, in the province. In the late 1980s, a "civil-war" mentality was approached, with brother confronting brother on the battle line. However, terrorism presents an even more disconcerting event for locals, in that a fellow villager's allegiances may not be readily identifiable by a uniform or lapel badge.

Proposition 8:   *Mutual distrust among the citizenry grows with the continuation of uncharacteristic change in group structure.*   Fluctuation in group membership logically intensifies the apprehension of group members and generally creates a sense of suspicion throughout the community. In the research setting, as is typical throughout much of the nation, a vast majority of the citizenry maintain traditional ties to local *barangays*. Social and geographic mobility for most has been minimal. Trust is built up over many years based upon close kinship and friendship ties which are also historically linked, in part, to the need for mutual cooperation among farmers in planting and harvesting.

However, as political and religious extremism leads to subversion and eventually flares into terrorist acts, individual villagers naturally become distrustful of insiders and outsiders alike. Even in a single *barangay*, groups and organizations abound which are associated with the various social institutions, including work, church, recreational, fraternal, educational, and political groups. Because numerous *barangays* cluster together to form a larger municipality, it is increasingly common for members of one *barangay* to associate with members of a nearby and often contiguous *barangay*.   That is, the fluctuation in group membership gradually makes one *barangay* less distinctive from another and such an increase in heterogeneity leads to distrust.

Such interaction and psychological changes have been customarily associated with folk-to-urban movements. However, in the research setting, terrorism clearly magnifies and amplifies such traditional changes. For example, changes in group membership in terrorist-prone regions of the Philippines can result in rather calamitous outcomes for the individual. If someone abandons group membership because of extreme differences in ideology, the former member runs the risk of being stereotyped as a potential troublemaker [i.e., agitator or traitor] by the original group. This is true because the dropout may retain inside information about the group's activities, including the membership, which the group or organization may not wish made public. As the group becomes increasingly suspicious of the ex-member, he or she may become the target of intimidation or even elimination.

A problematic circumstance commonly debated in the research setting in the late 1980s is what is feared to be a rather frequent shifting of allegiances by political activists from one agency of social control to another. As political defectors drift from military groups to city police forces and even to local rag-tag citizen vigilante organizations, it becomes increasingly difficult to separate friend from foe. Official and/or terrorist secrets cannot remain secrets for long with the prevalence of defectors who are also suspected as doubleagents. Although the fear of such military or police cases of infiltration is likely greater than the reality, it is clear that on a purely social or casual basis, similar role playing and intrigues may be rather frequent as members vacillate between various violent or corruption inclined organizations known to flourish in the research setting.

Fieldwork conducted in 1997 found that two highly sought after-rebel leaders who taunted police and military in 1988 had agreed to a cease-fire and subsequently each had been elevated to high public office [Gregorio "Gringo" Honasan is referred to as Senator Honasan, and Nur Misuari, is now Governor Misuari]. In 1997 an agreement was struck between Muslim rebels and the Philippine government to allow rebels who would surrender to officially enter the Philippine military. During the summer months of 1997, several thousand rebel soldiers of the MILF switched allegiances. Many of their fellow soldiers are suspicious of the loyalty of the former rebels who are now wearing uniforms of the Philippine military.

SITUATION

The situational context pertains to the stage on which the behavioral qualities of culture, interaction, and personality are carried out. Here, for example, concern is with the environmental elements or conditions [outside the specific individual], which affect overall behavior. In Lanao del Norte, a variety of situational conditions prevailed that influenced the way in which terrorism flourished. In some cases, terrorism first affects situational rather than individual qualities, and indirectly influences behavior. Four examples are especially notable.

Proposition 9: *Citizen mobility patterns are directly modified by the prevalence of terrorism.* It is true that as terrorist activity and the fear of terrorism increase, many villagers will withdraw from friend and foe alike as noted under the categories of "interaction" and "culture." That is, social interaction at the small-group level is generally repressed. Additionally, however, terrorism impacts upon the physical or geographic movement of peoples in a variety of ways, with negative consequences that are first felt at the larger community level. For example, the continuing presence of terrorism reduces the number of people immigrating into a region. Tourism and economic investment by outsiders came to a virtual halt in Lanao del Norte during the late 1980s and was only beginning to pull itself out of the down cycle in the late 1990s. Some adventurous risk takers were beginning to invest in industry and manufacturing in the region, but tourism remained basically at a standstill in Lanao Del Norte as late as 1997. Also, many locals limit their travel within the province. Bus passengers, for instance, have been a favorite target for ambush and subsequent robbery. At another level, mobility is affected as universities and industries have difficulty recruiting employees from outside the area, while highly qualified staff depart the region forcing a "brain drain" condition. Approximately a quarter of a million Filipino young adults—many college graduates—are working as servants to wealthy families in Hong Kong, Saudi Arabia and Singapore. This embarrassing condition became a political campaign issue in the presidential election of 1998 [see also Chapters 8 and 9 for further discussion of this social issue]. As terrorism is associated with death and destruction, occasionally victimizing innocent bystanders, it presents the ultimate impact upon mobility by bringing it to a standstill or by eliminating the means of livelihood through injury or property damage.

Proposition 10: *Terrorism more distinctly affects those at the economic extremes.* In a geographic sense, the diversity of separated and relatively autonomous islands in the Philippines may appear to offer easier targets for would-be terrorists. As suggested by Rubinstein (1988), it is difficult for the national government to offer strong central authority and protection to outlying populations who must, for the most part, fend for themselves. In the province of Lanao del Norte, and south of Iligan City, nine small municipalities are situated along the coast. Although systematic statistics are unavailable, locals insist that the poorer towns, rather than the more affluent, tend to be targeted by communist sympathizers seeking converts. The assumption is that locals who do not receive three square meals a day will be more apt to be persuaded by socialists reformers.

However, even the poorest municipality has a small number of more well-to-do citizens representing larger land holders, factory owners, leading merchants or professionals [physicians, lawyers, educators, etc.]. During the fieldwork, particularly in the summer of 1987 and 1988, a flurry of kidnapings occurred in the province which tended to center upon physicians. Such acts, whether by religious extremists or the communist-supported New Peoples Army, demanded relatively high ransoms while at the same time providing the terrorist organizations desired press coverage in the local weekly newspapers (see, for example, Quiranti, 1988). Locals posited that the kidnaping groups needed their own medical assistance, which made it even more appetizing to kidnap a physician once in a while.

Proposition 11: *Prevailing religious beliefs and practices tend to modify the impact of terrorism.* From a demographic perspective, at the community level, the proportion of Muslims and Christians residing in a village or municipality tends to modify the amount of hostility. Although this appears to make common sense, it deserves noting. That is, not only does the varying level of poverty appear to affect terrorism, but so does the relative diversity of religious factions among the villages and towns of the province. Those settings which are more purely Muslim and/or Christian are predictably freer from turmoil than the more religiously heterogeneous municipalities. It was rather common knowledge among longtime residents of the area that religiously diverse municipalities with subsequently higher levels of religious conflict, were also more regularly targeted by political revolutionaries [i.e., the New Peoples Army]. If locals are already in a state of confusion and turmoil, they are apt to be ripe for recruitment by an extremist group. If a municipality reflects both poverty as well as a composite of religious groups, then terrorist violence appears to be compounded.

Proposition 12: *Terrorism fluctuates with the style of social control and vice versa.* The relationship between terrorist activity and the style of social control is complex and few have addressed this issue. Although Black (1976) touched upon the related topic of social control in anarchic societies, the Philippine setting is not purely anarchic (i.e., without law). Rather, multiple styles of law and/or social regulations appear in varying degrees as one moves from small rural villages to large urban centers. Also, terrorism can, in fact, arise at both extremes. Having said this, it appears clear, at least in the research setting, that terrorism operates most easily in the city, where inefficient formal systems of government are charged with protecting the citizenry. Also, any abject poverty will be found in the cities. In rural tropical areas, afterall, residents can at least find food and water and are less likely to resort to begging for handouts. Terrorism is least likely to flourish in areas where informal social controls dominate. Rebel groups hideout in the mountain and rural areas, but do substantial recruitment in the cities.

Building upon the conceptual scheme of Black, for example, terrorism would be expected to increase with law [i.e., in urban areas filled with strangers]. Of course, extremist groups may and do move throughout rural areas seeking converts and intimidating locals by requesting money or food. To the extent that they are successful, they must be relatively unrecognizable by villagers. Locals are less likely to be intimidated or fearful of someone they know or recognize as having been reared in the area. In the city, a majority of the citizens are unrecognizable. In the rural areas of the province, local "anti-terrorist" groups are much more likely to arise. The well-publicized vigilante movement of the Philippines tended to prosper because the local citizenry, especially in the rural areas, maintain a long tradition of banning together for mutual protection. Accordingly, terrorism tends to be less apt to succeed in areas where local informal control mechanisms thrive.

In the research setting of Lanao del Norte, the problem appears not to be one of renegade vigilante groups. Indeed, they seem to be essential in a terrorist-prone region. The dilemma is the lack of trust and cooperation between local informal control groups and the more formal city police and military forces who, as outsiders [strangers] move rather freely throughout the region. Regardless, the point made is that terrorist activity most clearly fluctuates with the style of social control. Exactly how it adjusts in the face of varying styles of social control is confusing and presently unresearched.

This chapter has set forth general theoretical propositions pertaining to the impact of terrorism on individual and community life. Clearly, a logical follow-up is to contrast terrorist regions in diverse cultural areas of the Philippines and elsewhere around the world. Although the propositions appear to succeed in simplifying the predictable relationship between people and terrorism, the interplay still remains complex. For instance, both the macro and micro-level influences of terrorism are mixed. Precisely where and how such outside stimuli as terrorism and the fear of terrorism cross over from a purely personal impact to an organizational or communal impact is unclear. This is especially pertinent when it is observed that Filipinos maintain a tradition of clustering together at the village level in routine efforts to counter unruly insiders or outside encroachers. Since all Filipinos are closely tied to the *barangay* local village structure, every citizen, whether in urban or rural areas, at least potentially reaps the benefits of being part of a cohesive community. Possessing even a modicum of support groups undoubtedly aids the citizenry in the research setting who are forced to react to a terrorist environment. Regardless, whether the reaction to terrorism is personal or communal—or both—is still a gray area.

With regard to daily life in Lanao del Norte, the tone of this chapter seems grim, with people constantly looking over their shoulder and secretly wielding weapons. In fact, the mood in the research setting during the six months of fieldwork in 1997 was actually upbeat. This is undoubtedly due to the rise in economic growth throughout the nation over the previous three years. Iligan City appears as a boom town with building construction going on day and night throughout the area. "Help wanted" signs hang in many windows and fewer beggars panhandle on the sidewalks compared to 1993. Much of the anxiety toward terrorism has moved further south on the island of Mindanao, where Muslim and government forces continue to maintain a very fragile peace agreement. The New Peoples Army was not as hot a topic of conversation on the streets in 1997 as it had been earlier, and it was only occasionally discussed in local newspapers. Ex-president Marcos is now long dead, and although his many millions are still locked in Swiss banks, his earlier political compatriots are too old to stage political uprisings. Few seem to worry about them today. As is often observed with Northern Ireland, the region is enjoying itself during the good times, while they last. This is true even while suffering the label of the "kidnap capital of Asia," which after all, only victimizes the wealthy and leaves the masses to walk the streets relatively unscathed. The positive mood swing in the research setting does not detract from the twelve propositions discussed in this chapter. Each continues to provide theoretical launching points for research aimed at further exploring the impact of terrorism upon people and communities whether in the Philippines or other troubled world areas.

Chapter 6

Vigilante Activity

During the decade of the 1980s, international attention was placed on the way Filipinos struggled to withstand the impact of political transition, outside insurgency, economic strife, and Muslim-Christian conflict (Drozdiak & Richberg, 1987; Fallows, 1988; Ward, 1987). In a twelve-month period between 1986 and 1987, the single province of Lanao del Norte experienced 134 kidnapings victimizing wealthy adults, including foreigners (Timonera, 1987). Very little emphasis has been given to the subsequent voluntary restructuring of communities at the most local neighborhood level (Lluch, 1987; Santoalla, 1987). This chapter examines the social organizational nature of several Philippine police and vigilante networks operating in the research setting of Lanao del Norte and along the northwest region of Mindanao.

While news reports tend to concentrate on the social turmoil in the Philippines' major cities, such as Manila, Davao, and Cebu, the vast majority of the approximately 70 million Filipinos live outside the big cities in the rural villages or *barangays*. Life goes on in these 50,000 *barangays* at a more leisurely pace than depicted by outside news reports. Even when national political changes occur, several months or years may elapse before consequences are felt in some rural, outlying islands or regions. Nonetheless, in recent years the combined influences of political, economic, and socioreligious conflicts have been of sufficient intensity and duration to effect a noticeable rearrangement of local and even isolated communities. Such modifications appear to be organizational in character, representing clear efforts to maintain a sense of order and harmony at the village level. This is especially noticeable with regard to the establishment of neighborhood security groups.

Three categories of research questions must be addressed. First, from a descriptive point of view, how are the various formal and informal Philippine policing systems portrayed at the village level? For example, can a typology of social-control strategies be constructed, which reflects both official police systems and the more informal vigilante mechanisms of control? Second, what linkages, if any, exist between the informal vigilante organizations and the formal or official government agencies of control? For example, what is the form of the role relationships that bind the various social control systems to each other? Third, what is the relationship between the different styles of social control, and the larger village communities in which they are found? Specifically, do the vigilante groups appear to be isolated and renegade in character, or are they integrated into the social structure of the established communities?

The reader may find it helpful at this point to review Chapter 2 of this book, which provides an overview of altruistic values that tend to promote "self-help" groups traditional to the research area. The following discussion is important in explaining aspects of the setting during a most volatile era. Several theoretical assumptions help guide this discussion. The first derives from "self-help" theory. As formal agencies of social control are lost or withdrawn from a community, volunteer or self-help groups predictably emerge to satisfy the original aims of the agencies. Might it be found that based on the Philippine model the logic of purposely reducing the numbers of police personnel [i.e., "de-policing"] in order to generate voluntary organizations may have some plausibility (Baumgardner, 1980)? How a community strives to maintain control and harmony in the face of disasters, natural or otherwise, with the resulting loss of utilities and public services, appears to be a pertinent perspective (Mileti, Drabek, and Haas, 1975; Sennett, 1970). In the case of the Philippines during the 1980s, government police and military agencies of control were strained by persistent internal and external threats. Consequently, reports of a community upsurge in voluntary self-help groups seem reasonable, if not expected.

Second, related theoretical assumptions, as outlined by Donald Black, are also applicable. Black argues that "formal law varies inversely with other styles of social control" (1976:74, 107). That is, law [official police intervention, for example] becomes weaker, less prevalent, and even less necessary when people are tied more closely together by community bonds (see Diamond, 1971; cf. Rieder, 1984). If it is true that Filipino villagers are being drawn more closely together in the face of danger, does this mean they are inventing their own security systems out of self-protection, rather than solely relying upon official control systems? In this regard, Black argues that as a society increases in its quantity of organization, as during wartime, a corresponding increase is predicted in its level of law or quantity of policing systems (1976:86–87). The Republic of the Philippines, during the era of revolution and near civil war, provides a timely context for observing and assessing the nature of police and vigilante movements at the village level.

The field notes reflect at least six styles of social control. These police or community-security systems range from government police and military forces to unofficial vigilante organizations. An official system of social control is defined as one established by the national government. Several control systems tend to be situated between the two extremes and are categorized as semi-formal [endorsed but not established by the national government].

OFFICIAL POLICE SYSTEMS

Philippine Constabulary/Integrated National Police [PC/INP]

A young Filipino may enlist in the armed forces by choosing the Army, Navy, Air Force or the Philippine Constabulary [i.e., PC]. In fact, the PC, created in 1901, is the oldest of the nation's four armed services. It was established to preserve peace and order within the Philippines. In 1980 the Philippine Constabulary's strength was around 33,500 soldiers (Bunge, 1984). Given the geographic diversity of the Philippines, it was clear that the nation needed a centralized and mobile force to serve law enforcement functions to suppress major crimes. The Constabulary also includes a nationwide highway patrol force. The more traditional city and municipal police forces (i.e., Integrated National Police) have also existed side by side with the Constabulary for decades. However, compared to the Constabulary, the city and town police are typically concerned with lesser crimes and with more purely localized disturbances and issues. By 1980 there were about 51,000 INP officers throughout more than 1,500 cities and municipalities. In 1975, President Marcos established through decree the combined PC/INP, placing the Philippine Constabulary as the military authority over all city and municipal police forces. In effect, the president, as commander-in-chief, was able to maintain military control over all official policing in the nation.

Throughout the Aquino presidency, this aspect of martial law remained intact. Not surprisingly, some rift existed as to which unit [i.e., PC or INP] should actually be in charge at the small-town level. The city and town police, rather than the Constabulary, are more likely to know the citizenry and may feel more capable than their military superiors in handling local police problems. The history and relationship between the PC and the INP, while colorful and complex, are not within this chapter's scope. However, the relationship between the national forces and the village level security groups is of concern.

Civilian Home Defense Forces [CHDF]

Although the police officers of the various cities and towns are academy trained, their numbers are limited, given the nation's population [i.e., about one officer per 1,500 people]. Moreover, the combined PC/INP is primarily deployed in urban areas. Consequently, the bulk of the population residing in the thousands of rural villages is without protection of the Constabulary or the National Police. Because the political-religious conflicts in the Philippines occasionally unfold in the rural areas, a need has existed for additional community security. The Civilian Home Defense Force, numbering about 71,000, has helped to fill the law enforcement void in these isolated areas (see Jones, 1987a; Richberg, 1986a). In several villages within the research site, which were without a regular police presence, private civilians stepped forward to fill the positions of CHDF officers.

Respondents noted two categories of armed CHDF personnel, neither of which received formal police training. The first consisted of citizens who volunteered to be a part of the civilian force, but only for the specific purpose of protecting their own homes and families. Qualified citizens were authorized to keep handguns or, in some cases, were provided them by the PC. Second, should citizens volunteer for the more traditional police duties of the village (i.e., filling the roles of Integrated National Police), they might be given fatigue uniforms, a small salary of 200 pesos per month [about $10 U.S.], and high-powered weapons. These CHDF volunteers reported directly to the Philippine Constabulary.

Since the PC/INP staff were usually absent from the villages, the CHDF were left to perform police duties as best they could with only the barest amount of professional training. Citizens were quick to criticize the CHDF members, whom they often perceived as rag-tag police. Regardless, the CHDF acted as an official, though only semi-organized, policing unit at the village level. One respondent joked that the only uniform they have is one they take off an enemy soldier. Given the internal conflict in the Philippines, it is often difficult to tell who is the enemy simply by looking at a uniform. It was common for a PC officer and an INP officer riding in the same jeep to have different loyalties.

SEMI-OFFICIAL VILLAGE CONTROL SYSTEMS

The *Barangay Tanod*

The *tanod* is a security group operating at the village or *barangay* level very much like a "neighborhood watch" program. The Philippines is subdivided into cities, municipalities, and approximately 50,000 *barangays*. *Barangays* may be independent, isolated communities, as in the case of a rural hamlet or village, or they may be grouped together to form towns, cities, and large metropolitan areas. Nonetheless, every Filipino throughout the nation technically resides in, or is attached to, a particular *barangay*, in the same sense that all citizens in the United States live within a certain voting precinct. A vast majority of the *barangays* possess a variety of community organizations, one of which pertains to "*barangay* justice." Such a neighborhood based justice program maintains an informal court structure for dispute processing, and incorporates the "*barangay tanod*." Although the national government recognizes the *barangay* justice organization and keeps some records as to their activities, the *tanod* groups are only tacitly recognized and are best described as semi-official. Recruitment into the *tanod* security group is through appointment by the *barangay* captain. The members, who may number about six in an average-sized rural *barangay* of about 900 citizens, are not generally paid salaries, do not wear uniforms, and operate only under a most loosely structured set of rules.

Basically, the *tanod* members represent a group of male friends who have almost certainly been reared together in the same village, and who gain a sense of pride from being a part of the community organization. *Tanod* members of one *barangay* [in Munoz, Nueva Ecija], proudly   displayed old and tattered identifications made from cardboard on which were typed their name,   the statement "member of the *barangay tanod,*" and the name of the *barangay*. The *barangay* captain is elected by popular vote and maintains a substantial amount of community support, as well as influence over local town mayors and the Philippine Constabulary/Integrated National Police. The *tanod* members are extremely loyal to the *barangay* captain and would most likely not follow anyone's orders without the captain's approval. Although usually without official blessings, the *tanod* members occasionally possess firearms, generally homemade or furnished by the captain.   The captain, on the other hand, may be provided weapons by the Constabulary or a politically influential mayor [i.e., one who often has his or her own private security forces] who wishes to win the loyalty of the captain (Jones, 1987a). In turn, the *barangay* captain will appoint one of the more mature community members as chief of the *tanod.* The chief will often be provided weapons by the *barangay* captain. It is the *tanod* chief who will keep in close communication with the captain, reporting any security issues affecting the *barangay*.

Perhaps, even more than the Civilian Home Defense Force, the *tanod* members are aware of local gossip, friendship patterns, and daily neighborhood activities within the village. Whereas the CHDF may also be from the local area, they are organizationally tied to the military, thus potentially tarnishing their loyalty to the village, even if slightly so. The *tanod* members, however, remain within the confines of the village, ready to mobilize if called upon. The *tanod*, therefore, is closer to a community "self-help" activity.

Nakasaka

A second system of control, categorized as semi-official, is the "*Nakasaka*" [i.e., in the Cebuano "*Nagkahiusang katawhan alang sa kalinaw,*" or "unification of people for peace"]. The *Nakasaka* is national in scope, although with limited or no manifest qualities of organization. In fact, in 1987, the word *nakasaka* was used primarily as a slogan by politicians or other mission-oriented individuals to stir the citizenry to rise up in the name of peace and order. *Nakasaka* began as an idea or "ideal" encouraged to a great extent by then president Aquino. Most notable was the "people-power" movement, which clearly   became reality when thousands of citizens took to the streets of Manila to confront the troops and tanks of the faltering President Marcos. The dramatic display of "people power" was televised worldwide and was mentioned almost reverently by President Aquino's supporters as the "EDSA Revolution" (i.e., *Epifanio de los Santos Avenue* where the confrontation occurred;   see, Nemenzo, 1987). This ideal, at first only a visionary and abstract campaign goal, was infused with identity and credibility by being indirectly referenced in presidential speeches (Aquino, 1986).

It is difficult to articulate or categorize the *Nakasaka* movement and even more difficult to assess or measure it. At best, one can say it is a national enthusiasm or community cohesiveness [best described as *Gemeinschaft* in German], strongly felt by Aquino advocates and recognized as a force to be dealt with by government adversaries. Although it is probable that groups referred to as *Nakasaka* have organized in the Philippines, it is more likely that the "people-power" spirit has fueled various splinter groups that go by different names. It must also be noted that the same enthusiasm at the most local level that inspired one to join the CHDF, the *tanod*, or even the PC/INP, may also stimulate one to organize terrorist-oriented vigilante groups. Such crusading groups may kill in the name of *Nakasaka,* and sometimes embarrassed the Aquino administration (Mydans, 1987; Newsbriefs, 1987; Serrill, 1987).

UNOFFICIAL VIGILANTE GROUPS

The *Alsa Masa*

The *Alsa Masa* is a rather tightly organized group of citizens who have unofficially taken it upon themselves to combat the communist-inspired New Peoples Army [NPA]. The organization began in 1986 with a handful of enthusiastic individuals in Davao City, and by mid-1987, reportedly numbered in the thousands (Serrill, 1987; cf. Richberg, 1986b). *Alsa Masa* literally translates from the Tagalog language as "uprising of the masses." As such, it appears to at least logically connect with the larger, but more abstract, *Nakasaka* political ideal. Organizationally, the *Alsa Masa* movement, which has spread outside Davao into other areas of Mindanao, represents the more classic image of violence-oriented vigilante groups. In their professed aim to save democracy, they claim a good deal of popular support. However, their tactics are suspect, if not illegal, placing the PC/INP and the Aquino administration in the bind of having to denounce what may be a relatively successful defense against outside insurgents.
  The literature is scant regarding the *Alsa Masa*, but respondents claim their techniques include setting up highway checkpoints, armed patrols, and covert neighborhood surveillance. They are said to move from house to house soliciting donations for their cause [i.e., cash, food items, including animals that can be eaten]. The houses of those who contribute are marked so that future patrols will recognize sympathizers. To complicate matters, rebel NPA groups may also solicit help by moving from house to house and also placing their mark on households friendly to their cause. Not surprisingly, some residents feel intimidated, coerced, or frightened. At the checkpoints, the same tactics may be used to solicit items of value [the discussion of bribery and extortion in Chapter 7 will elaborate on this pattern]. As a result, the prevailing mood of the village is one of nervous anticipation mixed with deference to the vigilante [even if technically outlawed] groups, which at times claim more success than the PC/INP. If confronted by the Army or the Constabulary, the *Alsa Masa* groups may bring forward some of their members who also belong to the CHDF, thus adding confusion to the overall

Photo 6. Coconut-tree climber as lookout

picture of social control in the region.

The *Inpos*

A second style of vigilante control which must be categorized as purely unofficial and informal in character are the *inpos*. The term *inpo* is a shortened version of "informant." Provincial villagers, as do many Filipinos elsewhere, pronounce the "f" sound as "p," thus *inpos* rather than *infos*. Respondents in the research site emphatically stated that coconut-tree climbers [i.e., *mga manananggot* or coconut pickers] were the best *inpos* since they could see far from their treetop observation posts (see Photo 6).   Coconut tree climbers are primarily men [occasionally women] who climb the high trees to harvest the fruit.

Their precarious occupation requires them not only to be tree climbers, but also handy with a *bolo* [machete] and willing to work in the most rural areas of the province. The tree-climber *inpos* system must be defined as informal in group structure. The lone informant links with the community only sporadically and operates under loosely established rules. One local resident recalled that the tree climbers were known to sound out messages by tapping on the coconuts with their *bolos* when they spotted something of importance. They do not appear to be closely attached to other security groups and possess no organizational features identifying them with security systems. Their style was kiddingly referred to as *walay sapatos* [i.e., without shoes]. Local farmers of Lanao del Norte referred in jest to the coconut-picker *inpos* as "mp's" a play on words in that in the Philippines an "mp" is known to be "military police" ["mp" sounds like a blurred and rapid pronunciation of *inpos*].

The PC/INP, as well as other official or semi-official control systems, rely upon information from isolated villagers who farm in the outback regions of the province, and who are likely to observe guerrilla activities. It does not appear that the Philippine Constabulary or other policing agents actively recruit lone informants. Reportedly, isolated farm-worker informants, if they are so inclined, will voluntarily relay information regarding rebel movements by messenger or telephone or telegraph if they have access to provincial radio stations. In turn, it is the radio announcer who sifts through the information and then broadcasts the reported activities over the air. In this way, the location of rebels will be immediately known to rural citizenry, the CHDF, the Army and the PC/INP.   Such a system is advantageous to the citizenry by giving them time to prepare [i.e., lock doors or depart the area] should rebels be nearing the community. Ironically, the person most at risk is the radio announcer. It is not uncommon for announcers to be assassinated or stations bombed. The reason for such an unorthodox method of relaying information is not clear. Apparently, the citizenry feel more comfortable passing information to a friendly, though geographically detached announcer, rather than to the impersonal Army or Constabulary. This is particularly true if people do not fully trust the official control systems. Also, the *"inpos"* realize that they are, in effect, aiding their fellow villagers, regardless of whether or not the military finds the broadcasts useful.   Obviously, this network requires the volunteering of the radio announcer. Other than occasional newspaper reports, this complex network remains to be fully explored.

The emergence and interplay of the village control systems allow for further clarification of "self-help" principles. Regarding the villages in the research site, it is clear that in the summer of 1987, the citizens were not only much aware of the need to fill police roles in the absence of official government agencies, but also willing to take part in official, semi-official, or unofficial capacities. Whereas the formal police agencies (PC/INP) were constantly in need of recruits, such was not the case at the informal community level. Given the proliferation and persistence of the *tanod, inpos*, and *Alsa Masa*–type systems in the last few years, it appears clear that "self-help" networks in the research site are not only alive but robust.

Although the data did not permit quantitative analysis of police reports, the villagers did not complain of traditional crimes. Given the prevalence of various control agencies—official or not—rapid increases in street crime, even during times of turmoil, seem unlikely. The biggest fear was from those control agents who may overzealously demand donations for their cause [CHDF, *Alsa Masa*, and even the PC/INP)]. The kidnaping [i.e., hostage taking] and murder rates are high, but these are a result of rebel attacks rather than village-based self-help groups. With the exception of the *Alsa Masa*–type organizations, vigilantism in the research site generally pertains to showing vigilance rather than to seeking revenge.

News reports and field notes suggest that some unofficial vigilante groups do seek revenge. In order to gain membership into some extremist groups, initiates must kill a member of the communist New Peoples Army [NPA]. Members show faithfulness to the vigilante group by inflicting self-mutilation [i.e., cutting of arms or chest], leaving valued scars. The *Tad-tad* vigilante group [i.e., meaning "chop-chop"] is most notorious (see O'Neill, 1987), although quite friendly to the researcher, perhaps because members were hopping for publicity. Members of one extremist and unofficial vigilante group calling themselves the *Sagrado Corazon Senor* [i.e., "Holy or sacred heart"] would hide out on the beach at night where they would scavenge for food handouts. They felt their vengeful, terrorist acts would restore democracy and were approved of by the deity. In the safety of darkness they would visit PC or CHDF highway checkpoints to witness or pray for their cause [i.e., hopefully with an audience] prior to searching out individuals they perceived as enemies. There presence undoubtedly compounded the intimidating image of roadside checkpoints, where both officials and vigilante members solicited handouts from passers-by.

Other than the ongoing Muslim-Christian conflicts and political insurgents, life at the village level goes on about as usual. Rice is still planted and children still go to school. However, "life as usual" may still be a step backward given the prevailing economic instability in the area (Fallows, 1988). As noted, Donald Black's prediction of increased levels of organization during wartime appears to hold true in the research setting. Communities will become more involved and complex given the expansion of functions. A parallel increase was observed in the research site in various styles and diversities of policing systems. Black did not elaborate on the precise organizational nature of the control systems that would emerge during wartime. However, in Lanao del Norte, a variety of police styles surfaced as they were required to fulfill specific community needs. The degree of organization remains mixed and still unpredictable. "Self-help"– oriented systems persisted, or were established, which represented both clandestine and open policing systems. Also, vigilante groups appeared which were, on one extreme, highly individualistic [i.e., lone informants] and, on the other, rather structured, as in the case of the *Alsa Masa* or the *tanod*. The degree to which the various self-help groups are organized appears to be varied. That is, in the case of the *Nakasaka*, at least in the research site, there was no mention of actual citizen groups that convened, even on an irregular basis. Nonetheless, individual citizens are very much aware of the ideal or the cause and, if prompted, may rise up. No villagers were known to occupy any specific roles regarding the *Nakasaka* scenario. It must be characterized as an unorganized, latent system.

However, the *Alsa Masa* and *tanod* are more structured, complex groups. Both are made up of members who meet regularly and who fulfill specified roles within their groups. Furthermore, groups are hierarchically structured, with some roles being defined as higher or lower in status [i.e., chief of the *tanod*]. Although uniforms are not evident, on occasion a member may be seen wearing a T-shirt or cap on which is imprinted the word "*tanod*." *Alsa Masa*–type groups are well-structured, with status-oriented roles and specified locations for periodic gatherings. Whereas the *tanod* is integrated into the village social structure, the same cannot be said of the *Alsa Masa*. Such unofficial vigilante systems, although clearly structured, tend to be covert. This is particularly true of the more extremist groups that are inclined to use terrorist tactics.

Early in the administration of President Fidel Ramos [1992] the PC/INP [Philippine Constabulary and the Integrated National Police] were combined to form the Philippine National Police [PNP]. This placed all nationally based policing under a single organization. This restructuring was undoubtedly aimed at reducing the competition between the earlier PC and INP systems, whose members often bickered as to which system had, or should have, authority over the other, particularly when operating in local villages and towns. The PC, as a branch of the nationally organized "armed forces," and with authority equivalent to the military, felt it should have control. The INP, also nationally organized, argued for control over operations, especially since the officers were often more familiar than the PC with local institutions and influential citizenry. The unification appears to have taken hold, and other than the charges of corruption common throughout the government, appears to be accepted and successful. No complaints were voiced by locals to the researcher about this newly constructed system. This was one of President Ramos's first initiatives, and because he was commander of the Joint Chiefs of Staff of the military prior to being elected president, he was likely given the benefit of the doubt.

Between 1990 and 1995, the military and the PNP were effective in combating the communist rebels, so the *Alsa Masa* vigilante movement faded from view. However, by 1997 major newspapers were again reporting a regrouping and revamping of the New Peoples Army, and intense skirmishes resulting in deaths were again reported between the same old antagonists. It remains to be seen if the *Alsa Masa* will also reemerge, though its ultimate reestablishment seems likely.

Chapter 7

Bribery and Extortion

Coercing another person through intimidation to provide favors is prevalent in government and private sectors throughout the world (Heidenhein, 1970). The Philippines is no exception. In select areas of Mindanao, such activity appears to be so commonplace that it goes almost unnoticed. While technically remaining crimes, some extortion or bribery seems to have lost any earlier distinction as a cultural anomaly and appears as an expected behavior. Patterns of extortion, whether coercing another to provide something of value against his or her will, and the related practice of offering a bribe to elicit some advantage, beg to be more fully explored as prominent cultural features on the Mindanao landscape. This discussion provides some conceptual clarity to the changing character of these unique styles of illegal behavior and adds to our understanding of Filipino life ways.

It is beyond the scope of this chapter to give a wide-ranging comparative analysis of economic corruption. From a narrower perspective, this review analyzes accounts of prevalent but fluctuating extortion and bribery in the research setting of Mindanao. Three categories of research questions are addressed. First, what is the contemporary nature of extortion and bribery in the research setting? For example, how do these activities vary with regard to the type of favors offered or coerced from another and how do such behaviors differ from one social milieu to another? Second, what is the social organizational makeup of extortionate and briberous relationships? Specifically, what can be said about distinctions in role and status structures in different types of intimidating associations? Third, in what ways do local accounts depict a motivation or rationale for extortion and bribery, whether in the marketplace or, for example, in government offices? It is curious that given the substantial history of criminology and the longer development of anthropology, there remains today a relative paucity of literature on either extortion or bribery, both ancient and near-universal patterns of behavior. The Code of Hammurabi, the oldest known legal archive, dates from the twenty-second century BC and attests that extortionate relationships were notable in early Babylon (Driver & Miles, 1955:101). Historical reviews of criminal penalties portray extortion as a problem for Egyptians in the fourteenth century BC, for Old Testament Jews, as well as for early Chinese, Greeks, Romans, and Aztecs (Lasswell, 1963:690).

The deviant or unlawful quality of extortion could explain why it was rarely examined. Regarding Asian nations, Myrdal suggests that probing the sensitive topic of expansive corruption may have been taboo to outside researchers who likely biased their choice of topics away from embarrassing issues in an effort to remain diplomatic (1968:937–951). Regardless, the scholarly literature on official dishonesty and immorality, with particular emphasis on extorting and bribing behavior, is sporadic until perhaps the synthesis of works on political corruption by Heidenhein (1970). Even if extortion has been neglected as a research theme, it remains a fundamental type of illegal behavior, albeit variously enforced, among the diverse criminal codes of the world (compare Adas, 1981; Jain, 1979; and van den Berghe, 1975).

Both extortion and bribery represent deviant or unlawful styles of exerting influence or control over another. Unlawful or illegal acts refer to behavior in violation of the official government crime codes. Some extortionate and briberous activities may not technically be illegal but are still considered a violation of social norms and therefore deviant behavior, even if marginally so. Deviant activity may or may not involve violation of law. The issue is made more complex in that the two styles of influence [extortion and bribery] tend to overlap, creating conceptual confusion. Technically, extortion is "the obtaining or attempting to obtain something of value from another by compelling the other person to deliver it by threat of eventual physical injury or other harm to that person, his or her property, or a third party" (Rush, 1986:95). Extortion differs from robbery in that with robbery, there is an immediate confrontation between offender and victim and the threatened injury is physical and imminent [such as in an armed holdup]. Extortion is ordinarily considered a theft offense rather than a type of violence and thus would usually be viewed as a lesser crime than robbery. Bribery, on the other hand, is "the offering, giving, receiving, or soliciting of any thing of value to influence official action or the discharge of public duty" (Black, 1979:173).

Philippine definitions of extortion and bribery correspond to those in the U. S. Criminal Code after which they were likely modeled (Aquino, 1976). During martial law, the Philippines included bribery as one of the eleven crimes punishable by death, although no executions were known to have taken place. President Marcos apparently wished to depict his administration as one that would clean up corruption; thus the tough penalty for bribery. The death penalty was abolished in 1987 during the Aquino administration and reintroduced only for "heinous crimes" in 1993 during the regime of President Ramos (Morrison, 1994a). Bribery can pertain to illegal governmental operations such as police officials accepting payoffs. However, industrial or commercial bribery may also apply in the marginally private or quasi-government sectors when favors are solicited or offered to promote more efficient delivery of products or services, as in the case of electric and telephone utilities (Wertheim, 1970; Shleifer & Vishny, 1993). Confusion exists when one tries to determine exactly why a favor is offered. For instance, a bribe occurs if individuals of their own freewill, offer money under the table to reap special advantages from a government official. On the other hand, if individuals offer money surreptitiously because they feel intimidated and believe that not to do so would result in some disadvantage, it can be argued that they are being coerced or extorted. Accounts of influence peddling and intimidation among locals in Lanao del Norte allow probing of these conceptually gray areas.

A theoretical theme underlying this discussion is the presumption that peddling of favors [bribery] as well as compelling others to offer favors [extortion] are both types of social control. The growing literature on informal and unofficial styles of social control in folk and modern societies logically comes into play (Abel, 1982; Alper & Nichols, 1981; Nader & Todd, 1978). Of clear theoretical application is the early work of Donald Black (1976). In his recent work, *The Social Structure of Right and Wrong* (1993), the argument that social control may be considered a dependent variable is more fully developed. As such, numerous actions of individual and community emerge as independent variables, which influence social control. In addition to the establishment of laws that direct people to behave in specific ways, other actions may control the behavior of others, including crime itself (compare Black , 1983). Just as one may use physical force to control another [murder, assault], so can extortion and bribery act as mechanisms of social control. Following this theoretical argument, it is possible to analyze the social organization of extorting or bribing relationships. As the findings unfold, opportunity will be provided to view extorting and bribing activity from different vantage points and to further explore the viability of several of Black's concepts and propositions. For example, how do extortion and bribery vary with regard to the group structure in which they operate? What can be said of the number and direction of specialized roles, the duration of events, and whether or not extortion and bribery involve only the principals [offender and victim] or third parties as well. In this regard, Black introduces three types of relationships: unilateral [flowing in a single direction from offender to victim], bilateral [flowing in two directions at once], or trilateral [involving third-party intervention].

Additionally, in considering the style of social control, Black asks what are the varieties of motivations for independent variables such as extortion or bribery? Any style of deviance or crime may be viewed from the perspective of at least four incentives or inducements. These are penal, compensatory, therapeutic, and conciliatory. If extortion and bribery are viewed from a penal perspective, the deviant would be regarded as an offender who has violated a prohibition and who deserves punishment. The compensatory style depicts the offender as a debtor and liable for damages. In the therapeutic style, the offender is viewed as victim and in need of help. Finally, the conciliatory style sees the offender and victim as embroiled in a dispute in need of settlement (see Black, 1983:6–7). Such theoretical patterns will predictably give precision and clarity to an analysis of extortion and bribery in Lanao del Norte.

Close scrutiny of the field notes uncovered at least thirty episodes of extortion, most with allied accounts of bribery. These ranged from minor, spontaneous and almost trivial examples of coercion and influence peddling in daily interactions to major and long-term efforts to intimidate and gain advantage of highly placed government officials of the province. The variety of episodes can be roughly clustered into four categories, as shown in Table 7–1.

Table 7–1
Occurrence of Types of Extortion in Diverse Social Settings

Type Favor Demanded	Private Source	Public Quasi-official Source	Government: Appointed Source	Government: Elected Source
Cash payoffs	frequent	frequent	occasional	rare
Non-cash goods	occasional	rare	occasional	rare
Written endorsements	rare	rare	occasional	occasional
Status control	occasional	frequent	frequent	occasional

Each extortion category can also be arranged to show the type of social setting where its occurrence is most often observed. The occurrence of payola types as "frequent," "occasional," or "rare" does not reflect systematic quantification. The designations are based upon researcher identification of the subjective consensus of a team of six local expert informants. The four categories of cash payoffs, non-cash goods, written endorsement, and status control each deserve detailed explanation.

CASH PAYOFFS

A common type of extortion develops when someone's coercive efforts stimulate another to offer money. The amount of money could be large or small and the transaction may involve varying degrees of secrecy—sometimes under the table, sometimes not. Direct observation and informant accounts reveal that most cash payoffs in the Iligan region are nearly innocuous and have become sufficiently commonplace to have shed any earlier deviant label, at least as perceived by local citizenry. Pitching money out of a moving vehicle represents a minor but important example. What must appear rather bizarre to outsiders is the tossing of coins out the windows of vehicles by the more well-to-do citizens. This periodically occurred when a vehicle passed a military checkpoint or when a barricade was placed in a road to bottleneck vehicles, as when picket-line strikers wish to be seen by slow-moving traffic. Military as well as local police in Lanao del Norte have not in recent years routinely stopped vehicles during daylight hours. However, on past occasions they have been criticized for harassing vehicles' passengers. To be on the safe side some passengers throw money out the window to placate any potentially threatening troops. Or, when driving past a factory picket-line on the outskirts of Iligan City, the front-seat passenger near the window routinely tosses several pesos out the window to the road even while the car is moving. The primary purpose, it was learned, was not to give aid to out-of-work strikers but to mitigate any anger and rock-throwing tendency picketers may hold toward more affluent passers-by, especially if in an expensive vehicle. During such brief encounters the vehicle owners were responding to a perceived threat of the strikers or checkpoint guards. The strikers or troops must be defined as the initiators of extortion [requesting payoff's], even if covertly so. In the case of the checkpoint guards, the quiet but uniformed extorters could intimidate vehicle passengers through stares and wielding of shotguns or automatic rifles, even if from a distance.

Dropping money from vehicles can also be seen in the open markets of the town square, where elementary school–aged boys scamper for a few centavos. What appears on the surface to be a handout to street children can take a different turn. Youth will surround a vehicle and yell *bantay*, the Cebuano word for watch or guard. For a fee of pocket change, they will safeguard an automobile or jeep during the driver's absence. Upon approach of the *bantay* children, a vehicle driver either nods approvingly at the youth or quickly responds "no thank you." If approval is shown by the driver, nothing else is said. The driver walks away with the presumption that the vehicle will be guarded. Upon return of the driver, even several hours later, the boys will be close by and will approach the driver expecting payments. No amount is discussed and the driver will generally hand or toss several pesos or less to the boys. Local adults point out that the boys often organize themselves to the extent that they watch over multiple cars. There is substantial competition among the children to watch the vehicle of a prominent citizen, a tourist, or any foreigner.

Refusal to engage the services of the youngsters may encourage the children to vandalize the vehicle when the owner disappears into a nearby store. Even youth, due to their threat to property, can hold adults somewhat captive. Being coerced to pay for a public service [secure parking] is in Lanao del Norte a most rudimentary type of payoff. Such coin tossing appears to occur most often in private settings such as shopping districts or outside restaurants. It is easier and less expensive to placate the children than to run the risk of having the car stripped of valuable parts. The activity of the *bantay* youth appears analogous to windshield washers in Chicago and other large cities in the United States who, amidst traffic, intimidate drivers into paying for a service they do not want.

The *bantay* children are, for all practical purposes, street children or from low-income families. Whereas the *bantay* children may be respected for their enthusiasm and legitimate but rudimentary service, they are at least one step above the simpler form of begging which lures many children. Also, childhood begging can extend throughout life as an income source. Children beg on the street in greater numbers than adults and are much more persistent. Whereas the adult panhandler will, upon refusal of a handout, generally turn and walk away, the child often follows the adult target for many blocks and by nearly hanging onto the coattails of the annoyed adult will work to wear down the victim. The only way to escape seems to be either to turn with a vocal display of anger or to indeed offer up pocket change. The problem is that the youth are at every corner and even a single peso handed out each time becomes expensive. This begging scenario can be viewed as a mild form of extortion whereby the adult victim chooses to simply pay up rather than to be harassed for blocks. Another problem is that it may appear questionable for an adult to be seen loudly reprimanding an innocent-looking child who may have adult friends or relatives close by. It is common to see the child beggars hand over their profits to adults who remain in the shadows or hidden in the doorway of a crowded street. This operation is usually much better organized than first meets the eye. To avoid beggars by staying off the streets also victimizes some adults who are unable to move around the streets easily to carry out their own business transactions. Such is a most indirect and mild form of extortion.

Cash payments also occur in quasi-official settings when, for example, money is reluctantly exchanged for more efficient service. The surreptitious passing of a few pesos to encourage a utility company worker to fix a telephone or broken electrical line appears commonplace. Lack of an offer of money prior to the task could indefinitely postpone a service. Workers would not typically hold out a hand. Instead, money is secretly handed to service personnel, usually at the main telephone or electric company office. Only then can one be assured that repair workers will arrive at a private residence in a timely fashion. Locals would not approach a worker and brazenly say "Here is *hip-hip* [Cebuano for payola or bribe]." Rather, one might say "Here is a little extra." Just as likely, cash would be slipped into an employee's hand or pocket. Such payment should not be confused with a tip which would be offered after a service was rendered. Informants were single-minded in contending that such cash payments made prior to the service were payoffs or bribes and not tips or conventional fees for service. Oddly, the act of tipping after good service is relatively rare in the research setting. Locals often try to entice outsiders to not tip and remark, "It is their job to serve you." At the same time there is no hesitation to provide the *hip-hip*. Most likely, the term *hip-hip* originated from the action of an extorters [service providers, for example] touching their hand to their hip in the region of the wallet, reminding the victim of extortion that a little money may move things along more smoothly.

The necessity of offering payola to repair-shop employees was also commonplace. Unemployment is high in the Iligan area and many townspeople cannot afford new appliances. Instead, a radio or television set must be frequently repaired because of quick rusting and mildewing of electronic components in the equatorial zone. In such a repair-oriented economy, the routine trips to the service shops allow extortion and bribery to flourish. It is understood that if you want the appliance back quickly then you have to offer a little *hip-hip* up front. This amount would be in addition to any fee for service which would supposedly go to the repair-shop owner. What must be understood is that the service and repair workers hold customers at a disadvantage and can compel them to pay under the table. The customer is intimidated [or extorted], even if passively so, not because of a threat of violence but of being deprived of a necessary utility or repaired merchandise. At the same time, the payoff could in some cases be viewed as a bribe without intimidation.

Cash payoffs to government employees are common but a distinction must be made between elected and appointed officials. Elected officials, such as judges, town mayors or provincial governors, probably due to their higher public profile, would rarely solicit actual cash payoffs. Extorting and bribing activity involving such elected government employees would take other forms, as described later. Also, cash payments to elected officials, when they do occur, could likely be disguised as campaign contributions. It is with the numerous appointed bureaucrats of the province where one would at least occasionally encounter relatively small cash payoffs. Locals agree that appointed officials such as municipal police or *barangay* officials [neighborhood-level security officers] would occasionally accept cash bribes. These appointed officials receive meager salaries and often work at the street level side by side with citizenry, which increases opportunity for quick transfers of cash. Most common would be the passing of 10 to 50 pesos [about 50 cents to $2 U.S. in 1997] under the table to a minor government clerk who could control the processing of paperwork often critically important to citizens. Obviously, any such system discriminates against the poor who are unable to pay any extra bribe money.

On one occasion a sister was anxious to have a land deed transferred to her brother. Such transactions often proceed at a snail's pace and issues of who can legally farm a piece of land become confusing and problematic. The sister was observed stealthily handing a tightly folded 50-peso bill to the clerk while simultaneously saying "Can you 'personally' see this is taken care of?" The clerk quickly put the cash in her pocket without directly looking at the sister. Such transactions to stimulate processing of municipal or provincial papers, most of which is by hand and manual typewriter, appear widespread. Similarly, in Iligan City it is common to wait for hours before being assisted in banks by tellers. Some banks are becoming more orderly, with customers taking numbers and awaiting their turn. In other banks the tellers maintain a growing stack of paper petitions for service by customers who huddle in the lobby for hours waiting for their request to surface. A few pesos slipped to the teller can move a particular petition closer to the top. This practice of payoff to tellers could be viewed as either low-level extortion or simple bribery.

NON-CASH GOODS

Cash, easy to conceal and secretly implant, is more frequently handed out than other favors but it is not the only type of payoff. Three styles of non-cash favors were particularly notable in the region: rebel booty, squatting, and rewards to justice officials. For many decades the province has been a volatile area with regard to conflicting Muslim-Christian factions and opposing political rivals. Gang-land style violence is a recurring theme. Although a sporadic event, which occurs mainly on the outskirts of the city or in rural areas, rebel troops do band together as rag-tag mercenaries and are a menace to locals. One form of harassment well known in the area involves door-to-door soliciting for items of value to support religious or political uprisings. Such missions are prone to terrorist tactics; thus, when requested, villagers feel pressured to furnish donations. Food items such as rice or corn are sought after by the sometimes near-destitute renegades. Respondents report that payoffs also include cows, pigs, or chickens which are scurried off to rebel hideouts. Such items would likely be stolen if they were not handed over, according to longtime residents, so complying with the request is the lesser problem. The houses from which rebels acquired booty are earmarked so that allied dissidents passing by can detect the charitable from the unsympathetic residents. Those citizens who refuse must risk incurring the wrath of the rebels [see Chapter 5 on terrorism].

A related style of extortion, though never officially labeled as such, occurs when one refuses to pay required rent or to vacate a premise, thus becoming a "squatter." The demands of landlords are responded to by squatters with subtle or even blatant threats, sometimes reinforced with references to notorious rebel organizations. The property owner—typically a peaceful citizen who simply wants to make a living from rent—is left to seek satisfaction through the courts or else to take up arms in a dangerous attempt to counter squatter threats. Such illegal appropriation of land or housing can drag on for years in court; on occasion, even local officials become entangled with family or ethnic allegiances on one side or the other of the dispute.

This unusual type of non-cash extortion materializes when one party, for example, secretly builds a hut on a secluded piece of land. After several months a number of huts may arise, making their removal increasingly difficult. Sometimes a concrete walkway replaces a dirt path to give the appearance of permanence. Efforts by proprietors to collect rent are easily thwarted with threats against the rightful owner. On other occasions persons move into a house but simply refuse to pay rent. In one instance a Christian leased a house to a family he did not realize was Muslim. After several months elapsed with no rent money forthcoming, the landlord confronted the squatter who remarked "Take it to court and prove the house is really yours." It was learned that the judge was related to the squatter and it was clear that if any action were to be taken by the court, it would only be after a long delay. The landlord decided to take action himself to get rid of the squatter. He called together his sons and when they saw that the squatter was temporarily out of the house, the sons and father began to dismantle it piece by piece. When the squatter family returned and saw the house in pieces, and the original family owners standing angrily near, they fled and did not return. The owner then reconstructed the house, but at major expense. Such an encounter could have easily resulted in bloodshed.

In the research area an entire village arose on prime beachfront property mainly resulting from a collection of squatters. In time, with no resolution of property disputes against the squatter village—either legal or otherwise—the village incorporated, subdivided into *barangays*, and eventually became officially established as part of the city. Even though locals have owned a piece of land for generations, it may be difficult to produce original documentation in a court. Deeds dating from before World War II were often on non-durable paper and have long since deteriorated, even if they can be located. Even paperwork in the courts is subject to the most primitive storage and filing systems in non air-conditioned environments and waste away in the humid, tropical air.

Non-cash gifts to justice officials appear to be occasional or rare. Yet, as a distinct category they form a separate style of potential extortion or bribery. On infrequent occasions, food items were observed being placed by litigants on judge's desks in private chambers. It was unclear if these were offers to entice a particular judgment or rather in gratitude after a favorable judicial outcome. Respondents felt that such cases generally reflect families of defendants simply offering uncoerced favors after a settlement; the families likely did not think of such activity as unethical. One prominent judge who was present when gifts were placed on a desk shrugged his shoulders and remarked "That's just something they do." Informants recounted a different case of apparent extortion by justice officials when police officers, using personal vehicles, were observed acquiring gasoline from a station after hours when it was closed to the public. Such an incident would not generally be thought unusual. However, a politically motivated murder had occurred at that location in earlier months and informants were convinced gasoline was being provided to police as a favor or payoff for protection to the station owner. In this situation it would be difficult to separate extortion from giving or receiving a bribe.

WRITTEN ENDORSEMENTS

Respondents were quick to agree that a most disheartening type of extortion involves the control and manipulation of a fellow employee by withholding written endorsements, generally by a superior over a subordinate. A most clear type of intimidation pertains to government officials who refuse to sign [endorse] final separation papers for a retiring employee. One of the perks of government employment in the research area is that a portion of money is set aside each pay period by an agency to act as a kind of severance or "terminal-leave" pay. After decades of service, career workers may accumulate sums of 100,000 or more pesos. Employees carefully plan their exit from work fully expecting to advantage themselves of the funds to ease the transition to retirement. With an employee's retirement imminent, a superior or manager must declare in writing that the subordinate is leaving office in good standing and with no outstanding debts or obligations. Without this declaration the worker's terminal-leave pay remains in limbo. Locals are well aware of the pressure to stay on the good side of government supervisors as retirement approaches. All informants were mindful of the anxiety felt throughout the last year of government service when subordinates must walk a straight and narrow path. This anxiety is compounded in politically dynamic government agencies headed by unscrupulous officials.

Such an extortion style in the research area appears limited primarily to government service, whether municipal, city, or province. Private work settings may also experience such unsavory manipulations of terminal-leave but the laying aside of funds may not be as bureaucratized. Any details of money amounts and how pensions might be distributed to retiring employees is left up to private proprietors; this could also present problems for employees not on good terms with their supervisors. Many city and provincial politicians continue to represent wealthy and powerful family clans which have remained in office for decades and in some cases hold animosity for select subordinates of rival clans (Morrison, 1994b). This practice appears similar to cases in the United States and elsewhere whereby managers mysteriously release employees just prior to the date when the employee would be vested and due a pension. The potential exists for both extortion and bribery. Simple bribery would occur if the subordinate were to offer favors to the superior in hopes of winning a smooth release of terminal-leave pay.

Such cases appeared to be rare in the Lanao del Norte area. However, more recurrent and conspicuously unethical are cases whereby elected officials hold a retiring subordinate as hostage by demanding unrealistic tasks during the last few months or even weeks prior to retirement. In the case of one aging government employee, a son admonished his father with the words, "Don't upset the mayor. Remember, your terminal-leave is being processed." The father, who was an influential member of the community, was later denied terminal-leave after retirement for refusing to manipulate the supervision of the ballot boxes which would have proven favorable to a local politician. Even after several years had elapsed, cronies of the politician would continue to visit the retired employee and offer to have the terminal-leave processed if he would perform several illicit tasks. Especially problematic are cases of permanently assigned lower officials [government clerks] under supervision of more transient elected officials who may come and go with changing political tides. It behooves the subordinate to appear as a political ally of the transitory supervisor or at least to remain neutral. Complicating such scenarios in the area are ongoing social, class, and ethnic tensions, which tend to contaminate work relationships and indirectly influence the processing of terminal-leave papers. Muslim workers who are subordinate to Christian bosses may suffer, and the reverse is also true.

Informants of the province argued that it was common for persons approaching retirement to locate intermediaries to smooth the path toward successful endorsements. Occasionally, bribe money, such as a portion of the terminal-leave, may be offered to, or requested by, the go-between. Those retirees unwilling to engage in bribery may lose any chance of recovering their separation funds, at least until an antagonistic politician is replaced in subsequent elections. As a final insult to the suffering employee, the supervisor may be able to transfer the stockpiled funds into the agency's operating budget and thus indirectly gain access to the accumulated leave pay.

STATUS CONTROL

The field notes revealed instances where locals were influenced, and sometimes intimidated, not by money, goods, or endorsements, but simply by the presence of high-status individuals. Social control may be subtle in such cases. However, examples are evident whereby villagers and townsfolk are compelled to move or to act because of the elevated status of another entering the scene. Around Iligan City, rank appears to be a function of money, political connections, and family-ethnic heritage. These variables are not mutually exclusive, and overlap is the rule rather than the exception. Political prominence is often gained by persons with money and family connections. On the other hand, considerable status may be periodically wielded by persons of average income, such as academicians and religious leaders. By considering the relevance of status in social interaction, particularly in the marketplace and during other routine activities, a fourth category of extortion emerges among the residents of Lanao del Norte.

As shown in Table 7–1, status applies across a variety of social settings. In private encounters, social status plainly comes into play but informants suggest that bribery or extortion would be only occasional rather than frequent. A prominent individual entering a marketplace stall to purchase a mango would be expected to pay the advertised price just as any other shopper would. However, that same esteemed individual, upon entering a quasi-official agency such as a bank or utility company, would rarely sit in line with other locals. Instead, the high-status customer would be beckoned to a rear office where individualized service would be provided. It is common for prominent individuals to expect privileged responses to status. Similarly, one of high status would unlikely experience any delay in gaining rapid service from utility companies. High-ranking individuals would not personally make rude demands for special services. Instead, a person of prominence is accompanied by an entourage of hangers-on [bodyguards, drivers] who usually pave the way for the entrance of the high-ranked person. The approach of a prominent personage is announced by the appearance of an expensive vehicle [commonly a van with all windows tinted and disallowing any view inside the vehicle] with multiple passengers accompanying the celebrated party. Bodyguards casually display their weapons.

Thus, low-intensity extortion arguably occurs when an individual enters a workplace anticipating the offer of special favors. Such commonplace scenarios take on an increasingly deviant image when interactions involve official or government transactions. As an example, consider the prominent individual who presupposes that special indulgences will be forthcoming, as when police soft-pedal or ignore unlawful behavior. Informants claim that in addition to the substance of any dispute or illegal act, police officials ordinarily give careful attention to a party's personal identity. Such shifting and posturing in small groups in response to the varied rank of members is a natural process in all social settings. However, as this social-control mechanism reaps special favors and is observed among the citizenry in the research area to express threat and harassment, then a type of extortion must be presumed to exist.

A different style of status-related corruption develops with regard to religious distinctions. The mixture of Islamic and Christian Filipinos in the region intensifies extortionate relationships at the small-group level in daily affairs. Extremists prevail in both religious camps, with each convinced that members of the other religion exemplify distrusted infidels. Long-simmering prejudice between the two cultures, each perceiving the other as subordinate, results in numerous antagonistic encounters. At the marketplace both may be seen butting in line in front of the other.

The potential for extortion increases when hostility of one group toward the other includes suspicion and fear upon another's approach. This gives rise to the attitude of "Give them what they want to get rid of them." For instance, such a disposition is observed when a Muslim individual may have occasion to appear at a front gate in a Christian neighborhood. Such an encounter could reflect the unusual circumstance of a lower-status individual extorting one of a higher status for favors. For example, a poor individual may call from the front gate and request a handout of rice. The homeowner may provide rice out of fear of retaliation. Theoretically, the same incident would exist in a predominately Muslim neighborhood when the outsider is Christian. However, Christians argue they would never go into a Muslim area asking for rice handouts.   At any rate, without a specific purpose, ethnic outsiders would seldom linger within a neighborhood to which they do not belong.   Suspicion and sometimes fear result in rudeness based on an assumption that the outsider is up to no good. Many similar patterns can be found in diverse cultural areas of the world. See, for example, problems of off-reservation Crow Indians (Austin, 1984).

Caucasian outsiders, even if European or Australian, are generically referred to in Lanao del Norte as *Amerikanos* or simply as *kanos*. Such persons are few in number and are regularly given deference as high-status individuals. This results from the assumption they have U.S. dollars and are from a land many locals aspire to reach. Consequently, it is commonplace for special favors to be offered the outsider, whether or not requested. In the marketplace, they are sought after as valuable and popular customers. They are given special consideration in crowded lobbies and rarely expected to stand in line. Often a chair will be hurried over to an American guest while locals must remain standing, placing the guest in an awkward position. Refusal by the *kano* to accept special favors results in surprise and perplexity.

Locals claim that even traffic officers are apt to ignore infractions by *Amerikanos*. Field accounts portray traffic police at a busy intersection walking up to a vehicle to warn the driver. Upon seeing the driver is Caucasian, the officer immediately turns away. Since local police speak some English, it must be assumed that anxiety about having to speak English did not cause the officer to turn away. This pattern remains unclear. Perhaps Americans are accorded special exemptions because in past years local Catholic priests in the area have often come from the United States. It would be unusual for the Caucasian to exploit and thus extort such status-oriented favors. However, Filipino locals can attach themselves to *Amerikano* outsiders and through association indirectly realize special courtesies which spill over onto them. In such cases it is the hanger-on who becomes a discreet extorter by sustaining indirect-status enhancement. Such efforts are sometimes observed by potential victims as contrived. Attempts to gain derivative advantages may not always succeed and may reflect poorly on the high-status outsider.

INTERACTIONAL DYNAMICS OF INTIMIDATION

Deviance and crime occur in a social context and require an initiator of action [offender] and a victim. Extortion and bribery are not exceptions. A closer look at the descriptive accounts of intimidation provide clarification of the social structure of extortion and bribery in Lanao del Norte. Four features must be highlighted: role complexity and distance, role direction, duration of coercion, and rationale for intimidation.

Role Complexity and Distance

Extorting and bribing relationships range from simple to complex and occur in face-to-face encounters as well as from a distance. In their most rudimentary form bribery and extortion may involve one or more persons doing the victimizing without any face to face interaction with an extorter. For instance, citizens could suffer while patiently sitting in a bank lobby awaiting service as other customers give secret payoffs to tellers for quicker recognition. In such a case victimization could come about without the victims realizing what is going on in their immediate surroundings. Even if customers are aware of the exchange of favors, which is likely, but ignore such activity, they still experience longer waits in the bank lobby, which commonly extends throughout an entire morning. Thus, to provide payola to a teller is economically victimizing by being costly, and not to pay can also be frustrating and victimizing by being forced to remain in long lines. Without direct contact, an intimidating relationship can persist but with one party remaining only latently involved. As soon as one is compelled to offer favors or payola, then extortion becomes active and more complex, even if limited to two parties. Other examples apply. If a vehicle owner refuses to pay the *bantay* children for safekeeping a jeep, but worries about leaving the vehicle untended, the owner sustains passive victimization.

The reverse, of course, could also be true, whereby a driver gives cash to *bantay* boys when, in fact, the boys had no intention of harming the vehicle. Thus, it is possible an occupational position [*bantay* workers] may be conducive to extortion even if the person occupying the position has no intention to extort. The same argument holds true with police. If police in general are feared as extorters, it would not be surprising for locals to offer any particular police officer a bribe. This is also true of the checkpoint guards who may look intimidating but some of whom may not wish to extort passers-by. In the research area it is clear that most accounts recalled by informants reflected multiple offenders and victims. Picketers and checkpoint guards operated in small groups as did the *bantay* youth; the entourage attached to high-status individuals provided an aggregate extortionate force which could simultaneously intimidate multiple victims. Even when the retiring government employee fell victim to the recalcitrant supervisor, the entire family of the retiree grieved as victims, whether or not the extortionate relationship culminated with a victim offering payoffs.

Also, the proximity of victims to offenders may be distant or close and the relationship may vary in degrees of secrecy. With the exception of the clandestine transfer of cash to offer a bribe or to instantly appease an extorter, most victim-offender relationships occur at a distance [not face to face] and are relatively overt or unsecluded. This suggests that initiators of extortion commonly act as if they have nothing to hide by their intimidation of others and at the same time do not wish to associate with victims. Among the townsfolk, picketers and checkpoint guards operate from a distance and in the open, as do house or land squatters. The same can be said for utility employees or appliance-repair staff who passively coerce customers to pay extra for service. Radical religious factions, too, whether Muslim or Christian, can intimidate from a distance as from a front gate. Even the high-ranking politician who harasses a subordinate by delaying written endorsements may do so from a distance, via letters and memoranda, and at least for a time refrain from any face to face contact with victims.

In the research area no one wears a label as an extortioner, although it is well known in which settings extorters are likely to flourish. Secrecy seems to vary with the degree of deviance associated with a particular extortionate activity. The *bantay* boys are extorting but do not see it as such. It represents a low level of deviation typifying an unsophisticated style of coercion. Utility-service workers certainly do not advertise any eagerness to accept bribes or to extort others by delaying service. However, when payoffs are offered, they willingly receive the under-the-table *hip-hip* and are aware of their own secret identity. The most specialized of the extortionate types is clearly the supervisor who intimidates by manipulating a needed endorsement. Here the offender and victim relationship is most distinctive, with the extorter fully realizing how a subordinate can be intimidated. Even so, in this complicated scenario, attempts to extort or victimize an employee may be disguised. That is, the supervisor may fabricate explanations indicating that an employee holds unfulfilled obligations, thus encumbering retirement funds.

Role Direction

Following suggestions by Black (1993:5–6) any mechanism of social control varies with regard to direction and must also apply to extortion and bribery. As shown in Table 7–2, the direction of extorting and bribing relationships may be unilateral, bilateral, or trilateral.

Table 7–2
Incidence of Types of Extortion/Bribery by Pattern of Social Interaction

Interaction Pattern Offered/Received	Cash Payoffs	Non-cash Goods	Written Endorsements	Status Controls
Unilateral: one-way only	frequent	frequent	rare	frequent
Bilateral: clear offer and receipt of favor	occasional	occasional	occasional	rare
Trilateral: use of third-party fixer	rare	rare	occasional	rare

When an extortionate relationship flows only in one direction, as from offender to victim, a unilateral pattern is evident. Numerous such relationships persist in the research area, as portrayed whenever an extorter is unsuccessful. This would apply when one ignores another's attempt to extort. Also, if a bribe were offered but not accepted, then the attempt to influence was unilateral.

Table 7–2 indicates that cash payoffs, non-cash gifts, and status control are frequently unilateral, with only one party being actively engaged in the deviant or illegal enterprise. On the other hand, manipulation of an employee's terminal-leave is rarely unilateral. When both parties are consciously resourceful in an extortionate or bribing relationship, with interaction moving in both directions, a bilateral pattern exists. Such cases are more complex and at the same time appear to be associated with an increasingly deviant or severe style of lawbreaking. Severity of deviance is taken on face value. That is, manipulation of life savings is greater than loss of rent money, which in turn is greater than payoff to a utility-company worker, which is greater than paying *bantay* boys. Any case in the research area which shows two-way interaction would be bilateral. Tossing coins to pacify picketers is bilateral as is the case of the landlord who disassembled the house of the squatter. Table 7–2 shows three categories of extortion and bribery to be occasional; only status control is depicted as rarely bilateral.

Trilateral relationships arise when interaction involves the intervention of a third party. In the research area, the incidence of these more complex styles of extortion or bribery is rare compared to the simpler unilateral and bilateral styles. However, when government officials manipulate endorsements, third-party intervention is more likely. In the case described, the victim who refused to bow to the demands of the conniving politician was visited by several associates of the politician who attempted to persuade the retiring employee to concede and thereby gain endorsement of the extorting supervisor. At the same time, the victim called upon his own supporters for advice and assistance and to act as intermediaries to prompt the supervisor to approve release of terminal-leave pay. The case of the house squatter who refused to pay rent also involved trilateral interactions, which included both unofficial townspeople who were unsuccessful mediators and the court, which refused to take official action.

Duration of Coercion

Accounts of locals plainly distinguished between short and long-term extortion activity (see Table 7–3). Only cash payoffs and status control are depicted

Table 7–3
Duration of Coercive Impact of Distinct Types of Extortion

Type of Extortion	Tendency for Short-term Coercion	Tendency for Long-term Coercion
Cash payoffs	frequent	rare
Non-cash goods	occasional	rare
Written endorsements	rare	occasional
Status controls	frequent	rare

as frequent coercive forces in the short term. When cash is involved, the impact of intimidation appears to be brief. This is true whether tossing coins into the street to placate picketers or giving under-the-table payola to government clerks. When written endorsements are manipulated, the intimidation may be longlasting. Some cases extend for years without resolution. In fact, written endorsements as a type of extortion rarely occur in the short term at all.

Although a variety of types of extortion and bribery can be identified in Lanao del Norte, most types rarely occur over the long term. An argument can be made that extortion and bribery are widespread, but at the same time most such episodes of economic corruption pertain to brief encounters. Yet, a discussion of duration and frequency cannot reveal the magnitude or intensity that even a specific instance of extortion has upon an individual. For example, manipulation of written endorsements, not easily resolved, may greatly damage a retiree's quality of life. The same was found to be true in the case of land and house squatting. Predictably, therefore, the more routine and brief types of intimidation suggest milder forms of irritation with less long term impact. Also important but not surprising, the more multidirectional and severe the extortion, the longer the duration of the intimidation.

Rationale for Extortion and Bribery

The episodes of economic corruption among the citizenry may take the form of seeking inappropriate favors from a public official [bribery] or coercion of another to give payola [extortion] with each style of deviance overlapping the other. It is sometimes difficult to determine if one is offering a bribe or is being extorted. Confusion exists, for example, when the anticipation of extortion, whether authentic or not, prompts a bribe offer. However, the occurrence of any such activity appears to always involve intimidation, whether ranging from slight apprehension felt by one who is offering a bribe to harassment and threat felt by a victim of extortion. Also, it is clear that the rationale underlying such extortionate or bribing relationships may take multiple forms. That is, what motivates one person to extort and another person to respond to an extorter with payola is not readily implied or directly understood. However, following Black (1976; 1993), if extortion and bribery represent types of social control, then the various rationales given for social control must also apply. Thus, it should be possible to identify, even if roughly so, whether or not the underlying motivations for the various accounts and case studies reflect penal, compensatory, therapeutic, or conciliatory styles of control. In Lanao del Norte, motivations for intimidation include all of the four styles as predicted by Donald Black, some occurring more often than others and some in unexpected ways. Penal and compensatory rationales apply when relationships are accusatory. Therapeutic and conciliatory rationales involve remedial relationships (see Black, 1976:4)

Accusatory Responses. A penal rationale for extortion exists when one party wishes to punish or victimize the other. Such relationships would imply a vengeful posture in efforts to coerce and control another. In fact, a penal or punitive rationale is comparatively rare in the research setting. Punitive accounts that do surface, however, may be vicious. Land or house squatters do not appear to be motivated by vengeance, but the victimized landlord may respond punitively out of revenge. Similarly, the politician may not set out to punish a retiring employee but without question the victim feels punished and may be motivated to seek vengeance. More precisely, the notes reveal that usually one party of the extortionate relationship is motivated, for example, by a felt need for compensation, while the other may feel compelled to make a penal or punitive response. The squatter may argue that "The landowner does not need so much land" which is translated by the squatter as a right to be compensated for being poor.

Overlap between punitiveness and compensation is also observed in the case of rebels who solicit cash or food handouts from rural residents. The extremist groups, usually with weapons and in makeshift uniforms, present a fearful image. The extorted victims could take a punitive stance or, more likely, acquiesce and offer compensation to the extorters. When payola is given, the victims can rationalize being extorted as paying a debt to the disadvantaged rebels. Similarly, when using personal status as a lever to exert control over others, the underlying motivation would likely be compensatory rather than penal. That is, the individual who disrespects the subordinate position of others, as at queuing stations in department stores or some bank lobbies, is motivated not by vengeance but by a perceived right to be compensated. Here the extorter maintains an attitude of "get out of my way, I am more important than you." Victims tend to respond by yielding to the demands of the dominant figure.

Compensation, whether demanded, as in extortion, or offered, as in payola in the form of a bribe, appears to reflect the most prevalent underlying rationale for intimidation (see Table 7–4). If an extorter's threat is punitive, such as a rebel soldier demanding handouts, the victim commonly counters with compensation. When the extorter is motivated strictly by a need for compensation, as in the cases of the house squatter and the manipulating politician, the response is commonly punitive. If both parties are punitive, the relationship may turn violent, which only escalates the situation. An unverbalized motive may be to avoid responses which could lead to violent confrontations [fighting fire with fire] which is a last resort in the research setting.

Remedial Responses. Filipinos have a long tradition of attempting to informally resolve disputes and grievances outside official court. Extortionate and briberous relationships do include such examples although they are not as widespread as the more accusatory responses [penal and compensatory]. However, remedial [therapeutic and conciliatory] responses to intimidation do occur. For instance, therapeutic responses apply occasionally with regard to cash payoffs. Locals agree that when a few pesos are given to the *bantay* youth, a feeling of providing charity to street children prevails, even if victims felt somewhat coerced by a threat of vehicle vandalism. In this case, if compensation is also included as a motivation [more of a non-compassionate payment of debt to the less fortunate] it would be secondary to a therapeutic rationale. A therapeutic rationale may occasionally accent the giving of payola in the form of "non-cash goods." An example would be the case of religious extremists who, as dirt-poor rebel soldiers, extort handouts. Offering of goods as payola would generally be considered

Table 7–4
Incidence of Types of Intimidation by Rationale and Setting

Rationale for extortion/bribery	Cash Payoffs private public gov't			Non-cash Goods private public gov't			Written Endorsements private public gov't			Status Control private public gov't		
Penal	o	r	r	o	r	r	r	r	o	r	r	r
Compensatory	f	o	o	o	o	o	o	r	o	o	o	o
Therapeutic	f	o	r	o	r	o	r	r	r	n/a	n/a	n/a
Conciliatory	r	o	r	r	r	o	r	r	o	n/a	n/a	n/a

f = frequent, o = occasional, r = rare, n/a = not applicable compensation, although some locals who embrace rebel principles feel a therapeutic orientation applies in the sense of helping needy soldiers. A sense of compassion is likely more prevalent toward the street children compared to the adult rebels. A similar case is found with regard to money thrown to picketers, which would only in rare instances be considered an act of therapy rather than compensation. The unemployed strikers are adults and whereas some victims of extortion feel the strikers need help, the money is more accurately viewed as compensation. Extorters would rationalize their fate with statements such as "I deserve help due to my dedicated suffering while awaiting better working conditions."

Conciliation, on the other hand, as a remedial response presumes a motive to maintain social harmony or to encourage repair of a damaged relationship. In its most pure form, according to Black (1976:5), negotiation would prevail whereby the aggrieved parties together restore their broken relationship to its former condition. With regard to extortion among the residents of Lanao del Norte, this appears to only occur rarely. If one person reaches a point of extorting another, then negotiation as a remedy between offender and victim is unlikely. At the same time, taking the matter to court in the research area would probably reap few benefits. Representing oneself as a victim of extortion in formal court may be embarrassing to the victim and the case could be litigated for years with each side denouncing the other. The case of the house squatter who countered the victim of extortion with a "Prove you own the house" defense is a good case in point. Also, the case of the manipulation of terminal-leave pay was never resolved by negotiation or arbitration in formal court. It is not unusual for a judge to be indirectly linked politically to one of the parties of the dispute, making formal arbitration further problematic.

Mediation makes most sense in the more severe cases and is a style of informal control familiar to Filipinos of the province. Yet, even mediation appears to have only limited success in extortionate relationships. When complex cases become trilateral, and pertain to severe deviation from community norms, mediation is the choice of resolution style. However, as these cases extend for many months or years, the maneuver of "non-action" emerges, not so much as a specific resolution style but simply that as events unfold mediation takes so long to run its course. Extended delays certainly benefit the land squatter as well as the supervisor withholding endorsement of terminal-leave pay. In many instances a land owner gives up and a squatter eventually appropriates the property, even gaining support from others who squat in nearby areas. Victims of delayed terminal-leave funds, after an elapse of years, find themselves simmering over the lost capital, but still surviving day by day, albeit as poorer retirees.

The field notes have permitted a productive response to the research questions. This is notably true with regard to the quest for conceptual clarity of extortionate and briberous relationships in Lanao del Norte. Analyses of personal accounts of longtime residents provided a typology of favors, either offered or coerced, in a variety of intimidating circumstances. The social organizational makeup of extortionate scenarios is better understood. Examples of extortion and bribery are shown to vary in complexity and in the degree of distance and secrecy separating offenders from victims. The chapter offers further clarification of Donald Black's thinking on the behavior of law. Of particular importance is the consideration of extortion and bribery as modes of social control. Black's use of the concepts of penal, compensatory, therapeutic, and conciliatory styles of social control proved to be constructive in interpreting rationales of extortion and bribery. The same can be said of Black's prediction of unilateral versus multilateral relationships which are also shown to have utility in detailing extortionate relationships.

This chapter originated in part with a curiosity about a possible growing tolerance of bribery in the research area. However, any comprehensive interpretation of why extortion and bribery may be losing some of their deviant image was necessarily set aside in order to concentrate on description, typology construction, and basic social-structural patterns. Future inquiry into the likely progressive leniency and legitimization of some styles of bribery and extortion should pay attention to at least four factors. First, what is the impact of the unstable and sometimes grim economic conditions of northwest Mindanao on the nature and incidence of bribery and extortion?

Some evidence may support an assumption that low wages and underemployment tend to be associated with economic corruption. A bold attempt to extort cash would appear to apply more than other styles of extortion discussed here. For example, the likelihood that a lowly paid police officer may increase his income by coercing bribe money does seem plausible and is a widely held perception in the region. Second, the Filipinos of Lanao del Norte tend to maintain social control at the community level without reliance on formal or official police as has been described throughout this book. In what ways might the absence of police, and a heightened dependence on neighborhood self-help networks, based on wide discretionary powers of influential citizenry, cultivate an atmosphere conducive to extortion and bribery?

Third, does the long Filipino tradition of reciprocal gift exchange underlie a modern affinity for extortion and influence peddling? If so, when does a gift become a bribe? Also, in the cultural context, is there something in the early socialization of Filipinos in the region which fosters reckless competition between individuals and which can, if allowed to stray, lead to rule bending and violation of law? Finally, the poor in the research area logically feel the impact of victimization more than the rich. The well-to-do in the region need not concern themselves with the generally small amounts of money needed for most cash bribes. They have telephones, new kitchen appliances, servants, and chauffeurs. Compared to the poor, if they are extorted, they are either in a position to provide payola or, due to their higher social status, to more successfully challenge a case in formal court. Although perhaps a latent function, the customs of extortion and bribery work to perpetuate a subservient class of citizens. Such a conflict-theory orientation deserves closer scrutiny.   Earlier reports illustrate how formal law may either purposely or inadvertently target and adversely affect the poor   (Austin, 1987b; Diamond, 1971; Turk, 1976).

PART III

Toward Interpretations

P art III continues a discussion of themes but tends to move increasingly in the direction of deciphering and interpreting some of the descriptive accounts. This is not to say that the previous discussion of Special Themes in Part II is devoid of interpretation or that the remaining chapters are without descriptive accounts. Yet, with caution, several interpretations are initiated in Part III to further whet the appetite of those searching for theoretical explanations of some of the social problems in the research area.

Chapter 8 considers the youth of the region and combines official data with field notes to profile the juvenile delinquency issue. Also introduced here are the pervasive problems of neglected youth and several deviant occupations appealing to some youth in the research area. It must fall as somewhat of an embarrassment to Philippine society to be confronted with the social problem of detached youth. After all, a positive feature of island life has traditionally been a sense of cooperation and community. The plight of contemporary youth is briefly presented, in part as a negative fallout of an unstable economy.

Chapter 9 pursues relatively uncharted theoretical directions by suggesting that the research setting can be viewed as a culture where rule bending and, in some cases, flagrant disregard for law, approach normalization. A combination of diverse styles of rejecting social norms seems to present a chaotic social climate where disregard for law becomes firmly embedded in the local culture. Beginning with analogies of indifference to motor-vehicle laws, a case is made that other kinds of social apathy create an atmosphere of near anarchy in Lanao del Norte. Although to the outsider such lawlessness looks chaotic, the possibility remains that such chaos is sometimes functional to locals. A final chapter reviews the major conclusions and suggests needed directions for future inquiry.

Chapter 8

Considering Youth

A s with other Asian nations, most notably China and Singapore, the Philippines has not given extensive attention to either criminology or juvenile delinquency as areas of concentration in its universities compared to the United States and other Western nations. Departments of criminology are rare, and dissertations and theses do not commonly use, if at all, the terms criminology or delinquency in their titles. Discussions of problems of youth must be absorbed into the broader contexts of more generic social sciences, social work, and humanities. This is not necessarily bad or good, but a matter of academic orientation. In a similar way, prior to the emergence of criminology courses in the United States in the 1920s and 1930s, issues of youth were subsumed by anthropology, sociology, political science, and related disciplines. What criminology programs do exist in the Philippines often tend to portray a more "police science" perspective.

Another difficulty is that the Philippine government, compared to the West, has seen less need to maintain statistical data, or to establish official programs addressing problems of youth. Although this clearly frustrates statistical inquiry and quantitative analysis by the researcher, one should not jump to a conclusion that lack of government agencies necessarily poses a predicament for the child. In Europe and the United States, a case could be made for repealing many of the juvenile delinquency laws and dismantling many youth-oriented social-service agencies and returning to a time when nongovernment agencies managed problem youth. Asian nations that give limited governmental attention to juvenile delinquency would undoubtedly reflect less of an "official" problem with delinquency. As is true in other nations, it is difficult to decipher whether delinquency rates are an artifact of agency records or, in fact, they represent reality. Regardless, if available at all, systematic delinquency rates are not easily acquired in the Philippines and the outside observer could presume, whether valid or not, that delinquency is relatively inconsequential or one of the lesser problems facing the nation.

Even if indirect and somewhat latent, many features of crime and custom relevant to Filipino youth were alluded to in other chapters of this book. Certainly, for example, disruptive influences of terrorism, Muslim-Christian conflict, corruption and anarchy do not impact only upon adults. Based on the data, the following pages will reassemble and reconsider some of these observations and judgments made elsewhere to highlight Filipino youthful involvement in deviance and law-breaking in the research settings. First, however, what can be said about the official procedures for dealing with juvenile delinquency? While the official response is still sporadic and without national coordination to encompass outlying islands, the Philippines has not totally ignored the problem of youthful misbehavior and crime.

In 1906 a law was passed which recognized that juveniles require special and humane treatment, and should be dealt with differently than adult offenders (Esguerra, 1979:49). Undoubtedly influenced by the juvenile justice movement in the United States, the law was modified several times and by 1930 was established as the Juvenile Delinquency Law. However, even with the law intact, special courts to manage juvenile delinquency did not appear until 1955, more than half a century after they had begun to appear in the Western Hemisphere. Shoemaker and Austin (1996:240) write: "Currently, these courts are referred to as Juvenile and Domestic Relations Courts [JDRC's]. Not all the laws providing for separate juvenile courts are uniform and furthermore, juvenile courts have yet to be established in many metropolitan areas, such as Cagayan de Oro City, on Mindanao island."

During the martial law years of the presidency of Ferdinand Marcos, several significant adjustments to law were made by presidential decree. First, in 1974, the Child and Youth Welfare Code was established, setting forth procedures for juvenile justice in the Philippines. This law, gave the Department of Social Welfare and Development [DSWD] primary responsibility for the welfare of youth. The law also stipulates how the DSWD will be responsible for the processing of youthful offenders through the justice system and also for the detainment and institutionalization of youthful offenders (Albada-Lim, 1978). The Child and Youth Welfare Code stipulates that in cases involving more severe offenses, the *barangay* captain is to refer the case either to the police, the prosecutor [fiscal], or the Department of Social Welfare and Development. If and when the police are notified, or if they have directly observed a serious illegal act committed by a juvenile, they may make an arrest and may file cases directly with the court.

The fiscal then is supposed to schedule physical and mental evaluations for the juvenile before an official court hearing takes place. Youth found guilty by a court may be imprisoned. Judges have the authority to overturn an earlier court decision after appeal by the offender and with recommendations of the Department of Social Welfare and Development. As is the case in many Western nations, the juvenile may be incarcerated until reaching adulthood, which may vary from eighteen to twenty-one years of age. Presumably, most first offenders processed in court are turned over to the DSWD and if they are to be incarcerated, it is in a Regional Rehabilitation Center for Youth [RRCY]. In fact, any other home or facility considered suitable may also be used. Periodic progress reports on each detainee are provided the sentencing judge by the Department of Social Welfare and Development.

Shoemaker and Austin (1996:244) report that the records of the Department of Social Welfare and Development are limited yet more informative than other national data regarding juvenile offenders. Officials of the DSWD explained that there are ten Regional Rehabilitative Centers for Youth spread throughout the Philippines (see Shoemaker, 1996:39–52). Each has a capacity of 50 youth, and between 1990 and 1992 a total of 1,695 were held in these institutions. Although no details were given by the Department of Social Welfare and Development, they also stipulated that another 11,103 youthful offenders were being treated during the same period in "noninstitutional" settings. Less than 2,000 youth living in captive settings in a nation of 70 million people is an extremely low number by most Western standards. The illegal acts for which the incarcerated youth were convicted were mainly property crimes [about 78 percent], which includes robbery. So called "person crimes" comprised about 12 percent of the total [i.e., rape, assault, homicide] and another 10 percent represent miscellaneous and more minor acts such as possessing a weapon or disobeying parents.

Shoemaker and Austin point out that "Interestingly, no offender placed in a Regional Rehabilitation Center for Youth was convicted of a drug offense. It is unimaginable that drug offenses are not committed by youth in the Philippines" (1996:244). What happens to drug offenders is simply not a matter of clear public record. They could be managed informally at the community level by the DSWD but not referred to the rehabilitation centers, or perhaps dealt with by other agencies such as the military. Likely, they are managed behind the scenes within the *barangays*. Fieldwork in 1997 reveals that possession and sale of illegal drugs is, according to locals, a growing problem in the Mindanao region. Based on news reports, drug use thrives throughout the nation (Monterola, 1997:6). Given the meager law enforcement resources in the research area, and the fact that police keep busy with other issues [kidnaping, terrorism, Muslim-Christian hostilities], it is not surprising that slight attention is devoted to local drug problems, particularly as they involve youth.

Shoemaker (1996:41) reports that in the Philippines, a distinction is made between a "delinquent youth" and a "youthful offender." A delinquent youth pertains to anyone under eighteen years of age who has committed a minor offense, but whose case has not been officially processed by the Philippine judicial system. A delinquent youth in the Philippines would closely resemble the "status offender" in the United States. According to P.D. 603 [the Child and Youth Welfare Code for the Philippines] youth are expected to have at least an elementary education, but there is no provision for dealing with school absences or dropouts, and running away is not listed as an offense. In the United States both truancy and running-away from home have represented traditional styles of "status offenses." Showing disobedience toward parents may result in a "delinquent youth" designation against Filipino juveniles and also remains as a "status offense" in many parts of the United States. Although there is concern for youth who may not be receiving adequate care and nurturing, the "delinquent youth" is described as having "behavioral problems." Focus appears to be placed on problems of the youth rather than on the family or parents.

In contrast, Shoemaker clarifies that a "youthful offender" is one between the ages of nine and eighteen who has committed a felony and who has been processed through the formal machinery of juvenile justice. If all the mechanisms for handling this offender were utilized, the case would first be heard at the *barangay* level, before being referred to the police. The police would, in-turn, transfer the case over to the prosecutor [fiscal]. The fiscal is supposed to arrange for a mental and physical examination of the juvenile, and, upon determining probability of guilt and the absence of extenuating mental and/or physical disabilities, send the case to the DSWD for placement until a court hearing or trial can be established.

Shoemaker's account suggests that the "youthful offender" case in the Philippines would in the United States fall somewhere in the conceptually blurred area between juvenile and adult court. Even in the contemporary United States, some jurisdictions disagree when, or if, a youth should be arranged for a "trial" for the determination of guilt. It should be recalled that the original juvenile court philosophy in the United States shied away from the seeking of a "guilt" orientation for youthful offenders. At any rate, in the Philippines, even at the final judicial stage, juveniles may be released on their own recognizance, under the supervision of the *barangay* captain. Alternatively, the suspected offender may be released to the custody of parents or relatives, or confined in a detention center.

The official data is sketchy and, as mentioned by Shoemaker and Austin (1996), the records regarding juvenile detainees in one city of over 300,000 population was kept by one official on the backs of matchcovers. The bigger issue, is what happens to youth who commit delinquent acts but who are diverted from the scrutiny of a judge, the Department of Social Welfare and Development, and the police.

HARMONY GENERATING SCENARIOS

It would be a mistake to presume that everything is negative on the Philippine scene and that all youth are problem offenders. Numerous features of Philippine society operate to provide a cohesive community environment for the child. A number of such cultural themes have been noted in other sections of this book but deserve rethinking in the context of the juvenile.

Close Family Bonds

Much has been written about Filipino family cohesiveness. Against a background of overpopulation and underemployment, the family unit maintains well-documented traditions of altruism (Andres & Ilada-Andres, 1987; Espiritu, 1987; Quisumbing, 1964; 1987; Vreeland, 1976). Family members are quick to come to the aid of another member, and will organize to defend family members against danger [see Chapter 2, "Peacemaking Filipino Style"]. Unless a child has committed very severe violations of law, it must be concluded that community leaders would opt to keep a child under close supervision within the family, and thus to divert the problem child from any official intervention beyond the immediate community. If the delinquent act involves a dispute with another community member, it would be up to the neighborhood and *barangay* leadership, when at all possible, to keep the problem under wraps. Importantly, if numerous problems are referred outside the *barangay*, to the police and court, for example, then the elected *barangay* leaders would suffer in subsequent elections. Without question, this works to keep the official record of delinquency to a minimum and the number of incarcerated youth low, even if artificially so.

Barangay Structure as Family Extension

The *barangay* structure, and particularly its further subdivision into *puroks*, furnishes the developing child with a network of relationships even beyond the extended family system, itself expansive. The *purok*, which in Lanao del Norte, may be composed of about thirty to forty households, is organized into subcommittees, each with officers who oversee the needs of the neighborhood. These include health, education, recreation, and security. Although not always operating at highest efficiency and sometimes loosely structured, the *purok* nonetheless provides connecting points for the individuals and families who have problems or, specifically, a problem child. Other than the family unit, it would likely be the *purok* which would be aware of a problem youth and of delinquent activity in the immediate vicinity of the neighborhood (cf. Pido, 1986:19). The *purok* acts somewhat as a quasi-official structure linking the family household to the larger *barangay* which is headed by the captain. It is the captain who has the authority to manage delinquent activity and either to keep a problem hidden within the cover and protection of the *barangay*, or to officially refer an illegal act to other government authorities [police, courts, DSWD]. Unless a police officer directly catches a delinquent child in the act and makes an arrest, it is the *barangay* captain who would decide if a case should be registered with the municipal court or, in fact, should be settled in a purely informal manner.

Captains are elected officials and permanent residents of the community. They wear no official uniform and in a majority of cases have some livelihood within the immediate community other than serving as captain. Because the captain is an elected position, it is understood that one occupying such a position would be most popular and respected by the local residents. The captain's position is distinctive by being the official link between higher government and the local community. Local respondents claim that good captains, in their dual roles, show allegiances more toward the community than the government. For detailed discussion of the precise process of how the captain works to resolve conflicts, of both adults and minors, the reader should review Chapter 1 ["Islands and *Barangays*"]. Particular attention should be paid to how the captain has the authority, and often the motivation, to keep a case within the protective shield of the *barangay* and outside the formal system of higher government.

Culture-Personality Attributes

Although some of the old traditions are likely being lost on the young, there remain in the research area numerous customs which act to engender a spirit of community and altruism. The precise origins of altruism and emphasis on close cooperative schemes is unclear. Being forced into close quarters by island life, combined with historically heavy doses of Spanish Catholicism, are possibly pertinent factors. A series of features are embedded in the value system of the local citizenry which can be applied here to the socialization and control of youth. Lynch and Guzman (1970:9–10) remarked that one of the more important cultural values in Philippine society is "smooth interpersonal relations." Building upon this basic idea, Shoemaker and Austin (1996:247) explain that "SIR basically refers to the importance of getting along with others and not offending another's character or honor. SIR is supported by prescriptions such as promoting social acceptance, the notion that one is to be accepted as a person, rather than for possessions or wealth." The well-documented Cebuano concept of *pakig-uban-uban* [or *pakikisama* in the Tagalog] coincides with this value by requiring that one "go along with" or "give in" to the requests or desires of another. Inherent in this value is the wish to avoid placing another in stressful or unpleasant situations. On its face, this value orientation would tend to engender good will in social situations. A possible exception may be if one were to "go along with another" in order to not hurt another's feelings even if that required inappropriate behavior. Generally speaking, one who expresses much *pakig-uban-uban* would be soft-spoken, courteous, likable, and, by definition, "personable." Youth adhering to such a traditional value should be able to repel the lure of delinquent activity compared to youth who disregard traditional values.

The concepts of *utang kabubut-on* and *ka-ulaw* [or *hiya* in the Tagalog] logically have relevance in considering socialization patterns of youth. A juvenile who is taught to uphold the quality of *utang kabubut-on* will always pay off a debt and will try to reciprocate, in kind, any favor offered. Among Filipinos, refusing to behave in such expected ways would bring shame [or *ka-ulaw*] to an individual. These values tend to work in unison to effect smooth interpersonal relations (see also Bulatao, 1964; Hollnsteiner, 1963, 1970; Jocano, 1969; Kaut, 1961).

Other examples of altruism persist in the northwest region of Mindanao; these provide models of cooperative behavior and encourage the appropriate socialization of youth. Such examples had more impact in earlier and simpler times than they do today. These are the cooperative schemes of always first trying to reach an "amicable settlement" or *areglo* [i.e., derived from the Spanish *arreglo* for "arrangement"] by calling upon close friends to resolve a dispute rather than pursuing official redress for problems. Also, the early tradition of *yayong* ["lift or transfer"] still exists in spirit if not so much in practice. This is literally the case of locals cooperating to assist a neighbor in moving a thatched-roofed, bamboo house to a new location. In the eyes of the child, *yayong* was analogous to a ceremonial activity requiring the cooperation of many citizens of the village and in a mood of great excitement and gaiety, not unlike a village fiesta. Other examples, discussed in Chapter 2, include the *ronda,* helping neighbors explore the origin of any village disturbance, and *hunglos*, the pooling of farmers to assist in working another farmer's rice field. These illustrations prevail as models of helping behavior for the ever-present children of the *barangays*. If such harmony-producing features go unopposed, one would expect relatively high levels of peace and order among adults as well as children.

DEVIANCY GENERATING SCENARIOS

About forty years ago, in reference to the high crime rate in the United States, Walter C. Reckless observed that diverse cultural models for the child and citizen were in great abundance (1960). He was referring to the increasing rates of mobility of American people, the technological and communication revolution allowing even rural people to receive novel and confusing information, and extensive ethnic conflict in many regions. Today in the Philippines, these same conditions apply. On top of these challenging conditions are other Filipino scenarios alluded to elsewhere in this book, which undermine smooth interpersonal relations for adults and youth alike. These include a population which is too great for the present market economy. Unemployment has been consistently high for decades and underemployment makes it difficult for the average worker to legitimately earn a livelihood. Except for the top professionals and landed gentry, many ordinary workers cannot enjoy a secure lifestyle, with the average annual income only a little in excess of 26,000 pesos [$1,000 U.S. in 1997]. Corruption is rampant, as evidenced by even small children scrambling on the street to press passers-by for a quick peso, up to high-ranking police officials being arrested for extortion.

Scars remain from years of martial law under a tyrannical and perceived ruthless despot, even as more honest politicians struggle to climb out of the hole made by many years of corruption at the highest levels. Over the past decade, the citizenry have had to work, attend school, and play in what locals refer to as a terrorist-prone land resulting from the conflict between government and communist insurgents, and also from the enduring hostilities between Muslim and Christian segments of the population. None of these conditions can be hidden from the adolescent citizens and are, according to local respondents, disruptive to

Photo 7. Children playing in a garbage dump at the research site

the young Filipino in search of a life direction.   For the majority of Filipinos who are poor and who live either in the large urban ghettos or in the thatched nipa huts of the hinterlands, life must be relatively gloomy.

The Department of Social Welfare and Development reports that 100,000 street children now struggle to survive in Manila, a number which has doubled from the previous year (Arquiza, 1997:15).   Remaining unreported are the number of street children in the urban areas on the southern island of Mindanao, where most of these field notes were developed (see Photo 7).   Undoubtedly, "neglected children" represent a more fundamental issue than delinquency, and one about which even less is known.   As was shown to be the case in Iligan City [which has no separate juvenile court], street children will seek ways to make money. Statistical data is unavailable but a group of physicians and health workers interviewed in Iligan City claimed that "street children in the area are plentiful." Many enterprising and clever juveniles will rely upon their "street wise" skills [*abtik* and *bukong* behavior more fully developed in Chapter 9] to wrench a few coins from pedestrians. It is a short leap from being a *bantay* boy who can fleece rich car owners of 10 pesos [about 40 cents U.S. in 1997], to shoplifting and picking pockets.

Compulsory education does not exist in the research area. Even if national expectations to attend school are voiced in the nation's capital, enforcement of any such regulations would be presently unlikely given the limited resources in the rural barrios where the bulk of the population reside. Even in Manila, the problem of school attendance is obviously problematic given the excessive numbers of homeless street children in that metropolitan area. Also, it is likely any such regulation would be dismissed in the same manner as are vehicle regulations discussed in Chapter 9 ["Marching as to Anarchy"]. Locals in the research area claim that for those who have the money, children can be taught at home by a visiting teacher. One longtime resident, and mother of six children, noted that "After all, if the children go to school they will just join the ranks of the unemployed after graduation. It would be better to stay on the farm and grow crops."

On another and more dangerous level, it is common knowledge in the research area that children learn the use of various kinds of weapons, including firearms, from their elders. The question must be, if a child is going to learn how to compete for another's space or property at an early age [pa-unahay] and does so with a spirit of pa-abtikay ["out-smart" another], and is socialized to bend or break laws [pa-lusotay], what will happen if the same child carries a lethal weapon? These cultural patterns are reviewed in greater detail in the following chapter and should be studied in light of cultural patterns learned by children of the province.

Respondents report that in Lanao del Norte a great variety of guns are available for a price. Given the political and ethnic turmoil and the terrorist climate in the region over the past decade, this should surprise no one. Also, homemade handguns are easily acquired. Referred to as "paltiks," some are highly crafted, others are more primitive, but both are lethal. No systematic attempt is made to register guns and they easily pass from one individual to another without paperwork. Police have rounded up thousands of firearms by offering cash to anyone who turns in a gun. However, locals claim that cheap guns are submitted to police just for the cash, and then are quickly replaced by others.

During the last few weeks of fieldwork in 1997, the question was asked how a homicide would be dealt with if it involved both Muslim and Christian teenagers. The response from a longtime and respected informant was, "The parties would never go to court." He qualified the statement by saying, "Well, if they did, it would only be to try to get money." A major problem, such as a killing between Muslim and Christian teenagers would be dealt with informally, and would most likely eventually involve additional killings as revenge [refer to Chapter 4, "Muslim-Christian Disputes"]. Revenge killings may be initiated by both Muslims and Christians and, according to the informant, "often involve teenagers who become killers for hire, and who can be employed for as little as 300 pesos" [about $12 U.S in 1997].

Another area which has been touched upon elsewhere in these chapters and which reveals aspects of a deviance-generating scenario for young people is the Overseas Contract Worker [OCW] program. Through OCW, some of the youngest and brightest youth are lost through an extensive and sometimes illegitimate program of providing Filipino workers to the more well-to-do citizens of other nations. The embarrassment—and sometimes plight—of overseas contract workers, now approaching 1 million, also relates to the broad issue of criminality and incorporates the young, occasionally as victims. First, many of the workers are themselves very youthful [eighteen to twenty-one years of age] and likely even younger, with forged birth documents easily acquired. Unfortunately OCWs are periodically victimized by their employers, although no systematic study of this issue is cited in the literature. The process of becoming an OCW itself often involves large amounts of money passed under the table [or the loss of a percentage of the worker's paychecks] to dubious employment agencies.

A second and perhaps more grim fact is that many Filipino boys and girls are conditioned from early teen years to aspire to become overseas contract workers as household nannies and servants lured by the promise of bigger earnings than at home. Gordon (1997) announced that the Filipino child does not typically embrace any equivalency to "The American Dream." His point was not that they should become American, but that the youth do not even aspire to be "Filipino," and for many the ultimate aim is to escape the geography of the Philippines as an OCW, if possible, and illegally, if necessary. Fallows (1988) alluded to this growing mind set as reflective of a "damaged culture."

For an unknown number of young women in Lanao del Norte, another semi-legitimate alternative for those who remain in the local area is to become a bar maid or hostess, to solicit high-priced drinks from patrons, and to occasionally provide sexual favors for money. Some of the bars in Iligan City have tried to upscale the hostess occupation by calling these women "Guest Relations Officers," and a young woman "hostess" is now often referred to locally simply as a "gro." The issue has not been systematically researched in the communities of Lanao del Norte but the prevalence of such bars is directly observable with about two hole-in-the-wall nightclubs per city block [about 30 such bars in downtown Iligan City]. Often the youthful women [many of them teenagers, according to respondents] can be seen preened and groomed for work, sitting on the steps of the bars in the early evening before the crowds arrive and the loud music begins. Some of the local influential citizens are quick to point out that the "gros" are required to submit to weekly health examinations which include a check for AIDS [Acquired Immune Deficiency Syndrome]. Knowledgeable locals who frequent the bars and know the young girls argue that consistent enforcement of such health checks is lacking. The women tend to be conspicuous often against a backdrop of shanty houses and primitively boarded storefronts. At the entrance of the bars can often be seen signs which read "no weapons allowed."

Prostitution is well-known on the Asian landscape and the Philippines is no exception. In 1997 President Ramos initiated programs, with limited success, to suppress prostitution and streetwalking in Manila, with occasional raids and arrests by police. In the more distant island area of Mindanao, and within the research area, attempts to prohibit prostitution are non-existent. Late-night bars with "Guest Relations Officers" of questionable age keep busy even across the town square from the police station.   Rather obviously, the research area represents a composite of values and ethical standards. The family and community traditions of cohesiveness and altruism are seemingly countered for many by the need for money; an unknown number of youthful workers come from families living at a bare subsistence level. Ironically, the desire to assist the family and to carry on a tradition of altruism may push some youth to work in near-servitude conditions both overseas and also into quasi-legitimate activity for some of the young women who remain in the local area.

Only limited opportunity allowed conversations with the "gros." They tended to be quite assertive and vocal, although reluctant to disclose their personal backgrounds or motivations for pursuing the late-night bar life. Locals who had ongoing relationships with the "gros" volunteered to the researcher that the women considered themselves temporary workers and were motivated only by the lure for quick money.   Some youth who have not found opportunity to pursue higher education, aspire to open their own drinking establishments, which they see as a quick way to make money with little overhead.   One young women in her mid-twenties and with a small daughter was struggling, along with her husband, a part-time jitney driver, to maintain a meager subsistence. The couple   did not hesitate to boast that they aspired to someday open their own Karaoke bar.   In the poorer sections of the towns, such bars display only dirt floors and straight-back chairs, but also provide a microphone which is passed among the customers who can sing to lyrics appearing on a television set.   These bars are quite popular and customers, with "gros" close at hand, sing "blues" oriented tunes and drink into the early morning hours.   Such bars with young hostesses appear to have rapidly become a stable fixture in the local economy, whether viewed by the young women only as quick employment or as long-range occupational objectives.

This chapter cannot attempt to survey the wide-ranging subject of juvenile delinquency. The issue is not often spoken of as a serious area of Philippine research and is only beginning to find its way into some of the larger universities. Yet, as much as any topic alluded to in the broader arena of crime and custom, the issue of despair and anxiety among a growing youthful population looms as a most critical concern.

Chapter 9

Marching as to Anarchy

A narchy means society without law, or without government social control. All societies have areas which are relatively anarchic—very rural regions; friendship cliques, playgrounds, hobo jungles—and the degree of anarchy varies within each society and over time (Black, 1976:123–124). However, once a law is agreed upon it must be presumed that it will be obeyed by the citizenry, or at least that is the goal of the law. Over time, lack of confidence in, or disrespect for law may generate an anarchic atmosphere. Once formal law is established, why it would be disregarded lies at the root of criminological inquiry, but is not always addressed in ethnographic research. Certainly, following Durkheim's observations, no people can be totally law abiding (1912). Yet, some appear to have very limited appreciation for laws and often become law breakers, as depicted in these chapters.

This book describes a number of major themes which clearly reveal that for some Filipinos unlawful behavior appears to be approaching the norm. Breaking the law seems at times to be of little concern. Stealing property by squatting on another's land, kidnaping, terrorism, bribery and extortion, among other styles of deviance and crime, are initiated with little hesitation. Figure 9–1 shows an adaptation of a model from Bates and Harvey (1975), illustrating the relationship between such a near-anarchic condition and societal features which help explain such a state. Anarchy is established as the dependent variable with a variety of emergent negative features. Also, the model depicts "situation," "culture," and "personality," as independent variables which coalesce through a process of "social interaction" to produce the anarchic orientation. At this point, the model does not try to weight one independent variable differently than another, or to predict which independent variable precedes the other. For purely descriptive purposes, an assumption is made that situational conditions impact upon the cultural makeup of the citizenry and may also be observed as an expression of personality. Each of the independent variables deserves further scrutiny.

Figure 9–1
Social Organizational Variables and Resultant Filipino Anarchic Tendencies

Independent Variables	Intervening Link	Dependent Variables
Situation {i.e., turmoil, isolation} →		Manifestations of Anarchy:
Culture {i.e., de-policing, self-rule} →	Social Interaction →	pa-unahay {being first, greed} pa-abtikay {overactive, audacious} pa-lusotay {push through, defiant} pa-bukongay {brazenly defy norm}
Personality {i.e., competitive spirit, anguish} →		

Source: Adapted from Bates & Harvey (1975); cf. Nix & Bates (1962).

SITUATION

Certainly a number of unfortunate societal situations contribute to the swing toward anarchy in the research area of northwestern Mindanao. First, the Philippine economy over the past four decades has not kept pace with that of other Asian nations such as Singapore, South Korea, Taiwan, Japan, and Malaysia. Although it shows some improvement in the past few years, it still remains near the bottom of Asian nations in economic clout. At best, the unemployment rate is over 10 percent and many of those with jobs must be considered underemployed. The average annual wage is $1,130 (Morrison, 1997). Competition for scarce resources is intense. A half million young adults—many college graduates—have departed the Philippines to find employment in Hong Kong, Singapore, and other nations as servants to wealthier Asians. Being in near poverty and suffering the lack of ability to legitimately compete in the marketplace must be a primary motivation for economic crimes. If one cannot afford to purchase a parcel of land for a house, then squatting on another's land becomes an alternative. Obviously, only the poor tend to be land squatters. Kidnaping in the Philippines is purely economically driven. It is a quick and relatively successful way to make large sums of money. Being labeled as the kidnaping capital of Asia is an embarrassment to many Filipinos, although such a stereotype seems a reasonable one.

Second, political revolution and subsequent recovery, even with the celebrated overthrow of an authoritarian ruler, have been difficult. The near two decades of martial law disguised the siphoning of hundreds of millions of U.S. dollars from coffers earmarked for Philippine operational funds. Such an economic deprivation is still felt throughout the provinces. It is no wonder that paved roads outside the urban centers are a rarity and those that are paved are potholed. When corruption is perceived to be rampant at the highest level, it operates to give legitimacy to rule breaking at the lower levels. Corruption is linked to the economy and again tends to function in favor of the wealthy by maintaining a sizable class of people unable to escape poverty. Compounding this problem is the influx of communist insurgents who have had some success over the past several decades in recruiting sympathizers, especially from the ranks of the poor. The NPA [New Peoples Army] maintains a corps of armed rebel groups which have terrorized citizenry and have kept the Philippine Army on alert for years. This continuing atmosphere of impending terrorism has confused many citizens and undermined a strong belief in the Philippine system of government, creating for some a fractured political identity.

Third, almost as a corollary to the communist-democracy conflict, is the longer struggle between Muslim-Christian groups in Mindanao. In some provinces, communist insurgency and Muslim-Christian conflict persist simultaneously, doubling the difficulty for residents of the area. The two social movements compete for daily headlines as to which results in the greater number of casualties, as both engage in armed battles with the military. As late as the summer of 1997, the involvement of the Philippine military was routinely reported as being engaged in combat with one or both of these extremist groups, each of which maintain their own militia.

A faction of the several million Muslims in Mindanao, under the banner of the Moro Islamic Liberation Front has established an autonomous region incorporating four Mindanao provinces which provides a base [or homeland] for a portion of Muslims who voted in favor of its creation. This land area is referred to as the Autonomous Region of Muslim Mindanao [ARMM]. The Philippine government agreed, not without difficult negotiations, with the wishes of the MILF to create the separate region which will hold its own elections and will at the same time receive funding from the national government. Allowing the formation of an autonomous region was deemed by President Ramos a better solution than continuing the heated battlefield turmoil of the previous decades. The problem may be that such an autonomous region will produce a "reservation" atmosphere similar to that found on American Indian reservations. In addition, the establishment of this separate region may not put and end to cultural conflict and in some ways may inflame differences between the two adversaries.

The economic, political, and religious upheaval has made it difficult for the masses to maintain a strong national identity. As noted in Chapter 4, the Muslims in Mindanao do not commonly accept an identity as being Filipino, choosing instead to align themselves with one or more Islamic states. The bigger issue is that growing numbers of non-Muslim children lack any secure national identity or character. Substantial numbers of twelve-year-old Filipinos no longer aspire to remain in their home country. Rather, in their early teen years they learn of alternative avenues of income by becoming overseas contract workers [OCWs] (Gordon, 1997). The over four million young adults who are officially outside the country does not account for the unknown number of unlawful migrants who escaped from their would-be homeland to become illegal aliens in other nations.

This practice appears well known by all Filipinos by the Tagalog term [*tago ng tago*] and is referred to commonly as "TNT." When a sense of hopelessness is created for the youth, one must predict a rise in anarchy. Conceptions of the law itself may tend to become ambiguous and confusing. Magnifying these conditions is a burgeoning population, pushing larger numbers of working adults to compete for limited numbers of jobs. As in other Asian nations, the people of northwestern Mindanao are on the move, mainly to the cities, contributing to overcrowding in urban areas.

CULTURE

In the context of the model in Figure 9–1, culture refers to the rules or norms of conduct which direct how one is expected to behave. Such normative aspects of culture may pertain to both informal rules and formal law. In a society posturing toward the anarchic, as appears to be the case in the research setting, the rules themselves become ambiguous or confusing. As outlined in the previous chapters, the citizenry in Lanao del Norte tend to bend rules and in some cases break laws and local ordinances. If the breaking of minor laws can be justified, it is of course easier to move to a higher level of law breaking.

Four features of the local culture reflect [or in some cases contribute to] either norm bending or illegal behavior, and merit closer inspection. First is the *pa-unahay* system of competing for space.

Pa-unahay

One of the ways to observe how informal rules may be pushed to the limit and overlap with unlawful behavior is to concentrate on the city and town traffic patterns and how locals relate to and compete with one another when operating motor vehicles. After considering driving patterns, other forms of deviation and law breaking tend to acquire special meaning. A Westerner, traveling to the research area for the first time, must be shocked and likely frightened by the drivers of taxis and passenger jeeps [called "jeepneys" or "jitneys"]. The first jeepneys were refurbished U.S. military jeeps discarded and left in the Philippines after World War. II. Today, thousands of jeepneys and other vehicles drift around the crowded streets with no regard for lanes or to most of the driving regulations so common to Westerners. Indeed, a passenger jeepney in Iligan City will routinely travel on what would technically be the wrong side of the street, forcing opposing traffic to swing out of the way to avert head-on collisions.

When traffic is slight, as in early morning hours, vehicle movement is fast and furious. When traffic is crowded, which is most any other time, vehicles are jammed together with movement often at a snail's pace. A bumper-car mind set seems to emerge, with vehicles vying for space, as they squeeze in and out of

Photo 8. Horse-drawn transportation still competing for street space

tight spaces inch by inch, with horns blaring, and almost indiscriminately stopping to pick up or drop off passengers. Road signs and traffic lights are routinely ignored as is any signaling—manual or electric—of one's intentions from the vehicle. Moving into another's lane of traffic is accomplished simply by pushing the vehicle into any space, no matter how small, thus cutting off an oncoming vehicle. Drivers in the Philippines are accustomed to such antics, which would be considered insensitive and brazen in the Western world and would be met with anger from the victimized driver. Little anger is shown by Filipino drivers, however, and butting into another space is without question expected behavior. Confounding the problem are the horse-drawn carriages which still transport passengers for a few centavos—providing a link to the past—but an irritant to motorized vehicles (see Photo 8).

After analyzing Manila traffic patterns, Richard Stone (1973) concluded that the drivers were claiming, occupying, and in some cases defending space or "territory." By applying territorial principles to driving patterns, he argued that the first person in a space on the roadway, in fact, owned that space. Once occupying that space, the driver had substantial latitude to ignore other vehicles. Of course, at the same time, any other vehicle has the right to take the space and is expected to do so. In the research area, this continuous competition for roadway space is referred to in the Cebuano dialect as *pa-unahay* [literally from the root word "*una*" meaning first]. The word is used more to imply "being first" in the sense of the quickest to get to a limited but desired space. Locals claim that the concept really is closer to the spirit of "Let's see who can get there first," or "Ready or not, here

I come." Thus, the literal translation of "first to go ahead" has taken on additional meanings.   Most locals, including drivers, when referring to *pa-unahay* did so with a smile and gleam in their eye, suggesting some humor and seeing the cultural pattern as if it were a sporting event. The most popular sport in the research area was "cock fighting" which also embodies aspects of "getting into another's space."   One cannot help but think of the chaotic street scene as a "law of the jungle" manifestation. Even if governed by some inherent unwritten rules, *pa-unahay* has become suffused with a "fend for yourself" conviction, suggesting a "What's mine is mine and what's yours is mine" mentality. The important point is that it becomes difficult to distinguish between "taking another's space" and actual law breaking when it comes to rules of the road.

Historically, when a small number of farmers acquired vehicles and ventured to the local marketplace on dirt roads, it was unnecessary to have formal regulations. One could park almost anywhere and few were concerned. The scene becomes increasingly problematic as one moves from the small municipality to the larger city. With many farmers driving into the city, sometimes in jalopies pieced together out of junk parts, *pa-unahay* takes on even more flavor, but is increasingly dangerous.   Ordinances have been established to regulate Iligan City traffic, and in 1995 the first traffic lights appeared. As of 1997, they were basically ignored by both drivers and pedestrians, except for those major intersections where a traffic officer was precariously stationed, and even then the rules were often disregarded. It is clearly an example of advancing technology and emerging formal laws clashing with local culture and *pa-unahay*. Open competition for space can lead one to push the regulations to the limits and eventually to generate anxiety and irritation even among Filipino drivers, particularly those few who may be trying to obey the new city traffic signals. Fender benders are frequent and head-on collisions common in the research area. In general, the *pa-unahay* system is beginning to break down in jam-packed streets.

Any user of the street may compete for space. The National Highway is a two-lane road, often in disrepair, forming the main north–south artery on the east coast of Mindanao. It is used by buses, trucks, and jeeps, as well as automobiles, motorized tricycles, bicycles, carabao-carts, and people pulling wagons. As the highway nears a *barangay* or a municipality, people tend to use the highway as a sidewalk. All users of the street tend to hold the space until the last moment, and at great peril contest speeding buses for the space. Adults and small children alike can be seen walking slowly across the street refusing to hustle to avoid rapidly oncoming traffic. Often a companion can be seen grabbing a lone individual refusing to give way and only at the last moment being pulled from certain calamity.

Clearly, *pa-unahay* does not stop with jeepney drivers or with open competition for street space. It exists in the queuing behavior, or relative lack of such, at checkout counters of local stores, and is noticeable at postal-clerk stations where crowds gather to purchase stamps or have a letter weighed. If one does not squeeze into place and push against others to deprive them of their insecure space, the stamp will not be purchased and the letter never weighed. Standing in a line at a checkout counter with six inches of space between yourself and the next customer will most certainly result in your losing your space to an enterprising customer intent on exercising the right of *pa-unahay*. Women appear to be particularly effective at competing for space in department store checkout lines, possibly because they feel men will not push back as hard. Regardless, butting into line is a constant practice. Naturally, the problem and subsequent apparent confusion are exacerbated in the city, where outsiders are more prevalent.

Even sidewalk behavior is clearly subject to *pa-unahay*, as individuals fail to give way to approaching persons. One will not see the obvious dropping of the shoulder or turning to avoid approaching pedestrians common in other cultural areas of the world. Instead, only at the last minute, even after touching, will one or both parties almost imperceptibly bend or loosen their hold on the sidewalk space. Collisions are not generally problematic because walkers tend to stroll, often in small groups, and do not typically walk at hurried speeds more commonplace, for example, in large cities such as New York or Paris. Filipino sidewalk passers-by tend to meld together, amoeba-like, and unlike automobiles do not suffer discernible damage. A fast walker, such as a tourist, who is unfamiliar with this custom may have difficulty and may generate confusion and irritability among local walkers.

Pa-abtikay

Another local custom allied to *pa-unahay* pertains to one who behaves in a "smart" way, but in the sense of cleverly "outsmarting" the other [*pa-abtikay*, was probably absorbed into the Cebuano from the English word "active" or "overactive"]. Locals remarked that "*abtik*" meant acting smart in a "negative" or "derogatory" way. Stories told among locals about one who is very "abtik" are met with belly laughs. Furthermore, the connotation of "Take whatever you can" is suggested about one who is smart, particularly in making money, even if others are duped. If the allied concepts of *pa-unahay* and *pa-abtikay* are united, the result would be "Get the best position you can ahead of others" and "If you can outsmart the other to gain a better position to make money, then more power to you."

Examples of *abtik* behavior are numerous, among people of all ages, genders, and walks of life. It is particularly noticeable among the large poor segment of the population, because the custom implies being smart in the sense of acquiring easy money. Often the author would purchase a newspaper from any of a number of elementary school-aged children who roam the city streets with stacks of newspapers balanced on their heads. The transaction is quick so the young child will not lose balance of the papers. The paper cost 10 pesos but frequently the seller will say [to an outsider] the cost is 12 pesos. Newcomers to the area will not know they have been overcharged by two pesos. Overcharging in the marketplace is commonplace, and it is the buyer who must beware.

The *bantay* boys, discussed in Chapter 7, were very skillful in convincing motor-vehicle operators to permit them to keep watch over their cars for a few pesos while owners were inside a restaurant. In the meantime, the boys might disappear entirely to another neighborhood and perform the same service, collecting money from different car owners in different neighborhoods who believed their cars were being "watched" [protected] while they were inside the restaurant. Although petty and humorous, the pattern instills a sense of "getting something for nothing" and works to deter the development of a strong sense of honesty and responsibility. Being duped in the marketplace is undoubtedly universal. Still, it must be said that in the open markets of Lanao del Norte, and during difficult economic times, any outsider must be suspicious of any price quoted by a merchant. Local Filipinos were resolute in admonishing the researcher about shopping in the open-air markets.

One professional adult, while traveling abroad to an international conference, began to offer a 5-peso bill [currency] as a souvenir of the Philippines to people he would meet. In turn, as a courtesy many representatives of other nations would likewise offer an example of their own currency [franc, mark, pound, dollar, etc.]. In almost all cases the currency received was much more valuable than the 5-peso note, worth only about 20 cents. The professional, and all fellow professionals who heard the story found it to be outrageously funny. The professional traveler said next time he would take a greater stack of 5-peso notes with him, thus, being very *abtik*. In this case, the professional was quite wealthy and in no need of the money, but the case shows the general disposition toward the ability to dupe another. Middle-aged or elderly respondents occasionally tended to see *abtik* behavior as insulting or at least potentially malicious. Some youth failed to see what was so derogatory about being clever and, in fact, one who is clever at card playing, as in the case of a card sharp, would also be considered *abtik.*

Local educators saw *abtik* behavior more in a manner described by Miller in the "focal concern" for "smartness" (1957). Miller explained that lower-class gang behavior in the ghetto regions of Boston represented, in part, youth acting to "outsmart" one another in attempts to survive the street life. Such "smart" behavior, even if malicious, was a way of life for ghetto dwellers. Theoretically, according to Miller, they should not be blamed for their behavior even if it ran counter to the law because they were socialized as small children to consider such behavior as normal.   In Lanao del Norte, outsiders are more sensitive to these cultural patterns of trying to outsmart another; locals, on the other hand, view such incidents as part of daily life as usual, and to them the patterns do not stand out as anything remarkable.

Picking another's pocket on a crowded jeepney represents a more shameless and flagrant form of *pa-abtikay* behavior, which also happens to be illegal. As a style of theft it involves stealth, which incorporates a sport-like quality. As with haggling behavior in the marketplace, pocket-picking is universal. However, the craftiness of secretly withdrawing another's wallet takes on a game-like element of adventure which also, in the research area, includes *pa-abtikay* features. Pocket-pickers operate on the jeepneys and sit with other passengers awaiting an appropriate target. The thief will sit with a duffle bag positioned on the lap to hide any hand movements. An accomplice sitting elsewhere in the jeepney will drop coins to the floor, as if accidentally, close to the feet of the unsuspecting target. When the target bends over to assist in picking up the coins, the thief will cleverly lift the wallet. In several cases reported in detail to the researcher, the wallet was returned to the victim, with a look from the thief suggesting "Gotcha."

It is common for the thief to take only some of the cash and to leave money and any credit cards in the wallet before returning it to the victim. Other passengers watch the ordeal, remain calm, and do not interfere, realizing that the thief works in a group and any intervention would be fruitless and possibly dangerous. The thieves work in the highly transient sector of the towns near the bus stations, where jeepneys pick up travelers who are often strangers to the area. Also, the jeepney passengers do not generally represent close-knit groups who may in other circumstances intervene to discourage pocket-picking. One outsider, but long-time visitor to the research area, admitted to carrying two wallets, one a throwaway with only a few pesos, which, if lost or stolen, would be no great loss while the more valuable wallet is kept well hidden. It should be noted that it is not the act of theft that represents *pa-abtikay* behavior but the sport-like quality associated with the act of theft.

Pa-lusotay

Locals agree that the *pa-unahay* and the *pa-abtikay* can easily get out of hand and lead to rather flagrant violations of law. When it is clear that a driver departs from the open competition for space and boldly violates a law, as when one daringly runs a stop sign, that person is said to *pa-lusot* [literally meaning to "push through" in the Cebuano] or is acting in a *pa-lusotay* manner. It is closer to "intimidation" and "getting what you want," even if it means breaking the law. At this point it is clear that *pa-unahay* stretched to its limits can overlap with *pa-lusot,* and rather than talking about competing for space, one moves to a discussion of taking what belongs to another. One local explained *pa-lusotay* by referring to the Hollywood chase scenes, in which police cars in hot pursuit of speeding bandits both totally disregard pedestrians and vehicles as they blaze through the streets and down the sidewalks. Such activity would place the *pa-unahay* behavior as a milder form of roadway antics, even if it does result in frequent fender benders and head-on collisions.

In Iligan, jeepneys engage in much *pa-lusotay* practice, which is commonly overlooked by police as extensions of *pa-unahay*. Interestingly, in the Cebuano dialect, different words apply to more traditional crimes. Locals referred to the *pa-lusotay* as being milder forms of law breaking. The word for crime is *salaod* or *krimen* and for thief or robber the word is *kiriwan* or *kawatan,* all totally different from the root word of *losut* meaning to "push through" as in pushing a norm or law to the limits.

Pa-losutay behavior carries with it a suggestion of frenzy or "frenetic" action.   The pushing through to the point of breaking the norm or even a law suggests that the individual actor does so with an outburst of excitement or agitation. It would not generally be used in reference to heavily pre-planned criminal activity; rather, it would likely refer to involuntary rule violations. If a group of youthful newspaper-carriers excitedly rush between cars across a crowded street to see if they can swindle a few extra pesos out of a group of tourists, they may be engaging in *pa-losutay* activity. Indeed, they are combining both *pa-unahay* and *pa-abtikay* behaviors to push through and at the last moment raise the price of the newspaper.

On occasion, a person may exhibit *pa-lusotay* which does not actually violate a norm, although such may be supposed or expected by others. One respondent provided the example of a person who was always able to come up with an alibi for any event and thus escape disapproval. Always having an alibi appeared incredulous.   In this case, the comment "There you go again with your alibi" carries with it a negative insinuation and the sense that one is fabricating an excuse for what was, in fact, misbehavior. Again, the alibi would appear to be quickly made up, as if frenetically or desperately concocted. Theoretically, this would also represent a departure from the norm by the one creating the alibi.

Pa-bukongay

Upon splitting open a coconut only to find it is dried up, without milk, and useless for eating, one feels cheated. *Bukong* literally means "dry coconut" in the Cebuano dialect and its meaning also extends to persons who cheat others. For example, one may act in a *bukong* manner if one purposely cheats another out of money. The use is not generally in reference to duping another as in being *abtik,* but is reserved for those who boldly refuse to pay, even if one has the money. Thus, *bukong* behavior can refer to both poor and rich alike who refuse to pay the bill, but usually pertains most often to the poor, who by virtue of their economic plight have more reason than the wealthy to refuse payment. The closest English translation appears to be "bolting" as when, after completing a meal, a customer darts past the cashier without paying and leaves the restaurant. In the United States such behavior may apply primarily to college-student pranksters. The Cebuano word *marama* pertains more to the professional swindler or cheater whereas *bukong* appears to refer more simply to impromptu but illegal actions of even well-heeled people looking to get away without paying a bill.

In the research area, such overt cheating of another was commonplace, and a variety of merchants, jeepney drivers, and other professionals were quick to provide examples. Importantly, along with the other cultural patterns reflective of deviant or illegal behavior, *bukong* exists as a common practice which can, for some, provide an additional negative model which encourages disregard for law. Some examples are quite minor, but represent unlawful acts. A person jumps onto the back bumper of a passenger jeep, rides for a few blocks, and jumps off, defying any expectation to pay the fare. Not paying the two pesos [4 cents U.S.]

seems trivial yet is disconcerting and belittling to the jeepney operator if it occurs frequently. Such hangers-on were observed to be both children and adults. Sneaking into movie houses in the middle of a group is another example. The practice has been sufficiently notorious to require one or more security guards, with automatic shotguns, checking for tickets at the entrance. The wielding of such firepower appears to represent excessive force or threat, yet is common in many Asian countries and widespread in the Philippines.

A hospital owner relayed many instances of patients who would wander out of the hospital without paying the bill. At times, a newborn baby would be hidden in a box, placed under an arm like a shopping container, and casually carried past the nurses' station and out of the hospital without the parents making payment. The hospital administrator claims such *bukong* offenders tend to be Muslims from the distant mountain towns of the province. The hospital was noted for catering to Muslim patients even though the patients were suspected of *bukong* behavior patterns. Muslim sympathizers argue that Christian lowlanders are guilty of the same behavior [compare to Chapter 4 on Muslim-Christian disputes].

Another example is provided by a modern, fast-moving passenger boat which began docking at the Iligan port in about 1996, and made frequent trips to nearby islands. The new boat—a waterjet—was well received by local residents who had long complained of the lengthy time inter-island travel had taken on the less modern and outdated passenger boats. However, in less than a year the boat stopped docking in the city, and management explained that, in part, the problem was *bukong*. Too many passengers were obtaining tickets without payment, and others would reportedly board the new waterjet and refuse to leave even without purchasing tickets. Because some of the lawless passengers were armed and intimidating, the boat's officers were unable or unwilling to use force. It was simpler to bypass Iligan and dock at another more peaceful port. This was a most flagrant example of *pa-bukongay*–styled activity.

Trying to get something for nothing seems customary in the research setting and provides a negative model for the child and adult. Although locals claim that such practices are prevalent, and many such examples can be directly observed, some residents speak critically of such actions. *Bukong* is clearly contrary to fundamental religious beliefs, whether Muslim or Christian, as well as being illegal. Because the vast majority of Filipinos profess religious affiliation [85 percent are Catholic], attend religious functions, and wear symbolic jewelry, one must presume that the prevalence of *pa-abtikay*, *pa-lusotay*, and *pa-bukongay* patterns generates substantial normative confusion among the citizenry.

PERSONALITY

Personality pertains to attitudes, beliefs, and values, and is difficult, if not impossible, to fully detach from cultural patterns of individuals. Surely culture and personality are interactive. For purely analytical purposes, the *pa-unahay* and *pa-abtikay* each have a facet or perspective which clearly implies personality attributes. Without fail, discussions of *pa-unahay*, which often took place in cafes or beer halls, were met with the same zeal expected if the topic of discussion were the local cock fights. Both men and women eagerly joined a discussion of how vehicles and people contested for space on and off the roadway. In all cases, respondents were animated and enthusiastic in relating their own experiences in the struggle for position and progress in the *pa-unahay* arenas.

Taken together, *pa-unahay* and *pa-abtikay* combine traits of daring with craftiness. Personality may be at least somewhat detached from culture when the attributes of enthusiasm, delight, and zeal are evident in the enactment of the behavior patterns. A fanciful spirit is associated with the cultural examples and, as noted, discussion by locals about *bukong* behavior was accompanied by much jest and humor. When one computer programmer of the area was asked "What is the difference between *pa-unahay* and *pa-lusotay*?" he paused for a few seconds and, smiling, said "Nothing." *Pa-lusotay,* roughly suggesting indiscriminate norm breaking, combines qualities of audacity with thoughtlessness, in the sense of not caring about victims. Distinctions between the three concepts are blurred, with some overlap between *pa-unahay* and *pa-lusotay*. Also, it is evident that some overlap exists between *pa-lusotay* and *pa-bukongay* activity.

ANARCHIC ALLIANCES

The four cultural features all possess potential negative components and it remains reasonable to conclude that the sequence of negatives originate with the *pa-unahay*. The goal of "being first," appears to become problematic only when carried to the extreme, as in traffic. The origin of *pa-unahay* is unclear. Why would even a small child practice the well-known game of daring called "chicken" [i.e., who is the first to give up space] by refusing to quickly move to the side of the road when trucks are approaching? Local accounts tell of small boys living in the Divisoria section of Manila, an area known for its densely populated ghettos, who play a game on the railroad tracks to see who can jump off at the last moment before the train rushes by. It may be that the personality trait of "machismo," symbolized by the fearless Spanish matador, remains a vestige associated with over 300 years of Spanish occupation (see Mirande, 1997). Such a deduction remains unexplored.

This discourse becomes more compelling when it is noted that young children are conditioned—even while sitting in a parent's lap on the jeepney—to adopt the *pa-unahay* and even the *pa-abtikay* behavior patterns. Not surprisingly, locals agree that as children grow older, it is easier for them to justify the more severe forms of law breaking. Land squatters can rationalize that "I moved in when you were not around, so what is wrong with that? Now it is my space, and you can try to take it from me." If squatters demand, "Prove to me in court that it is yours," they are exhibiting the *pa-abtikay* behavior.

Much theft, in general, can be so rationalized, and even kidnaping can be seen simply as impermanent theft [i.e., "I have taken something of value from you when you were not looking. If you want your property or individual back, you can pay for it [him or her.]" Indeed, some crime takes on a game or prank quality of "outsmarting" the victim. Kidnaping is such an event, where the offender must be very *abtik* [quick and smart] and must rely on ingenuity to reap any ransom. In most cases in the Philippines, the kidnap victim is returned unharmed. It is no exaggeration to claim that many locals in Lanao del Norte argue that kidnap victims bring such a fate upon themselves; that is, victims precipitate kidnaping. Everyone in the province knows the game, and adult outsiders are constantly reminded of the possibility that they will be nabbed off the street on the assumption that any outsider must have money by virtue of the fact that they are travelers. The game must be played by both sides, in the sense that any potential victim must take precautions to thwart the kidnapers. Both offenders and potential victims must remain street smart.

This discussion began with an assumption that evidence exists in the research area of what Donald Black specifies as anarchy or at least "near anarchy." The social problems of economic survival, political corruption, and religious turmoil, lay a foundation where many, especially the poor, experience hopelessness. Those in lower income jobs, who barely make ends meet, if at all, can easily rationalize ways to make extra money or to succeed through "smart," and sometimes illegitimate, means. Following Donald Black (1976, 123–137), anarchy is used here as an analytical concept which applies to all nations and which, during their history, fluctuates between varying levels of anarchy and smooth governmental control.

Being anarchic might not be all bad. That is, if it is possible to resolve interpersonal problems without formal, official government control, then an anarchic direction might be acceptable and desirable. This chapter has described the darker side of social problems in a specific Philippine setting, but makes no claim that the research area is doomed or that it cannot reverse directions, should the citizenry so desire. If life in the research setting is viewed as a game, with all aware of the rules, then the apparent anarchy or chaos may only appear as such to outsiders. All local citizens are intimately familiar with *pa-unahay*, and it is not a pattern many think of as unusual.

A plausible explanation for the anarchic nature of the northwestern Mindanao province under scrutiny is that, like most Philippine provinces [or isolated Philippine islands], life in the very rural hinterlands was always relatively anarchic, with little need for government control and certainly limited dependence on the seat of government in Manila. This is likely true of very rural communities anywhere in the nation. As populations grew in size and density, and social institutions expanded, along with advancing technology, there was also a need for increasing government social control. Perhaps, as much or more than with most nations, the Philippines today reflects a clear mix of both provincial and urban ideologies. As portrayed in Chapter 3, the *barangay* and *purok* systems, even in the large cities, push the nation's people toward a rural mind set. Among other things, this accentuates local neighborhood and non-governmental patterns of control. As noted in Chapter 1, government regulations purposefully discourage lawyers from legislating *barangay* justice disputes and any local grievances are expected to remain outside the parameters of government, at least for a period of time. This being true, it appears to pave the way for a rather casual attitude toward such quasi-legitimate or norm-breaking features as discussed here.

Figure 9–1 reflects the dependent variables of anarchic manifestations as a whole or in the aggregate. That is, no attempt is made to suggest in the illustration that one dependent variable is any more or less important or critical than another. The argument is simply that these manifestations or tendencies toward anarchy do exist and result from the major independent variables of situation, culture, and personality. Although it may seem obvious, it must also be said that the various anarchic tendencies are mobilized through social interaction. Although each of the anarchic tendencies exists as mental constructs, either as rules of expected behavior [culture] or as values and attitudes [personality], they are also sociological in the sense that they can be observed as overt patterns of social action.

However, the various scenarios of anarchic manifestations as discussed here do allow at least for implications of the sequencing of specific dependent variables. That is, which tends to precede the other and is one manifestation more anarchic than the another? Consider the following proposition: *Pa-unahay, once established, sets the stage for pa-lusotay behavior patterns.* An argument can be made, even if hypothetical, that one independent variable is antecedent to the another. In other words, a struggle to be first [*pa-unahay*] serves as a launching point for a struggle to "push through [*pa-lusotay*]," thus leading to norm breaking or illegal conduct.

Pa-unahay, with regard to the roadway, appears on first glance as total confusion. However, according to the unwritten rules of the road, squeezing inch by inch into a tight street space is acceptable, although it appears at best to the uninitiated outsider as orderly chaos. Yet, when one driver makes the frenzied leap to "push through" traffic, even if that mean striking the bumper of another vehicle, *pa-lusotay* prevails. The transition is a gray area and some locals describe *pa-unahay* as "Here I come, ready or not," which itself implies the anticipation of *pa-lusotay*. At the very point that *pa-lusotay* is activated, a rule of proper driving technique is breached.

Whereas vehicular-traffic patterns depict a single example that can be rather clearly visualized, the possibilities of explaining the juncture of these two cultural features appear endless. The case provided earlier of butting in line also reflects the sequence of *pa-unahay* and *pa-lusotay*. Squeezing into a space, no matter how small, in a department store checkout line is one thing, but frenetically pushing one's way past others to the front, even if allowable, forces one to redefine rudeness. Should pushing give way to shoving, as would be a logical extension if persons in a crowd are all competing with one other, then simple assault is approached at least in a technical sense. The pushing and shoving, which would likely bring about cries of foul play as improper queuing etiquette in other cultural areas, seems to have become customary in Lanao del Norte.

In the Philippines, some infractions rather than others tend to result from the joining of *pa-unahay* and *pa-lusotay*. For instance, land squatting is commonplace in the research setting and exemplifies a logical extension of these two cultural features. In fact, depending upon one's perspective, land squatting can be rationalized as appropriate, even though someone certainly is being victimized or made to be a loser in the game-like event. Admittedly, upon first glance, it would appear odd to consider land squatting as an example of *pa-unahay*. However, if one considers that entire villages have sprung up as a result of people competing for and squeezing onto unoccupied land space owned by others, then the *pa-unahay* scenario may apply. It is also common for land owners to counteract squatters, which can lead to a feverish pushing by the original squatter to remain firm, which is characteristic of *pa-lusotay* attributes and which can trigger court action or attempts to resolve such matters informally within the *barangays*.

Even kidnaping, although more of a theoretical stretch, may be illustrative of the end result of *pa-unahay* and *pa-lusotay*. As many potential victims walk the streets of the research setting, opportunists see these victims as money- making ventures. It is common knowledge that numerous kidnap bands exist and that these bands in fact compete for particularly lucrative victims, and in so doing engage in a *pa-unahay*–styled exercise. In such competition, the first band to successfully compete for and to nab a non-vigilant or negligent victim off the street is the first to score. To the extent that the act involves intensity and frenetic activity to be first [to kidnap a particular victim], the activity can also be viewed as *pa-lusotay* or "pushing through" toward norm or law breaking.

Some actions can be said to be "*abtik*" and to represent, in and of themselves, wise-guy or smartalecky behaviors. Yet, *pa-abtikay* appears to make most sense when allied with other, sometimes negative or illegal, activities to include *pa-lusotay* and *pa-bukongay* operations. A second proposition is in order. *Pa-abtikay tendencies tend to amplify seeds of norm breaking inspired by pa-lusotay or pa-bukongay behaviors.* The so-called brash "hyperactivity" of *pa-abtikay* tendencies could either precede or parallel norm-breaking acts.

In this regard, *pa-abtikay* behavior may not necessarily be inappropriate per se but works as an attitude or disposition which fans the fire of already established norm violations. Being smart in a negative sense is bad enough, but adding trickery and subterfuge—often affiliated with *pa-abtikay*—to an already-established *pa-lusotay* or *pa-bukongay* activity can work to make the norm breaking increasingly acute. For example, bypassing the cashier and bolting from a restaurant without paying the bill would be *bukong*, but such norm breaking is intensified if an offender becomes crafty and expert at the infraction which moves in the direction of prior thought and planing. *Bukong* generally carries with it a connotation of furtiveness and spontaneity. If one is also *abtik*, then a suggestion applies that the culprit is developing a more permanent cunning ability and sentiment at carrying out the particular action.

Consider the following proposition. *Anarchy flourishes to the extent that pa-unahay and pa-abtikay converge with pa-lusotay and pa-bukongay manifestations.* The "occurrence" of norm breaking, in and of itself, is insufficient for anarchy. However, once the race toward norm breaking [*pa-unahay*] becomes part of a cunning mind set [*pa-abtikay*] of the citizenry, law and order in any traditional sense is undermined. In such an instance, the adage that rules are only made to be broken would appear to apply. In a number of ways, already detailed, the research setting represents a place where scurrying to break the law has become customary. Thus, the diversity of extortion and bribery opportunities can easily pertain to the culturally anarchic manifestations. Here, for example, offering bribes or demanding payola may be analyzed in terms of the extent to which the activity includes, *pa-abtikay* or perhaps *pa-lusotay* dispositions.

Moreover, at the risk of stating the obvious, it follows that *advancing anarchic tendencies parallel a decrease in effectiveness of social controls.* In Lanao del Norte, loss of social controls appears a necessary precondition for the anarchic manifestations, although the condition of "de-policing" does allow anarchic activities to proceed unabated. What is pertinent is that once the four anarchic activities persist over time, agencies of social control also lose their legitimacy and effectiveness. For instance, *pa-lusotay* and *pa-bukongay* acts recur with little noticeable impediments from either formal police or informal community controls. Local reports and direct observations suggest that official police agencies are the first to lose citizen trust. As late as 1997, uniformed police in the research setting were the butt of jokes and were commonly referred to as corrupt.

On the other hand, even the time-honored traditions of out-of-court conflict resolution, so common to the Philippines, also appears to be deteriorating in Lanao del Norte. It is true that remnants of an earlier and effective system of informal dispute processing remain. The case of calling upon the mestizo fixers to assist in the resolution of workplace disputes represents such a remnant, itself shown only as a partially effective solution. The structured *barangay* justice system persists, but to the extent that it is also allied with government, even if at the lowest level, it also suffers a loss of credibility. That is, even the *barangay* officials can be influenced by political favors and cannot be expected to actively pursue the kinds of anarchic manifestations discussed here.

The next decade will have to address the damaged Philippine culture (see Fallows, 1988), which is reflected, in part, in the aspiring of youth for careers outside the Philippines. The economic and political turmoil is fixable, and the religious antagonists may forge a truce, as is being organized in 1997 as this chapter is written. However, the anarchic mind set which depicts law bending or breaking almost as if they were sporting events, will take longer to repair and will have to wait for the resolution of the other problematic conditions examined in this chapter.

Chapter 10

Summing Up

S ummaries are not generally written with gusto. Some authors are burned out by this stage and see the final chapter as an afterthought. Perhaps with some justification, writers may be peeved that readers might find here a cursory review of the contents and thus avoid reading the book altogether. Yet, summaries provide a necessary capstone. They allow the writer to inventory the central points made throughout the previous pages and, without redrafting the detail, to synthesize the primary findings. Finally, in the tradition of scientific inquiry, it is in the summary where the researcher can suggest directions for future exploration.

THE INVENTORY

Six central points need to be highlighted. First, this book explains issues which are of value to researchers interested in Philippine history. Social and cultural change is continuous, and by the time this book finds its way into print, many of the issues described here may have already shifted. The Philippine economy may continue to improve, highland Muslims and lowland Christians may work out a truce, overseas contract workers may return home, and kidnapings may go on a decline. Any such changes would in no way diminish the importance of the findings presented in these chapters. It is critical to know the nature of crime and custom in the research area during an important period of recent history—the last two decades of the twentieth century—in order to make better sense of what the future brings. Depending upon one's outlook, this book furnishes either a snapshot of Philippine crime and custom or a longitudinal view of nearly twenty years. In looking at kidnaping rates, twenty years is a long time and major changes may be expected. On the other hand, examining changes in language patterns and, for example, watching for adjustments in the meaning of *pa-unahay* and its relationship to anarchy [as described in Chapter 9], twenty years may be brief. Generations may have to come and go before significant changes can be seen in such fundamental quasi-anarchic mind sets.

Also, the discussion of vigilante movements [Chapter 6] is most conducive to swift changes. As was pointed out earlier, the names of specific groups quickly fluctuate as one community network replaces another. Thus, the Civilian Home Defense Force [CHDF], discussed in Chapter 6, has now faded from view, only to be replaced by the Civilian Army Force Geographic Unit [CAFGU], briefly described in Chapter 2. The communist party influence has waxed and waned over the past twenty years. This has had a direct impact on the nature and extent of terrorism in the research area which, in turn, has impacted on the style of policing and peacemaking strategies evident in the *barangays*. All these relevant points involve history, although the foregoing essays are meant to provide more than historical accounts.

Second, resulting strictly from author preference, this book has presented various themes of crime and custom primarily from a social-psychological or "social interactionist" point of view. Thus, for example, each of the chapters, beginning with "Islands and *Barangays*" [Chapter 1], offers a small-group perspective whereby concern is chiefly with daily activity of individuals and/or groups. Emphasis is on describing a *barangay* and explaining how it operates with respect to the dynamics of justice processing. Similarly, regarding peacemaking in Chapter 2, care has been taken to detail how persons and groups work together to secure peace at the grass-roots, neighborhood level.

Chapter 3 introduced a variety of unanticipated measures which emerged during the fieldwork and which unexpectedly fostered social control. Again, from a small-group perspective, it was explained how technology [for example, radio transceivers and cellular phones] impacted on villagers to provide safety and, in some ways, upset their custom of face-to-face interactions. The high rate of unemployment and underemployment allows for the unusual presence of adults in the community during the daytime who pass the hours at the *sari-sari* stores, providing unforeseen neighborhood security. Chapter 4 tackles the multifaceted theme of Muslim-Christian conflict and provides case studies of how selected disputes are managed in the workplace. In this manner, attention was placed on how cultural conflict functions in small-group settings in communities comprising peoples long antagonistic toward each other.

Chapter 5 demonstrates how terrorism impacts on individuals, and how, in some instances, individuals are apprehensive about making new acquaintances or even about which friends to keep given the complex mix of competing political allegiances. Throughout the chapter, terrorism was considered as a constant variable which influenced the behavior of individuals and groups. In a similar manner, bribery and extortion are viewed as types of deviant or criminal behaviors which depict how one person interacts with another in a victim/offender relationship. Each example presents a micro-sociological approach. This can be seen in the case of small children moderately intimidating adults with the threat of vandalism if a few pesos are not given to watch a vehicle during its owner's brief absence. Or, face-to-face interactions are scrutinized in the instance represented by intimidated adults "tossing coins" to guards at police checkpoints. Concern is primarily on social interaction and the meaning certain briberous or extortionate actions have for group members.

Chapter 8 considers the youth of the region. Limited reports are reviewed regarding the official perspective, followed by descriptions of a few of the unfortunate circumstances befalling the youthful citizens of the research area. The mood of the chapter is necessarily downbeat by pointing out the harsh reality for the bulk of the children of the area who struggle to escape poverty and enter a middle class where the quality of life remains austere by standards of more economically affluent nations. An issue which perhaps needs consideration is whether much of the Philippines should not be judged by, for example, Singaporean or Japanese standards. Many elders of Lanao del Norte long for a return to barrio life, when times were peaceful and the food supply plentiful. Returning to these days is far removed from the minds of the youth who have had a taste, even if from a distance, of some of the cultural artifacts available only in an aggressive market economy. In the poorest barrio of the research area can be found advertisements for high-priced Air Jordan basketball shoes, the price of which would equal for many a year's wages.

In Chapter 9, the final theme of Part III, a case is made that an anarchic mind set of the citizenry is conditioned early in life to accept intense competition for space. This is illustrated by adult driving habits, queuing behavior, even the maneuvering for sidewalk space. For many, ownership of property appears to be fluid and impermanent, as seen in the rather facile and nonchalant manner in which squatters appropriate another's property. In the research setting, property ownership does not appear to imply an inviolable or even an ultimately protected right. Not only is property ownership itself slippery, but the norm itself is mobile. It is certainly understood that different approaches to the study of crime and deviance in northwestern Mindanao, other than the social psychological, may also provide useful findings. Among these other approaches are demographic, legalistic, theological, human ecological, or national political orientations to name a few. These can only be alluded to here.

Third, as reflected in the title, this book presents field notes as well as other commentary on crime and custom in the Philippine setting. Criminological theorists realize that one cannot effectively limit inquiry specifically to the "criminal" in trying to explain deviant or unlawful behavior. Consequently, as space permitted, some digressions away from criminality were taken to relate the systemic nature of law breaking in the research setting. For example, effective discussion of Filipino crime, or the absence of crime, must take into account the family and community structure, as outlined in Chapters 2 and 3. Ultimately, the nature of criminal and deviant behavior can only be understood by integrating the variables of culture, personality, and situation as they coalesce through a process of social interaction. This process is best illustrated in Chapter 2, which outlines cultural and personality features of Filipinos with respect to the traditions of peacemaking, and Chapter 3, which presents a number of situational factors in the research setting, which influence security and social control at the neighborhood level.

Fourth, in several ways this book was written with an eye toward criminological theory. For example, the careful reader will note that throughout the chapters, aspects of the predictions of Donald Black are clarified or given partial test through the Philippine examples. In a most basic way, it appears clear that the research setting, and especially the rural *sitios*, illustrate "self-help" theory, as citizens arise to take care of themselves in the absence of police and government social control. The evolution and persistence of the *barangay* concept itself fosters an explicit sense of community, which has become an integral component of Filipino society, providing facets of security to its members. Black's and Baumgardner's concept of "de-policing" comes to life in the instance of *sitio* residents having to fend for themselves without formal police or governmental social control [Chapter 3].

The discussion of vigilante networks [Chapter 6] attests to Black's principle that law is less necessary with the advent of other kinds of social control. That is, social organization becomes increasingly complex in times of turmoil, and with the emergence of self-help "vigilante groups," formal law becomes less necessary. Stated differently, these chapters provide examples of the durability, if not the inevitability, of altruism in the face of turmoil. Granted, it does appear that volunteerism and cooperation are sorely tested in the research setting. Black's intricate and somewhat cryptic discussion of anarchy (1976:123–137) is considered in Chapter 9 by suggesting that the way some Filipinos define public and personal space may promote fertile conditions for anarchy. The time-honored Filipino traditions of self-help and altruism have been colliding with advancing legalistic society, creating a near-anarchic setting [partial disregard for law] for years. The outcome may not be known for some time.

The folk ideal typical of rural and isolated settings has been put to the test in the research area in the face of advancing mobility and technology. Television antennas sit atop squatter huts. At the same time, economic instability, corruption, extremist insurgency, and Muslim-Christian conflict have taken their toll, even if sleepy and friendly villages lay slightly beneath the surface. Confusion and anxiety lead to resentment and anger and for some this results in a lack of respect for law. Confusing settings persist, as is noted in the case of *pa-unahay* [competitiveness for space in the streets, on sidewalks, and in queuing lines] and *pa-abtikay* [unscrupulous money-grabbing]. These culturally complex patterns are detailed in Chapter 9. At the same time, one can witness an opposite pattern of behavior whereby cooperation replaces competition.

While the jeepneys are breaking all local traffic ordinances [as outlined in Chapter 9], the passengers, aware of the vehicle's reckless struggle for space, still cooperate among themselves. That is, all passengers work in concert to assure that a passenger sitting at the back of the jeep can pay the fare by transferring money from one passenger to the next and finally to the driver. The driver gives any change back to a passenger and the money eventually finds its way back to the original traveler. Unfortunately, this orderly and helpful system not only occurs during chaotic *pa-unahay* but at times while a passenger's pocket is being picked. Pocket-picking of jeepney commuters is well-organized. Mixing of values is obvious and widespread and must generate role conflict among youth and adults alike. These issues deserve more in-depth examination.

Although Donald Black's work provides a logical guide for much of the fieldwork portrayed in these chapters, it would be a mistake to assume the field-work projects were initiated only to formally test sociological theory. Rather, most of the ventures were undertaken in a spirit of describing and explaining systems of behavior under the assumption that social patterns would emerge from the raw data. This clearly occurs, and it is these patterns which comprise the heart of each chapter. In some instances—for example, Chapter 5 on the impact of terrorism and Chapter 7 on bribery and extortion—the patterns are stated in proposition form. This should benefit future ethnographers in a quest for researchable relationships. When not in proposition format, the relationship between critical variables is profiled in case studies or in a discussion section at the end of a chapter.

A fifth central point highlighted in this book is the Filipino tradition of struggling to maintain a sense of community. This point is noted in some detail in previous pages and needs only brief reiteration. The quality is accentuated in a number of ways throughout the chapters. If the celebrated community spirit among the islanders, which has been lauded as pre-dating the Spanish occupation [see Chapter 3], is suppressed in one region or time, it reappears elsewhere. It flourishes, as would be expected, not only in the isolated *sitios*, but also in the middle of Manila because of the nationwide networking of the unique *barangay* and *purok* systems. By design, all citizens anywhere in the Philippines are interconnected, and thus secured, through a web of neighborhood-based political units or *barangays*. The advantages and possible drawbacks of this system are also discussed in Chapter 1 ["Islands and *Barangays*"].

Sixth, as noted early in the Introduction of this book, the Philippine field projects began, in part, as a way to periodically escape the classroom in hopes of discovering and describing systems of justice far removed from Pennsylvania. This has been accomplished and, without question, any attempts to explain American systems of crime and custom [among other diverse models], while in the classroom, have been enhanced by an awareness of and an appreciation for the Philippine scene. The subjects of concern are applicable in most nations of the world. All would agree, for example, that corruption, terrorism, religious extremism, disrespect for law [anarchy], or the plight of youth, have their counterparts on the global scene.

All of the findings presented in these pages apply to comparative approaches of crime. The findings are of theoretical relevance to comparative criminology and should assist future researchers in understanding how one justice system contrasts with another even if they are on separate continents. For instance, the chapter on terrorism only happens to have originated with the Philippine illustration. Even with the voluminous literature on terrorism, very few citations address its impacts on people, individually or collectively. Any future dialogue on terrorism, in any world region, should include this neglected perspective. Having said this, it remains true that those specifically interested in understanding Filipino culture will find of consequence this discussion on the influence of terrorism and how residents of northwestern Mindanao are adapting to life in a region of the world which has seen its share of turmoil.

Similarly, the brief case studies presented in the chapter on Muslim-Christian conflict only touch upon an extensive and complex problem of diverse religion-based cultures living and working in the same locale. Still, at the workplace level, such basic explanations bring us to a closer understanding of cultural conflict and potential remedies, and are directly pertinent to the study of comparative justice systems. It is appropriate for comparative criminologists and other social scientists to search for cross-cultural analogs. The anticipation is high that a pattern found in one part of the world may provide a key for better understanding other world regions. Surely, this is a worthy pursuit. At the same time, some argue that a sufficient quantity of ethnographic descriptions of diverse justice systems are already at hand, and that additional accounts of unexplored or frontier regions of the world would be of minimal additional value. This author counters that most world cultures remain untouched by ethnographers, which is to the obvious detriment of a subjective understanding of dispersed and fluctuating cultures.

Ethnography conducted in one year may result in varied findings a year later. Cultures shift as quickly as do a nation's political boundaries, and cultures as well as nations are born and die out. This makes it even more compelling that additional ethnographic fieldwork be continuously undertaken. Just as important, those nations which have previously provided rich accounts, including the Philippines, need cross-observer reliability checks. Replication remains one of the hallmarks of science but one that is often glossed over.

To this author, the facts presented in these chapters represent, are of extremely high validity. However, even with the attention given to reliability concerns discussed in the Introduction, it remains to be seen if another researcher in the same or a comparable region of the Philippines would arrive at corresponding data and interpretations. Such a mission is of primary concern and is welcomed. Each of these chapters has provided a series of testable hypotheses. In some cases, sociological or criminological theory is partially clarified by the Philippine scenarios presented in these chapters. Much is left undone and is a task for subsequent research.

Glossary

Alsa Masa. In the Tagalog, "uprising of the masses." A name associated with a strong, popular, and sometimes illegal vigilante movement which began in Davao City on the island of Mindanao.

Amerikano. Colloquial expression commonly given to any Americans in the Philippines. Often, the simplified expression "kano" is heard.

Amicable settlement. The process of resolving disputes and minor crimes outside of court and within the community. The practice probably originated with the Spanish ideal of *areglo,* meaning to arrange things unofficially. The Spanish *arreglo* is spelled as *areglo* in the Cebuano.

Anarchy. Variously defined but used here to imply a disregard for government or the rule of law.

Anting-anting. An amulet often worn around the neck or on the upper arm which is believed to ward off evil spirits, and thus protect the wearer from danger.

ARRM [Autonomous Region for Muslim Mindano]. Four provinces of Mindanao [Maguindanao, Sulu, Tawi-Tawi, and Lanao del Sur] which have established by popular vote an autonomous geopolitical region in Mindanao.

Balanghais. Literally meaning "boat" in the Malayan language and used here in reference to boat communities which were originally brought by sea from the Malay Peninsula to what are now the Philippines..

Bantay. Translates as "watch" in Cebuano and is used to refer, for example, to "*bantay* boys" who will keep watch over a vehicle for a fee while the owner is away.

Bantay ng Bayan. A Tagalog phrase which literally translates as "watch of the country" and refers to a security network of vigilant citizens who communicate with each other primarily by hand-held two-way radio transceivers.

Barangay. Originally the name given to communal settlements of the indigenous Philippine people at the time of the Spanish arrival. After 1973 the term was used to denote the citizens' assemblies established in each barrio. In mid-1974, by Presidential Decree, the term *barangay* replaced barrio.

Barrio. Pertains to a village. Often consists of a primary hamlet and several satellite hamlets. Generally considered the principal settlement form of the country. Later renamed *barangay* in mid-1974.

Bribery. Generally refers to the offering, giving, receiving, or soliciting of any- thing of value to influence official action or the discharge of public duty.

Bukong. Literally means "dry coconut" and in the Cebuano refers to one who refuses to pay, as in one who jumps off a jeepney without paying fare to the driver.

One who opens a coconut to find it is dry, is cheated. [See **Pa-bukongay**.]

CAFGU [Civilian Army Force Geographic Unit]. Citizens who volunteer to be attached to military units but who also reside within the local community.

CHDF [Civilian Home Defense Force]. A loosely structured volunteer force, later replaced by the CAFGU.

Compadre/compadreism [*kumpadre* in the Cebuano]. The act of functioning as a godfather to another and thus creating a bond of obligation, and usually closeness, between the two individuals. Having a godfather is believed to make one more secure.

Companion. A common Philippine expression which refers to a close friend who often accompanies one during everyday activities. One with a companion is felt to be more secure [as from danger].

Comparative Justice. A subdivision of criminology which focuses on and contrasts the hundreds of diverse justice systems around the world.

CPP [Communist Party of the Philippines]. A Maoist-oriented communist movement which caused political turmoil in many regions of the Philippines. In the early 1970s, the CPP, along with other political insurgencies, reportedly inspired President Marcos to declare martial law.

De-policing. Refers to reducing the size of the police force and is often associated with informal justice perspectives.

EDSA Revolution. Refers to the rising up of masses and the beginning of the people-power movement which started with a revolt by the citizenry on a Manila thoroughfare named *Epifanio de los Santos Avenue*. The revolt ended with the forced departure of President Ferdinand Marcos.

Extortion. Obtaining or attempting to obtain something of value from another by compelling the other person to deliver it by threat of eventual physical injury or other harm to that person, his or her property, or a third party. Extortion typically lacks immediate confrontation, as is the case in robbery.

Familism. A general concept referring to a condition of family cohesiveness and willingness to assist any individual member. Usually associated with closeness of family members at the rural or village level rather than in the more detached simple nuclear families often typical of urban areas.

Filial piety. A near-religious devotion between sons and daughters to the family or parents. Also refers to one's duty to assist in any way possible a family member in need. A specific form of familism.

Filipino. A person native to the Republic of the Philippines. The feminine form of the word—Filipina—is often used to refer to any female native to the country.

Fixer. Colloquial term given to a person who acts as a "go-between" or mediator of disputes in the Philippines.

GRO [Guest Relations Officer]. A name given to "bar maids" or "cocktail waitresses" in the mid-1990s. Commonly the primary activity is to entice male customers to purchase drinks by offering and providing sexual favors although that is technically illegal.

Hip-hip. Rough translation from the Cebuano meaning "payola"; probably derives from the act of one placing a hand on the back wallet pocket, suggesting the desire to give or receive bribe money.

Hiya. [See Cebuano term *Ka-ulaw*.] Feeling shame or loss of face. One who does not exhibit *pakig-uban-uban* or fulfil obligations of *utang kabubut-on* should feel shame.

Hunglos. A cooperative scheme whereby rice farmers, for example, assist each other in planting or harvesting rice.

Inpos. An abbreviated term adapted from the word "informant." A most unofficial information source, sometimes used to refer to coconut tree climbers who can act as lookouts.

Intrigues. Social scenarios, commonly office based, which involve gossip and/or backbiting.

Islam. Refers to the faith held by Muslims and worshipers of Mohammad.

Kabisig. An anagram from "ka" [link] and "bisig" [arm] meaning "linking arms" in Tagalog. A program established by President Corazon Aquino to provide funding to help local organizations link up with each other and with the national government in a countrywide effort to solve social problems.

Kapher [or *Kaper*]. In Arabic, an infidel. Slang for one who defies Muslim beliefs. A swine-eater.

Katarungang pambarangay. Translates from the Tagalog as "community justice." Refers to the official program of local justice established in 1978 by President Ferdinand Marcos.

Ka-ulaw. [See Tagalog term *Hiya*.] From the Cebuano meaning a feeling of shame or loss of face.

Kufer. In Arabic, the fact that one does not believe in Islamic principles [belief that pork eating is appropriate.]

Lupon tagapayapa. Appointed group of citizens in the *barangay* who initiate peace and order. This group would be most analogous in the United States to a jury pool from which a jury is selected. Usually made up of 10 to 20 persons.

Luzon. The largest geographic region of the Philippines; situated to the north. Manila, the nation's capital is located on the southwestern coast of Luzon.

Maranao. A subdivision of Muslim people in northwestern Mindanao. The Maranao language.

Maratabat. A deep sense of self-esteem held by Maranao and other Muslims. Damage to a Muslim's sense of self-esteem may be grounds for future revenge.

Mestizo. A person of mixed blood or ethnic heritage. In the Philippines, a person with one Muslim parent and one Christian parent is referred to as a mestizo.

Mga manananggot. Cebuano term for coconut tree climbers who are occasionally used as lookouts for vigilante organizations.

MILF [Moro Islamic Liberation Front]. A branch of the Moro National Liberation Front.

Mindanao. Refers to the largest island in the southern Philippines and one of the three major geographic and cultural divisions of the country, along with Luzon and the Visayan islands.

MNLF [Moro National Liberation Front]. Islamic movement primarily situated in central and southern Mindanao.

Moro. A name given to Muslims of Mindanao or a region inhabited by Muslims [morolandia]. Coined by the early Spanish who believed the Philippine Muslims were as warlike as the African Moors, a tribal people of northern Africa.

Muslim. A person of the Islamic faith. Several million Muslims reside in Mindanao.

Nakasaka. An anagram formed from the Cebuano expression *Nagkahiusang katawhan alang sa kalinaw* [unification of people for peace]. A slogan used during the presidency of Corazon Aquino signifying a people-power movement.

Non-action. Refers to the ability of the *barangay* captain to delay any action on a case for a period of time and by so doing allows a dispute to cool down.

NPA [New Peoples Army]. Military arm of the Communist Party of the Philippines.

OCW [Overseas Contract Worker]. Refers to young adults who find employment outside the Philippines and who work for predetermined periods of time.

Pa-abtikay. In the Cebuano an expression meaning "overly active" and generally associated with inappropriate behavior though not necessarily illegal. Probably derives from the English "active."

Pa-bukongay. Whereas **"bukong"** literally means "dry coconut" thus "cheated," attaching the prefix *"pa"* with **"bukongay"** adjusts the meaning to "the act of being cheated."

Pakig-uban-uban. The Cebuano term for *Pakisama,* and with the same meaning.

Pakisama. [See Cebuano term *Pakig-uban-uban.*] To go along with, as in the sense of feeling an obligation to please others. A feeling expected among colleagues, comrades, or friends.

Pakyaw. An economic contract, as, for example, between rice-farm owner and laborers, whereby workers are paid based on the amount of work performed.

Palo-apon. Means "to follow up" in the sense of checking up on the progress of some transaction. Forcing one to continuously "follow up" on any business transaction often requires face-to-face dialogue.

Paltik. A homemade gun; often a crude one-shot pistol.

Pa-lusotay In the Cebuano an expression meaning "to push through" in the sense of forcing one's way even if against the law. One who breaks traffic laws by speeding through red traffic signals. An extension of *pa-unahay.*

Pangkat ng taga pagkasundo. In the Tagalog this translates as "committee of persons, selected from the *lupon,* who when mobilized, decide the outcome of a dispute or minor crime in the *barangay.* Similar to a jury but never referred to as such. Comprising three persons and generally shortened to simply the *"pangkat."*

Pa-unahay. Translates from the Cebuano as "to go ahead" or "I will go ahead no matter what," and is generally used in reference to driving practices in busy streets. **PC/INP [Philippine Constabulary and Integrated National Police]** The Philippine Constabulary was the first armed service of the Philippines and acted as a national police force, analogous to the military. The Integrated National Police was non-military and referred to the nationwide organization of municipal and city [civilian] police.

Peacemaking. A recent subdivision of criminology, which emphasizes models of conciliation rather than guilt and revenge-oriented systems of control.

Peso. Philippine currency. In 1980 the exchange rate was eight pesos to one U.S. dollar and had by 1998 reached forty pesos to the dollar.

Pilipino. Refers to the national language and is generally interchangeable with Tagalog.

PNP [Philippine National Police]. In the mid-1990s President Ramos combined the Philippine Constabulatory with the Integrated National Police to form the PNP.

P're. In everyday speech in the Philippines, the term compadre or "kumpadre" is often shortened to "p're."

Purok. A political subdivision of a *barangay:* similar to a neighborhood. In the Philippines, a *purok* may be represented by numerous community organizations.

Redo. To repeat a harm done in the sense of "doing again" what one has done to you in an effort to gain revenge.

Ronda. The mobilization of a group of neighbors to investigate any disturbance in the community.

Sagrado Corazon Senor. Means "Holy or sacred heart"; a name taken by a vigilante group in the 1980s operating in Mindanao.

Sakop. One's immediate work group. Refers to obligations between worker and employer and derives from the feudal relationship still prevalent in much of the Philippines. Possessing an extensive *sakop* may make one more secure in the sense of having persons who may provide assistance in time of need.

Salvage. To kill another as in "putting another in his/her place."

Sangguni-an. Municipal government panel appointed by the mayor.

Sari-sari. Literally "variety-variety"; pertains to neighborhood-based roadside stores, which sell sundry items.

Self-help. A process, usually altruistic, whereby community members take action on an issue without reliance upon official government agencies [for example, vigilante groups or neighborhood-based dispute-processing activities].

Sitio. A hamlet and part of a *purok* and *barangay*. Generally geographically detached from other population clusters of a *purok* or *barangay*.

Snowball sampling. Sometimes referred to as networking, whereby the researcher locates a single interviewee who in turn suggests another who could provide useful information and so on. The researcher may stop interviewing when a point of redundancy is reached; that is, when no new information is forthcoming.

Squatter. A person who illegally lays claim to another's property by physically occupying the property and refusing to move.

Tad-Tad. Literally means "chop-chop"; a name taken by a violence-prone vigilante group operating in Mindanao in the 1980s.

Tagalog. Lowland Christian group located in Luzon and centered in Manila. The Tagalog language, now considered the national language of the Philippines, is also referred to as Pilipino.

Tago ng tago. Well known throughout the Philippines as "TNT"; literally translates as "hide and hide." Reference is made here to one who illegally remains in a foreign country, without visa, and must remain a fugitive and thus "hide and hide."

Tanod. Defined in the Tagalog as "watch" or "guard." A group of citizens selected by the *barangay* captain to act as security guards for the community.

Terrorism. Variously defined, but discussed here as illegal violence or destruction, or threats of such, linked to political or political-religious extremism and subversion.

Tig-atiman. A person who will follow up any paperwork for another, thus relieving one from the time-consuming effort associated with many business transactions. More formally expressed in the Cebuano as *Taga-atiman*.

Tigs. An abbreviated expression referring to any of the occupational types discussed under "*tig-salmon*," "*tig-say-say*" or *tig sulti*" [etc]. In northwestern Mindanoa the role of "*tig*" has assumed some deviant connotations.

Tig-salmot. A person who will attend a meeting in place of another. More formally in the Cebuano as *Taga-salmot*.

Tig-say-say [or ***Tig sulti***]. A person who will speak on behalf of another.

Trapos. An anagram formed from the English "traditional" and "politician" meaning "traditional politicians." Because the word *trapos* also means "rags" in Tagalog, the word has been used in a derogatory manner to refer in non-progressive members of congress.

Utang kabubut-on. Translated from the Cebuano language as "inner debt." One who receives a favor or gift is obliged to repay the favor or gift in the future; thus, a form of reciprocal exchange. Sometimes one may be obliged to offer assistance to another who has earlier provided a favor or service.

Utang na loob. Tagalog translation of "inner debt"; holds the same meaning as *utang kabubut-on*.

Vigilantism. A social activity, often at the small-group or village level, which emphasizes a vigilant citizenry and is sometimes reflected by a group of citizens who voluntarily patrol the community and watch for danger or intruders.

Visaya. Refers to the central region of islands groups between Luzon to the north and Mindanao to the south. Colloquially, many persons living in this region refer to *Visaya* as a language, as in speaking Visayan [language of the Visayan islands], although more accurately, dialects are specific to islands, as in the case of Cebuano being spoken on the island of Cebu, and elsewhere.

Walay sapatos. Translates as "without shoes" and used as an expression which describes the sometimes poverty-stricken lifestyle of rebel soldiers.

Yayong. The process of assisting another, as in transporting a house from one location in the village to another.

References

ABA (American Bar Association). 1986. "Dispute Resolution." Special Commemorative Issue. Special Committee on Dispute Resolution, No. 19: 11.

Abel, Richard. I. 1982. *The Politics of Informal Justice*. Volumes I & II, New York: Academic Press.

Adas, Michael. 1981. "From Avoidance to Conformity: Peasant Protest in Precolonial and Colonial Southeast Asia." *Comparative Studies in Society and History*. 23 (2):217–247.

Albada-Lim, Estefania. 1978. "Care of the Juvenile Offenders in the Philippines." *International Journal of Offender Therapy and Comparative Criminology*. 22:239–243.

Almonte, J. 1988. "A Perspective on National Security" *Manila Bulletin* 187 (21): 7, 35.

Alper, Benedict S., and Nichols, L. T. 1981 *Programs in Community Justice and Conflict Resolution*. Lexington: Lexington Books.

Anderson, Harry, and Vokey, Richard. 1993. "A Make or Break Year: It's Now or Never If the Philippines Is to Bloom." *Newsweek.* (February 8): 11.

Andres, T., and P. Ilada-Andres, P. 1987. *Understanding the Filipino*. Quezon City: New Day Publications.

Aquino, Corazon. 1976. "Tapping the Unarmed Forces of the Philippines." in *Speeches of President Corazon Aquino*. Manila: National Books.

Aquino, R. C. 1976. *The Revised Penal Code of the Philippines*. Manila: Central Books.

Arce, Wilfredo F. 1973. "The Structural Basis of Compadre Characteristics in a Bikol Town." *Philippine Sociological Review*. 21: 51–71.

Arquiza, Rey. 1997. "Number of Street Children on the Rise." *The Philippine Star.* (April 22): 15.

Austin, Timothy. 1984. "Crow Indian Justice: Strategies of Informal Social Control." *Deviant Behavior.* 5: 31–46.

———. 1987a. "Conceptual Confusion Among Rural Filipinos in Adapting to Modern Procedures of Amicable Settlement." *International Journal of Comparative and Applied Criminal Justice*. 11 (2): 241–250.

———. 1987b. "Crime and Custom in an Orderly Society: The Singapore Prototype." *Criminology.* 25 (2): 279–294.

———. 1988. "Field Notes on the Vigilante Movement in Mindanao: A Mix of Self-Help and Formal Policing Networks." *International Journal of Comparative and Applied Criminal Justice.* 12 (2): 205–217.

———1989. "Living on the Edge: The Impact of Terrorism upon Philippine Villagers." *International Journal of Offender Therapy and Comparative Criminology.*

———. 1991. "Toward a Theory on the Impact of Terrorism: The Philippine Scenario." *International Journal of Comparative and Applied Criminal Justice.* 15 (1): 33–48.

———. 1994. "Unexpected Dimensions of Informal Social Control: A View from the Philippine Sitio." *International Journal of Offender Therapy and Comparative Criminology.* 38 (4): 355–365.

———. 1995a. "Filipino Self-Help and Peacemaking Strategies: A View from the Mindanao Hinterland." *Human Organization.* 54 (1): 10–19.

———. 1995b. "Patterns of Extortion and Bribery among the Hiligaynon of Northwestern Mindanao." Presented at the Center for Philippine Studies Seminar. University of Hawaii at Manoa (Spring Semester). Honolulu, Hawaii.

———. 1996a. "Banana Justice in Moroland: Peacemaking in Mixed Muslim-Christian Towns in the Southern Philippines." In *Comparative Justice Systems: Traditional and Nontraditional Systems of Law and Order.* Charles B. Fields and Richter H. Moore, eds. Pp. 270-291. Prospect Heights, IL: Waveland Press. Pp. 270–291.

———. 1996b "A Rejoinder: In Regards to Critiques of My Research on Filipino Self-Help and Peacemaking in the Mindanao Hinterland." *Human Organization.* 55 (2): 248–249.

Balacuit, Sr. Jimmy Y. 1994. "Muslim Rebellion in Southern Philippines Revisited." *Mindanao Forum.* 9 (1): 1–53. Iligan City, Philippines: Official Journal of the MSU-Iligan Institute of Technology.

Baradas, David B. 1974. "Maranao Law: A Study of Conflict and Its Resolution in a Multi-Centric Power System." In *On the Codification of Muslim Customary Adat and Quranic Laws.* Papers of the 6th Annual Seminar on Islam in the Philippines and Asia. Davao: Ateneo de Davao.

———. 1977. "Vendetta: The Maranao's System of Social Justice." In *Filipino Heritage.* Vol. 2. Manila: Lahing Filipino Publishing, Inc.

Bates, Frederick L. 1963. *The Social and Psychological Consequences of a Natural Disaster: A Longitudinal Study of Hurricane Audrey.* National Disaster Study No. 18. Washington, D.C.: National Academy of Sciences.

———. 1982. *Recovery, Change and Development: A Longitudinal Study of the 1976 Guatemalan Earthquake.* Athens: Department of Sociology, University of Georgia.

Bates, Frederick L., and Harvey, Clyde C. 1975. *The Structure of Social Systems.* New York: Gardner Press.

Baumgardner, M. P. 1980. "On Self-help in Modern Society." In Donald Black, *The Manners and Customs of the Police.* New York: Academic Press.

Berg, Bruce L. 1989. *Qualitative Research Methods for the Social Sciences.* Boston: Allyn and Bacon.

Berger, Warren E. 1982. "Unclogging the Courts: Chief Justice Speaks Out." *U. S. News and World Report.* February 22.

Bergonia, T. 1988. "65,748 Armed Civilians Fighting Mindanao Rebs." *Philippine Daily Inquirer.* (July 14): 1, 8.

Black, Donald. 1976. *The Behavior of Law.* New York: Academic Press.

———. 1983. "Crime as Social Control." *American Sociological Review*. 48: 34–45.

———. 1993. *The Social Structure of Right and Wrong*. New York: Academic Press.

Black, H. C. 1979. *Black's Law Dictionary*. Minneapolis: West Publishing Company.

Bulatao, Jaime C. 1964 "Hiya." *Philippine Studies*. 12: 424–438.

Bunge, F. 1984. *Philippines: A Country Study. Area Handbook Series.* Washington, DC: U. S. Government Printing Office.

Capadocia, J. 1988. "Sparrows Gun Down Two Cops in Malate." *The Manila Times*. 29 June: 1,6.

Casino, Eric S. 1988. "The Anthropology of Christianity and Islam in the Philippines: A Bipolar Approach to Adversity." In *Understanding Islam and Muslims in the Philippines*. Peter Gowing, ed. Quezon City, Philippines: New Day Publishers.

Curran, Daniel J. and Renzetti, Claire M. 1994. *Theories of Crime*. Boston: Allyn and Bacon.

Danao, Efren. 1997. "Kabisig Groups Sought in South." *The Philippine Star*. March 16:12.

De La Cruz, Bobby. 1997. "First Kabisig Mindanao Congress Opens Today." *The Philippine Star*. March 14: 20.

Diamond, Stanley. 1971. "The Rule of Law Versus the Order of Custom," In *The Rule of Law*. Robert Paul Wolff, ed. New York: Simon & Schuster.

Driver, G. R. and Miles, J. C., eds. 1955. *The Babylonian Laws*. London: Oxford University Press.

Drozdiak, William and Richberg, Keith B. 1987. "Aquino Scores Victories in Year." *The Washington Post*. February 25: A: 1.

Durkheim, Emile. 1938. *The Rules of Sociological Methods*. Chicago: University of Chicago Press [first published in 1895. Paris: Felix Alcan.]

Enriquez, Virilio. 1988. "Filipino Values: Towards a New Interpretation." *Philippine Studies Newsletter*. Center for Philippine Studies, University of Hawaii at Manoa (November): 29–34.

Esguerra, Ramon. 1979. "The Youthful Offender before the Juvenile Courts." *Philippine Law Journal*. 54: 45–62.

Espino, C., and Sampana, A. 1988. "24 Sparrows Nabbed in Quezon City Raids." *Philippine Daily Inquirer*. July 8: 1, 8.

Espiritu, Socorro. 1987. "The Family." In *Sociology in the Philippine Setting: A Modular Approach*. 4th ed. Chester L. Hunt et al., eds. Quezon City: Phoenix Publishing House.

Fallows, James. 1988. "A Damaged Culture." *The Atlantic Monthly* 260 (5): 48–58.

Feleciano, Jay. 1993a. "Marines Kill 8 Moro Rebs in 2 Clashes." *Philippine Daily Inquirer*. February 11: 1, 11.

———. 1993b. "MNLF Areas Bombed: Marine General Sacked." *Philippine Daily Inquirer*. February 13: 1, 13.

Felson, Marcus. 1998. *Crime & Everyday Life*. 2nd. ed. Thousand Oaks, CA: Pine Forge.

Fields, Charles B., and Moore, Richter H. 1996. *Comparative Justice Systems: Traditional and Nontraditional Systems of Law and Order*. Prospect Heights, IL: Waveland Press.

Flores, Nelson F., and Agnote, Mario. 1993. "Government Ineptness vs. Crime Scored." *Philippine Daily Inquirer*. February 13:1,14.

Francisco, J. 1988, "CPP-NPA Drive Faltering in Countryside—Ramos." *The Philippine Star*. July 14: 1,4.

George, T.J.S. 1980. *Revolt in Mindanao: The Rise of Islam in Philippine Politics.* New York: Oxford University Press.

Gibbs, Jack P. 1989. "Conceptualization of Terrorism." American Sociological Review. 54 June: 329–340.

Giron, O. 1988. "CPP Infiltration Movements Cited." *Manila Bulletin.* July 18: 1, 17.

Gordon, Richard. 1997. "The State of the Philippines." Speech at Regional Meeting of Rotary Clubs. March 21. Maria Christina Hotel, Iligan City.

Gorospe, Vitaliano R. 1966. "Selected Bibliography on Filipino values." *Philippine Sociological Review.* 14: 173–179.

———. 1977. "Sources of Filipino Moral Consciousness." *Philippine Studies.* 25: 278–301.

Gouldner, Alvin. 1960. "The Norm of Reciprocity: A Preliminary Statement." *American Sociological Review.* 25: 161–178.

Gowing, Peter G. 1971. "The White Man and the Moro: A Comparison of Spanish and American Politics Toward Muslim Filipinos." *Solidarity.* 6 (3) (March).

———. 1975. "Christian-Muslim Relations in Insular Southeast Asia." *Solidarity.* 10 (6) (July-August): 2–17.

———. 1977. *Mandate in Moroland: The American Government of Muslim Filipinos, 1899–1920.* Quezon City: Philippine Center for Advanced Studies.

———. 1988. *Understanding Islam and Muslims in the Philippines.* Quezon City, Philippines: New Day Publishers.

Gowing, Peter G., and McAmis, Robert D. 1974. *The Muslim Filipinos.* Manila: Solidaridad Publication House.

Greisman, Harvey. 1977. "Social Meaning of Terrorism: Reification, Violence and Social Control." *Contemporary Crisis.* July: 303–318.

Guerrero, Leon Ma. 1972. *Encounter of Cultures: The Muslims in the Philippines.* Manila: National Media Production Center for the Department of Foreign Affairs.

Hart, Donn V. 1977. *Compadrinazgo: Ritual Kinship in the Philippines.* DeKalb, IL: Northern Illinois Press.

Heidenhein, A. J. 1970. *Political Corruption: Readings in Comparative Analysis.* New Brunswick, NJ: Transaction Books.

Hennig, Robert P. 1983. "Philippine Values in Perspective: An Analytical Framework." *Philippine Sociological Review.* 31: 55–64.

Hollnsteiner, Mary R. 1963. "Social Control in Filipino Personality." *Philippine Sociological Review.* 2: 184–189.

———. 1970. "Reciprocity in the Lowland Philippines." In *Four Readings on Philippine Values,* 3rd ed. Frank Lynch and Alfonso de Guzman II, eds. Quezon City: Ateneo de Manila University Press.

Jain, Ravindra K. 1979. "Sociology of Corruption in the Developing Societies: Morality in Theory and Practice." *Philosophy and Social Action.* 5 (3–4): 33–48.

Jardiniano, P. F. 1989. *Handbook on Barangay Administration.* Manila: Joris Trading Company.

Jimenez-Magsanae, Letty. 1993. "Kabisig Forms Working Committees." *Philippine Daily Inquirer.* March 31: 8, 32.

Jocano, F. Landa. 1966. "Rethinking Smooth Interpersonal Relations." *Philippine Sociological Review.* 31: 55–64.

———. 1969. *Growing Up in a Philippine Barrio.* New York: Holt, Rinehart and Winston.

Jones, Gregg. 1987a. "Aquino Orders Militia, Private Armies Disbanded." *The Washington*

Post. March 17: E: 19.

―――― . 1987b. "Civilians Aiding Fight Against Rebels." *The Washington Post*. April 1: A: 15.

Kaut, Charles. 1961. "Utang na Loob: A System of Contractual Obligations among Tagalogs." *Southwestern Journal of Anthropology*. 17: 256–272.

Kelley, K. 1982. *The Longest War: Northern Island and the IRA*. Westport, CT: Lawrence Hill.

Lacar, Luis Q. 1987. "Neglected Dimensions in the Development of Filipino Muslims." *Solidarity*. 113 (July-August): 8–16.

―――― . 1988. "Neglected Dimensions in the Development of Muslim Mindanao and the Continuing Struggle of the Moro People for Self Determination." *Journal of the Institute of Muslim Minority Affairs*. 9 (2) July.

―――― . 1993. "Culture Contact and National Identification among Philippine Muslims." Report prepared while a Visiting Research Fellow at the Centre for the Study of Islam and Christian-Muslim Relations. Selly Oak Colleges, Birmingham, United Kingdom.

Lasswell, H. D. 1963. "Bribery." *The Encyclopedia of the Social Sciences*. New York: Macmillan.

Lawless, R. 1966. "A Comparative Analysis of Two Studies on Utang na Loob." *Philippine Sociological Review*. 14: 168–172.

Lebow, R. 1978. "The Origins of Sectarian Assassination: The Case of Belfast." *Journal of International Affairs*. 32: 43–61.

Lee, A. 1984. *Terrorism in Northern Island*. New York: General Hall, Inc.

Ligo-Ralph, Vivian. 1990. "Some Theses Concerning the Filipino Value System." *Philippine Quarterly of Culture and Society*. 18: 149-161.

Lluch, Pacificador M. 1987. "Vigilantes Group Against the NPA—Three Views." *Mindanao Week*. 1 (10). (April 27–May 3): 11.

Locsin, Joel. 1997a. "MILF Threatens to Quit Peace Talks." *The Philippine Star*. (March 20): 40.

―――― . 1997b. "MNLF Threatens to Return to the Hills due to Poor Government Services." *The Philippine Star*. (April 23): 17.

Lynch, Frank, and de Guzman, Alfonso. 1970. *Four Readings on Philippine Values*. 3rd ed. Quezon City: Ateneo de Manila University Press.

Macalangcom, Capal M. 1974. "The Muslim-Christian Conflict in Mindanao and Sulu: Its Implications to National Integration." *Philippine Military Digest*. 11 (2): 70–77.

Madale, Nagasura T. 1990. *Possibilities for a Peace in Southern Philippines*. Zamboanga City, Philippines: Silsilah Publications.

Magdalena, Federico. 1977. "Intergroup Conflict in the Southern Philippines." *Journal of Peace Research* 14 (4): 299–313.

―――― . 1990. "Peace or Conflict in Muslim Mindanao?" *Philippine Studies Newsletter*. 18 (1): 1, 3. Honolulu, HA: University of Hawaii Center for Philippine Studies.

Majul, Cesar A. 1966. "Islamic and Arab Cultural Influences in the South of the Philippines." *Journal of Southeast Asian History*. 7 (2) (September): 1–10.

Man, W. K. Che. 1990. *Muslim Separatism: The Moros of Southern Philippines and the Malays of Southern Thailand*. Singapore: Oxford University Press.

Marapao, Alan. 1991. "Rebel Group Threatens to Blow Up NPC Plant, Burn Christian Workers." *The Mindanao Scoop*. 24 (8) (May 12): 1, 5.

Mileti, Dennis S., Drabek, Thomas E., and Haas, Eugene. 1975. *Human Systems in the Philippine Extreme Environments: A Sociological Perspective*. Boulder: Institute of Behavioral Science, University of Colorado. Program on Technology,

Environment and Man, Monograph Number 21.

Miller, Walter B.   1957.   "Lower-Class Culture as a Generating Milieu of   Gang Delinquency." *Journal of Social Issues*. 14 (3): 5–13.

Ministry of Justice.   1983.   *Five Year Summary Report on the Katarungang Pambarangay. 1979–1983.* Quezon City, Philippines: Bureau of Local Government Supervision.

Mirande, Alfredo.   1997.   *Hombres y Machos: Masculinity and Latino Culture*. Boulder: Westview Press.

Molloy, Ivan.   1988.   "The Decline of the Moro National Liberation Front in   the Southern Philippines." *Journal of Contemporary Asia*. 188 (1): 59–76.

Monterola, Archie O.   1997.   "Drug Lords Using Minors as Shield from Prosecution." *Manila Bulletin*. (March 12): C 6.

Morais, Robert J.   1980.   "Dealing with Scarce Resources: Reciprocity in Alternative Form and Ritual." *Philippine Sociological Review*. 28: 73–80.

Morgan, David L.   1993.   *Successful Focus Groups: Advancing the State of Art*. Thousand Oaks, CA: Sage.

Morrison, Ann M.   1997.   "Bottom Line (demographics)." *Asiaweek.* (March 28): 72.

Morrison, S. W. 1994a. "The Ultimate Price." *Asiaweek*. 20 (11): 28.

————. Morrison, S. W.   1994b.   "All in the Family: 'People Power' Has Failed to Sweep Away Clan Politics." *Asiaweek*. 20 (15): 28–32.

Mydans,   Seth.   1987.   "Right-Wing Vigilantes Spreading in Philippines." *New   York Times*. (April 4): A 5.

Myrdal, Gunnar.   1968.   *Asian Drama: An Enquiry into the Poverty of Nations*.   Vol. II. New York: Twentieth Century Publications.

Nadeau, Kathy and Vel J. Suminguit. 1996.   "A Critique of Austin." *Human Organization*. 55 (2): 245–247.

Nader, Laura, and Todd,   Harry F., Jr.,   eds., 1978. *The Disputing Process: Law in Ten Societies*. Columbia University Press.

National Census and Statistical Board.   1993. *A Monograph for the Estimation of Poverty and   Subsistence Thresholds and Incidences*. Quezon City,   Philippines.

Nemenzo, Francisco.   1987. "A Season of Coups: Reflections on the Military in   Politics." *Philippine   Studies   Newsletter*.   15   (3):   8–20.   Honolulu, Hawaii: University of   Hawaii Center for   Philippine Studies.

Newsbriefs.   1987.   "Aquino Endorses Anti-Communist Groups." *The Penn*. (March 30): 2. Indiana, PA: Indiana University   of   Pennsylvania.

Nix, Harold L.,   and Bates, Frederick L.   1962. "Occupational Role Stresses: A Structural Approach." *Rural Sociology*. 27: 7–17.

Noble, Lela G.   1976.   "The Moro National Liberation Front in the   Philippines." *Pacific Affairs*. 49 (Fall): 405–424.

————   . 1977. "Muslim-Christian   Conflicts—Its Religious   Background."   *Solidarity*. 11 (2)(March-April): 1–10.

O'Neill, M. 1987.   "Cults of War." *Asiaweek*. 13 (June):32–43.

Orendain, Antonio.   1979. *Barangay Justice*. Manila: Alpha Omega Publications

Padilla, Cesar B.   1989.   "From the Publisher: Still no Ransom?" *The Mindanao Scoop*. November 12: 1.

Pano, Antonio R.   1997a. "12 NPA Rebels in Bataan Yield after the Death of their   Leader." *The Philippine Star*. (March 16): 4.

————.   1997b. "United   Nations   Extends   Aid to MNLF Members." *The Philippine Star*. (April 21): 4.

Pascual, F.   1988.   "70,000 Vigilantes." *Philippine Daily Inquirer*. (July 19): 3, 4.

Pascual, F. 1988. "70,000 Vigilantes." *Philippine Daily Inquirer.* (July 19): 3, 4.

Pe, Cecilio L., and Tadiar, Alfredo F. 1979. *Katarungang Pambarangay Dynamics of Compulsory Conciliation.* Manila: UST Press.

Pido, Antonio J. A. 1986. *The Filipinos in America: Macro-Micro Dimension of Immigration.* New York: Center of Migration Studies.

Platt, Anthony. 1969. *The Child Savers.* University of Chicago Press.

Quinney, Richard. 1991. "The Way of Peace on Crime, Suffering and Service." In *Criminology as Peacemaking.* Harold L. Pepinski and Richard Quinney, eds. Bloomington: University of Indiana Press.

Quiranti, A. 1988. "Lanao Doctor Condemn Kidnaping for Ransom." *The Mindanao Scoop.* (June 5): 1

Quisumbing, Lourdes R. 1964. "Child-Rearing Practices in the Cebuano Extended Family." *Philippine Sociological Review.* 12: 109–114.

———. 1987. "Philippine Values." In *Sociology in the Philippine Setting: A Modular Approach.* 4th ed. Chester L. Hunt et al., eds. Quezon City: Phoenix Publishing House.

Reckless, Walter C. 1960. *The Crime Problem.* New York: Appleton-Century-Crofts.

Regalado, Edith, and Bagares, Romel. 1997. "MILF Official Confirms Defection of 5,000 MNLF Rebels." *The Philippine Star.* (April 28): 12.

Richberg, Keith B. 1986a. "Philippines Debates Keeping Controversial Civilian Militias." *The Washington Post.* (November 13): A: 31, 33.

———. 1986b "Irregular Troops Battle Philippine Guerrillas." *The Washington Post.* (November 7): A: 29.

Rieder, Jonathan. 1984. "The Social Organization of Vengeance." In *Toward a General Theory of Social Control.* Richard Abel, ed. New York: Academic Press.

Roces, Alejandro R. 1997a. "Kidnap Capital of Asia." *The Philippine Star.* (March 12): 9.

———. 1997b. "6.2 Percent of Students Hooked on Drugs?" *The Philippine Star.* (29 April): 9.

Rodil, B. R. 1994. "Update on the Peace Process Between the Government and the Moro National Liberation Front." *Mindanao Forum.* 9 (1): 95–101. Iligan City, Philippines: Official Publication of the MSU-Iligan Institute of Technology.

Rodriguez, Ben F. 1993. "Action Sought on Abalos Killing in Lanao." *Manila Bulletin.* 242 (25): 16. (February 25).

Rubinstein, Richard. 1988. *Alchemists of Revolution: Terrorism in the Modern World.* New York: Basic Books.

Rush, George F. 1986. *The Dictionary of Criminal Justice.* Guilford, CT: The Dushkin Publishing Group.

Saber, Mamitua, Tamano, Mauyag M., and Warriner, Charles K. 1960. "The Maritabat of the Maranao." *Philippine Sociological Review.* 8 (1 & 2): 10–15.

Saber, Mamitua, and Madale, A. T. 1975. *The Maranao.* Manila: Solidaridad Publishing House.

Santoalla, Ed L. 1987. "Vigilantism in Moroland." *Magazine of Malaya.* (August 23): 4–6.

Sennett, Richard. 1970. *The Uses of Disorder: Personal Identity & City Life.* New York: Alfred A. Knopf.

Serrill, Michael S. 1987. "Rise of Vigilantes: New Anti-communist Groups Present Prickly Political Problems." *Time.* (May 11): 40.

Shleifer, A., and Vishny, R. W. 1993. "Corruption." *The Quarterly Journal of Economics.* (August): 599–617.

Shoemaker, Donald J. 1996. "Juvenile Corrections in the Philippines: The *Barangay* System." *Journal of Offender Rehabilitation.* 24 (1/2): 39–52.

Shoemaker, Donald J., and Austin, W. T. 1996. "The Republic of the Philippines." In *International Handbook on Juvenile Justice.* Donald J. Shoemaker, ed. Westport, CT: Greenwood Press.

Silliman, G. Sidney. 1991. "A Political Analysis of the Philippines' Katarungang Pambarangay System of Informal Justice through Mediation." *Law & Society Review.* 19 (2): 279–301.

———. 1985. "Transnational Relations and Human Rights in the Philippines." *Pilipinas.* 16 (Spring): 64–80.

Simmons, C. H., and Mitch, J. R. 1985. "Labeling Public Aggression: When Is It Terrorism?" *Journal of Social Psychology.* 125 (2): 245–251.

Sorokin, Pitirim A., Zimmerman, Carle C., and Galpin, C. J. 1930. *A Systematic Source Book in Rural Sociology.* Minneapolis: University of Minnesota Press.

Smith, T. Lynn, and Zopf, Paul E., Jr. 1970. *Principles of Inductive Rural Sociology.* Philadelphia: F. A. Davis Company.

Soliven, Max V. 1997a. "The Shame of Our Being Labeled 'Kidnap Capital'." *The Philippine Star.* (March 7): 8, 9.

———. 1997b. "Solon Warns of Potential Risk Areas RP Could Face." *The Philippine Star.* (April 28): 41.

Stark, Rodney. 1987. "Deviant Places: A Theory of the Ecology of Crime." *Criminology.* 25 (4): 893–909.

Stone, Richard. 1973. Philippine Urbanization: The Politics of Public and Private Property in Greater Manila. (Unpublished Manuscript). DeKalb, IL: Northern Illinois University.

Tamano, Mamintal. 1973. "How to Solve the Muslim Problem Without Bullets." *Solidarity.* 8 (6)(December): 1-10.

Tarroza, Alvin. 1997. "MILF Group Kidnaps 3 Farmers in Zambo." *The Philippine Star.* (February 26): 6.

Timonera, M. 1988. "30 Killed in 12 Days in Lanao." *The Mindanao Scoop.* (July 17): 1.

Todd, Harry F., Jr. 1978. "Litigious Marginals: Character and Disputing in a Bavarian Village." In *The Disputing Process: Law in Ten Societies.* Laura Nader and Harry F. Todd, Jr., eds. New York: Columbia University Press.

Turk, Austin T. 1976. "Law as a Weapon in Social Conflict." *Social Problems.* 23 (3): 276–291.

———. 1982. *Political Criminality: The Defiance and Defense of Authority.* Beverly Hills: Sage.

Udarbe, Processo U. 1989. "The Transforming Power of Agape Love." In *Alternatives to Violence: Interdisciplinary Perspectives on Filipino People Power.* Douglas J. Elwood, ed. Quezon City, Philippines: New Day Publishers.

Usman, Ed K. 1997. "MNLF Rebels' Most Pressing Needs Bared: Steps to Fast-Track Solutions Proposed." *Manila Bulletin.* (March 10): 34.

van den Berghe, Pierre L. 1975. "Integration and Conflict in Multinational States." *Social Dynamics.* 1 (1): 3–10.

Vreeland, Nena. 1976. *Area Handbook for the Philippines.* Washington, DC: U.S. Government Printing Office.

Walter, Eugene V. 1964. "Violence and the Process of Terror." *American Sociological Review.* 29: 248–257 (April).

Ward, Richard. 1987. "A Fragile Democracy Hangs On." *C. J. International*.
    3 (25): 3, 5.
Wertheim, W. F. 1970. "Sociological Aspects of Corruption in Southeast Asia."
    In *Political Corruption: Readings in Comparative Analysis*. A. J. Heidenhein, ed.
    New Brunswick, NJ: Transaction Books.
Whitehall, A. 1981. "Seduction, Intimidation and Terror in the Philippines." *P a c i f i c
    Defense Reporter*. (October): 49–50.
Ynvessen, Barbara. 1978. "Responses to grievance Behavior: Extended Cases
    in a Fishing Community." *American Ethnologist*. 3 (2).
Zaide, S. M. 1990. "The First Kingdom in Mindanao." In *Butuan: The First
    Kingdom*. Monograph for the City Government of Butuan, Philippines: 3–53.
Zwick, J. 1984. "Militarism and Repression in the Philippines." In *State as Terrorist*. M.
    Stohl and G. Lopez, eds. Westport, CT: Greenwood Press: 123–143.

Index

About the Author

W. TIMOTHY AUSTIN is Professor of Criminology at Indiana University, Pennsylvania. His teaching specialties include theoretical criminology and comparative justice systems. He has completed twenty years of research on Southeast Asia, particularly concerning the Philippines and the southern island of Mindanao.

ISBN 0-275-96204-0

90000>

EAN

9 780275 962043

HARDCOVER BAR CODE